The Sandbridge

DANCE TUNE COLLECTION

ARRANGEMENTS OF
REELS, JIGS, HORNPIPES, POLKAS AND RAGS FOR THE
HAMMERED DULCIMER

By Ken Kolodner

Nine years ago, I launched a weeklong retreat in Sandbridge Beach, Virginia for hammered dulcimer players. I started "Sandbridge" to provide an intensive learning environment in a relaxed setting. Since its inception, Sandbridge has evolved into three weeklong workshops that draw 50 intermediate and advanced players from around the U.S. and beyond. This collection draws heavily from arrangements developed at Sandbridge and over the course of my 30-year career as a hammered dulcimer performer and instructor.

1 2

Visit us on the Web at www.melbay.com — E-mail us at email@melbay.com

The Sandbridge
DANCE TUNE COLLECTION

Arrangements of Reels, Jigs, Hornpipes, Polkas and Rags for the Hammered Dulcimer

Arrangements of traditional and original tunes including fiddle tunes, reels, jigs, hornpipes, rags and polkas. Repertoire draws from Old-Time, French-Canadian and Celtic traditions. Includes basic tunes and one or more arrangement for each tune. The arrangements offer a wide range of levels of complexity. Backup and harmony parts are provided for many of the pieces. Includes a discussion of arranging ideas.

Photo cover: ©2011 Laurie McCarriar: www.stoppingtolook.com
Photo backcover: Alison Brown
Graphic Design: Kathy Sanderson, Washington D.C.

To order copies of the book, please contact:

Ken Kolodner
3806 Fenchurch Rd.
Baltimore, MD 21218
410-746-8387
www.kenkolodner.com
kenkolodner@aol.com

TABLE OF CONTENTS

THE TUNES

APPENDICES

ACKNOWLEDGEMENTS

This book would not have been possible without all those who have taken lessons or workshops from me, motivating me to write out many hundreds of arrangements. Much thanks goes to all those musicians from whom I have learned these tunes and countless others. Thanks to Kathy Sanderson for her invaluable assistance in putting this book together. And to Alison, Bradley and Hillary!

INTRODUCTION

How I chose the tunes

My interest in music is broad but my focus has been on traditional music from a wide variety of cultures and sources. In the two-book companion collection, I include a healthy dose of Old-Time, Celtic (mostly Irish and Scottish) and Québécois tunes, as well as some traditional pieces from around the world. For "The Sandbridge Dance Collection," I selected reels, jigs, hornpipes, some Irish polkas and rags. For "The Sandbridge Waltzes and Airs Collection" I selected a slower repertoire of a wide variety of waltzes, slow airs and marches. To keep the repertoire focused, I chose not to include hymns, Christmas tunes, popular and classical music but hope to save those for a future collection.

I prefer teaching less complex pieces of music to create arrangements of varying levels of difficulty. Thus, I included mostly straightforward tunes, with some notable exceptions such as *Carnaval*, **Loftus Jones*, and **Sir Sydney Smith*. For some tunes, I have included multiple versions of the arrangements ranging from very simple to considerably more complex. My intent is to present arrangements appropriate for a wide range of playing abilities.

Please consider the written notation as a guide. Ultimately, it is essential to listen to examples of the arrangements. Over my thirty plus years of playing the hammered dulcimer, I've recorded or performed many of these tunes. Jump on YouTube and look for me! If you have some of my recordings or instructional CDs, please listen to the tune that you are considering learning. (You may refer to the index of tunes in this book to see which tunes I have recorded.)

* *MB30441 "The Sandbridge Waltz and Slow Air Collection"*

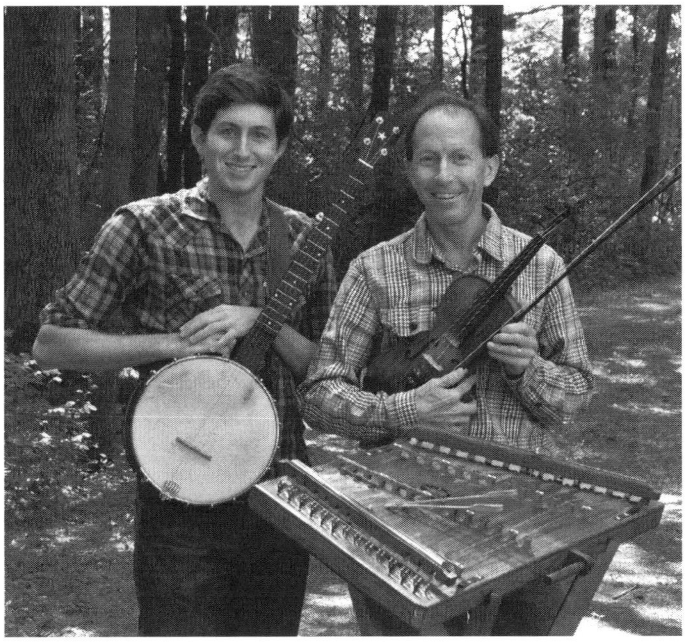

Brad and Ken Kolodner in Vermont, 2012 Photo:Hank Schless

Four skill areas

If I may preach for a moment, I like to think of four general skill areas to develop in playing music.

(1.) Technical skills. This is perhaps where we tend to spend most of our time and effort – mastering the many techniques used in playing our instruments.

(2.) Listening skills. Developing listening skills is arguably the most important tool to master. Many people equate "listening skills" with learning to play by ear. Learning how to play by ear is a great skill to master and it is one of the many skills to acquire under the umbrella of "listening." But we can be more specific regarding the many components of "learning by ear." First, we need to learn to hear how tunes are

structured in terms of parts and phrases. How many parts does the piece have? Within each part, are there "question and answer" phrases or repeating sections that we can identify? We need to be able to identify the tonal center in a piece of music. Having done so, we can learn to hear whether the piece is major, minor or in some other mode. We can learn to hear the many scalar patterns, arpeggios and intervals that typically make up a piece of music. A higher level of hearing is to hear the many subtleties of phrasing like swing, and dynamics.

Additionally, listening skills include learning how to pick up tunes on the fly in a jam. This may involve all the skills listed above but also how to identify the critical anchors or notes in a phrase, how to hear chord changes, how to play backup in a jam, and how to selectively tune out "the clutter." I often hear the complaint that "I can't hear myself in a jam." While it may be difficult at times to hear yourself, most of the time, it is more a question of learning how to listen to that which is important. This involves selectively listening only to those who are actually playing the tune correctly. Simultaneously, we must strive to tune out the distractions of those who are may be playing lots of wrong notes or chords.

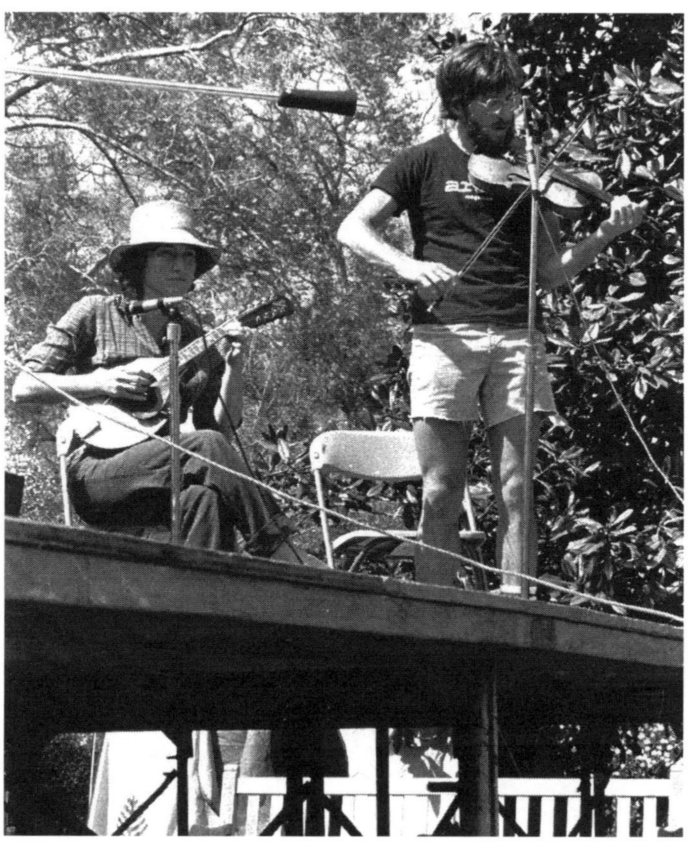

Perhaps you aren't interested so much in jamming but you still play with others. A critical listening skill to develop is to learn to divide your focus between hearing your instrument and hearing your playing partners. This involves staying focused on your playing while listening and communicating musically in terms of tempo, phrasing and dynamics with your playing partners.

(3.) Understanding and applying theory. It is possible to play music without understanding all that much about the big picture. However, understanding keys, modes (especially modes!), how tunes are structured, how to form simple and more complex chords, and how chords move (chord progressions) all greatly increase one's ability to learn, process and retain music. First, we identify the tonal center and whether it is in a major key or possibly a mode, the most common being Dorian, Aeolian and Mixolydian. In analyzing the structure of a tune, the first and most obvious components are the big sections, the number of parts and the phrases within each part, especially identifying those phrases that repeat in a "question" and "answer" manner. Beyond that, many tunes involve pieces of arpeggios and scales put together in interesting ways, along with longer notes and movement in intervals such as thirds. Learning to see these pieces helps us to identify and process the supporting harmonic structure of the music, otherwise known as the chord progression. I learn every tune not only by memorizing the specific notes, but also by identifying the chord structure, arpeggios, scales and intervals that exist in the tune. This may seem like an awful lot of processing and thinking, but I find that it greatly speeds up my learning and retention.

(4.) Musicality. Mastering the mechanics of playing a tune and an arrangement is only part of the battle. The real art of playing comes when we master how we play each note and communicate a story with that phrasing. Musicality includes a wide range of elements such as how to phrase and shape a tune in terms of dynamics, the amount of swing to add, when

Maggie Sansone and Ken Kolodner, performing at the Deer Creek Fiddler's Convention in Westminster, MD, in 1979, before either of us played the hammered dulcimer!

to shift accents, and where to place the pulse of the tune. I have heard the argument that musicality is so subjective that it cannot be taught. I disagree. I always state my case about how to play a tune and why. You don't have to agree with my statement but I am going to put it out there and provide a guide.

Backup and harmony parts

My main focus in this book is on solo arrangements. However, for many of the tunes, I have included a backup and/or a harmony part. Many of the harmony parts are likely more appropriate for an instrument capable of sustaining a note, like a fiddle or flute. I included them hoping that you will share them with others with whom you may play.

Over the years, I have learned so much more from developing accompaniment parts than from developing leads. In fact, backup is my favorite place to be, working in the chord progressions and in rhythm. My hope is that you will learn a lot about the tunes if you spend some time exploring the backup parts. I improvise frequently in creating a backup just as I do while playing my arrangements. But what I have written down should offer a good start.

My three arranging approaches: Individual techniques, the full model and the kitchen sink

I like to approach teaching arranging using three general methods. I have presented many examples of each of these in this volume.

First is a technique-driven approach where I use *only* one idea and present it in the entire tune. The idea here is to master that one idea so that it will be available to you to use in a wide variety of tunes. While using just a single idea can sometimes be a bit tedious to play, one idea can be quite effective. For example, I use only two-note chords in one version of **Fanny Power*. In this version, I demonstrate the use of two-note chords to create ascending and

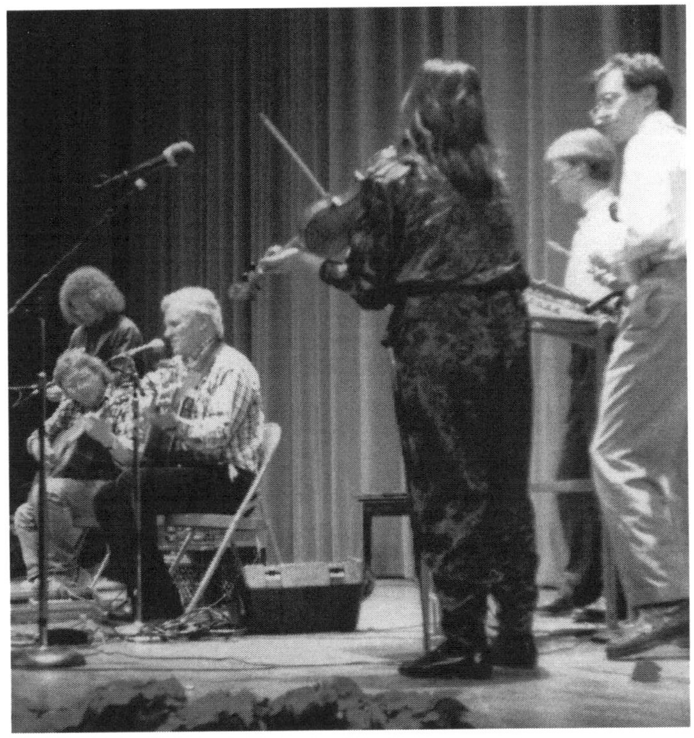

Playing "St. Anne's Reel" for an NPR broadcast with Robin Bullock, Jack Lawrence, Doc Watson, Freyda Epstein, Chris Norman, and Ken Kolodner, at Helicon's Winter Solstice Concert, 1989. Photo: Paul Hartman

descending bass lines and to separate the harmony in physical distance from the melody. I might not play the tune ever with *only* two-note chords, but I think that you will find this version surprisingly successful. In **Southwind*, I present three versions that each use a single idea, using "two-note chords," "three-note chords," and "fills". I also include a more adventurous version that combines ideas. In practice, I rarely play a tune using only one idea, but it is excellent practice to be able to master each idea separately. Ultimately, by mastering each idea, my hope is that you will be able to create your own arrangement that incorporates each technique.

In my second approach, I present a full model of how I might play the tune at least one time through. Here I use a variety of ideas to embellish the tune, while allowing you to still clearly hear the melody. There are many examples of this approach, but to highlight a few check out **Bonny at Morn*, **The Down Home Waltz* and **The Clock Waltz*. Although I typically only present one pass of the tune, these "full model" arrangements work as stand-alone arrangements, unlike the third approach that I offer in the book.

* *MB30441 "The Sandbridge Waltz and Slow Air Collection"*

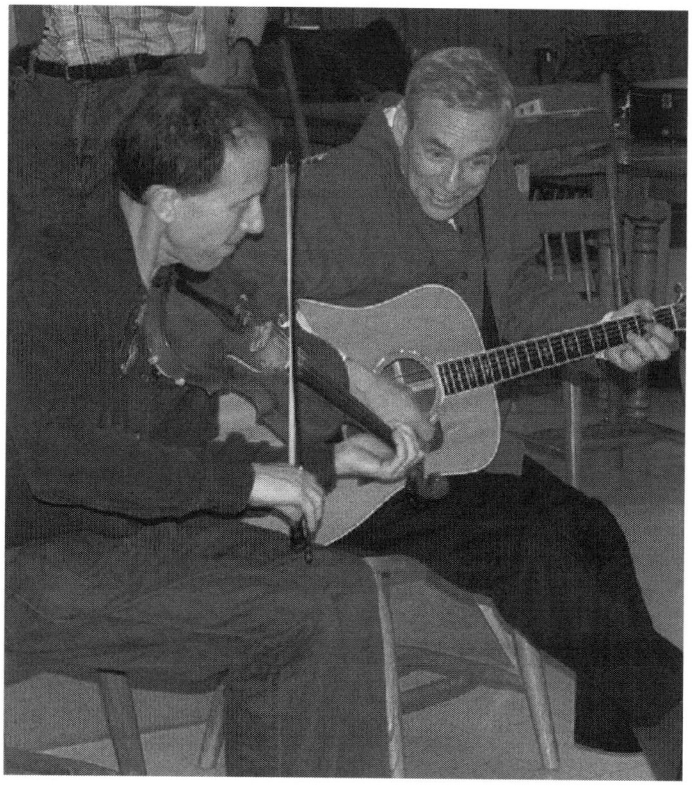

Rick Thum trying to decipher one of Ken's crooked tunes, Mountain View, Arkansas, 2011 Photo: Ilace Mears

In this last approach, I cram in as many ideas as I can on a single page. I often write out the repeats of the A and B parts and present a new idea in each couple of measures. I like to think of this as the "kitchen sink" approach that is meant to be a collection of ideas. Rarely would I play all these ideas together as it would likely obscure and overwhelm the tune. My goal is that you will eventually be able to pick and choose from the many ideas to create multiple arrangements of the tune.

For the most part, I do not play memorized arrangements. Instead, I first develop many ideas for each tune. In performance, I have a general plan for presenting the tune, but leave room to improvise so that each performance is completely unique, at least to some extent. And in the best case scenario, I come up with new ideas on the spot. This means that I take risks. This improvisational approach likely will not work for most players as it is a difficult way to go!

I think of these "kitchen sink" transcriptions as collections of ideas from which you can draw. Feel free to pick and choose which ideas work for you. In learning the more complicated "arrangements" presented here, I hope that you develop at least one simple arrangement for each tune.

My goal is that you will eventually be able to draw from the many ideas to create multiple arrangements of the tune.

Caution: always learn just the melody and keep moving!

This is an obvious point, but so often I see folks have nailed a complicated arrangement and the listener can barely tell what the tune is. My thinking is that you should always be able to play the basic tune with no embellishments. First, it can be refreshing and rewarding to play through the basic tune simply, and focus on phrasing and musicality. Second, you should have some concept of how the ideas were developed by always keeping the basic tune in sight.

A further word of encouragement: do not focus on your mistakes. Especially as you begin to add ideas and master the arrangements, try to practice without "correcting." It is easy to fall in the trap of trying to master an arrangement and sacrificing the flow of the tune. If a particular idea seems too difficult, simplify or adapt it. Ultimately, some wrong notes do not matter, but losing the rhythm does. Learning to never stop is a difficult lesson, but the most important one!

Hammering choices

When I first started to play the dulcimer, I was unaware of any *systems* or philosophies of hammering. Because of the set-up of the instrument with the lower notes on the right, I thought that it made sense to try to put as much melody in my left hand as possible so that my right hand was free to add chords and bass lines. I especially thought that it made sense to develop my hands equally. While I will not venture into a discussion of pros and cons of the many "systems" of hammering, I'd like to highlight a few of the more prominent. (1.) *Alternation.* Simply put, when learning a new tune, always alternate. (2.) *Dominant hand* leads by using your dominant hand on the "primary" counts of the tune. The basic idea is that it will be easier to keep the rhythm of the tune if you use your dominant hand for the primary counts. If you are playing in 4/4, the dominant hand is used on the counts of "one, two, three, four" and the non-dominant hand plays the count of "and." (3.) *Right vs. left hand lead.* Many players suggest that sticking to a right (e.g. Rick Thum) or left hand lead (e.g. Bill Spence) has certain advantages or sounds better for certain types of tunes. Some players (e.g. Ken Kolodner!) suggest that handedness should not play a significant role in determining one's ability to use a consistent lead. Just to be sure of our definition what a lead hand means, in a left hand lead in 4/4, the left hand plays the primary counts of "one, two, three, four" while the right hand plays the "and" counts. (4.) *Whatever works best* based on the tune and the player. This last philosophy leaves it up to each player to find their own way for each tune and typically features no clear "leading" of hands. Typically, alternation is also not used.

I am a proponent in certain types of tunes (waltzes, reels, fast tunes in 4/4) of using a left-hand lead for a variety of reasons. Most notably, a left hand lead "frees" my right hand to add bass lines and widely spaced harmonies. It is a misconception that you have to be left-handed to use a left-hand lead. On the contrary, in using a left hand lead, my right hand often moves far greater distances than my left. I have found that most right-hand lead players who give left-hand lead a try for a few months can strengthen their left to accomplish what their right used to do.

If you have used a right-hand lead for a long time, you may decide it isn't worth the trouble to try left-hand lead. In many of the arrangements, some of the ideas presented here may not work well or at all when played with a right-hand lead, at least not as written. But you can probably find other ways to play most of the ideas presented in the arrangements. Ultimately, you are on your own to navigate your way through the arrangements, as I decided not to complicate the transcriptions by adding suggested hammerings. It will often be obvious when the left must take the melody. You should be fine if you use the duplicated notes and carefully explore alternate approaches to choreographing the hammering.

Using the arrangements

I hesitate to use the word "arrangement" to describe what I have presented in this volume. Most of the "arrangements" are collections of ideas from which I hope you will learn to incorporate into your own new arrangements. Much of my arranging is actually conceived "on the fly" and is often partially improvised. Certainly, I spend a lot of practice time working out ideas and sometimes develop a formal arrangement. But for most tunes, I hope that every performance of a tune varies. While I usually have a general plan in a performance, I like to experiment and see what happens. When I write "arranging ideas," I have written down a collection of ideas that I could fit on one page. I did not intend that the entire page be played exactly as written. Rather, I have condensed into one page a variety of ideas that could perhaps be thought of as a library of ideas that you might use in different passes of the tune. For example, I would never play *Frenchie's Reel: aranging ideas* as my first or *any* pass through the tune. Rather, I might pull in those ideas as I play the tune multiple times. In contrast, when I have written "arrangement #1," or simply "arrangement," I think of this as a stand-alone presentation of the tune that I might play in total.

Wes Chapell, Randy Marchany, Ken Kolodner, as always, in shorts and Hawaiian shirts, fiddling "Hangman's" at the Swannanoa Gathering, 2002.

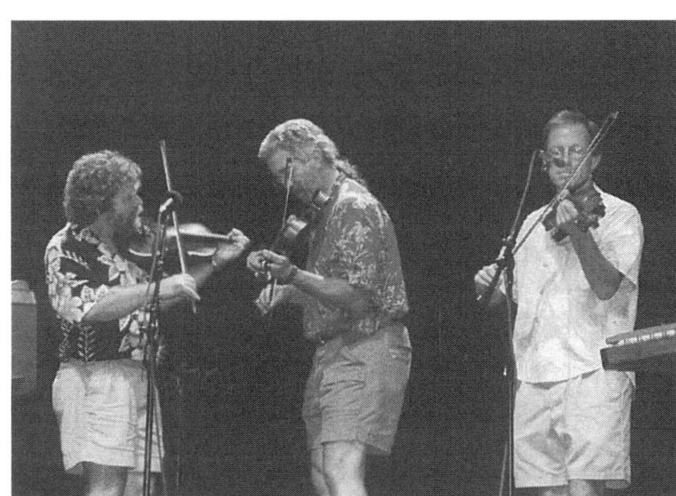

The discussion that follows is not intended to be a full treatise on how to arrange, but includes an explanation of the most common ideas that I present in the transcriptions. I have included descriptions of the ideas in some of the arrangements such as **Bonny at Morn: arrangement; *The Down Home Waltz; *Polska: arranging ideas; Lonesome John: arranging ideas; North Carolina Breakdown: variations;* and *Oklahoma Rooster: variations*. It may be informative to look at these annotated arrangements in order to understand the ideas and notation.

* *MB30441 "The Sandbridge Waltz and Slow Air Collection"*

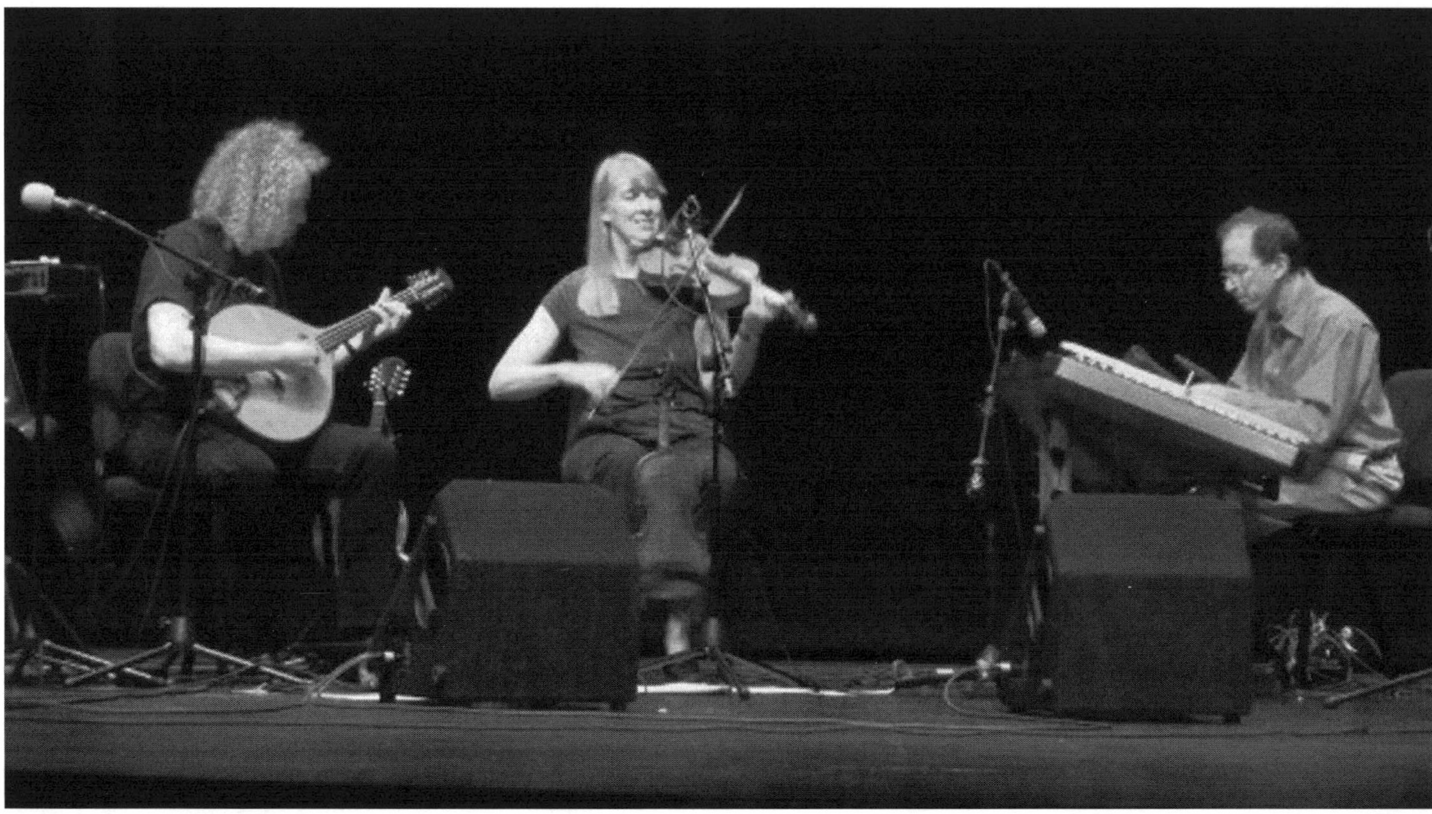

Robin Bullock, Scottish National Fiddler Champion Elke Baker, and Ken, Shepherdstown, WV 2009. Photo: Joanie Blanton

TWENTY (or more!) ARRANGING IDEAS

Here are some of the more prominent ideas presented in the volume. There really are many more than twenty, but who's counting?

(1.) Use the full range of your instrument

This is an obvious, but surprisingly often overlooked, idea. It is often quite easy simply to move a melody to a lower or higher octave for the entire tune or at least a few sections of the piece. Aside from sounding good, we may discover new ideas and ways to play the piece. In anticipation of using the full range of the instrument, I try to choreograph my hammering so that it is easy to move from one octave to the next. (See the B part of *The Black Nag: variations*.)

(2.) Hand separation or hand independence

Here, one hand is devoted to playing the melody while the other hand plays an accompaniment. Typically, the left hand plays the melody while the right hand plays the accompaniment. The challenge here is to play the melody stronger than the accompaniment and to play both the right and left hand dynamically, including sometimes contrasting dynamic lines between the two hands. (See **The Cradle Song* and **Evening of Roses* for examples).

(3.) Two-note chords

Two-note chords are often undervalued as a simple but effective arranging idea. Three general uses of two-notes chords are presented throughout the arrangements: first using two-note chords to clearly separate harmony from melody; second using two-note chords to create bass lines; and third using two-note chords on less obvious counts in the music to move the accents in unexpected ways.

I tend to use a wide variety of intervals but I especially emphasize separating harmony from melody in physical distance. Rather than using a close harmony, I often opt for playing the harmony notes far away from the melody notes. This greatly opens up the instrument.

I am especially fond of using two-note chords to create simple rising and descending bass lines. This may be obvious, but I like to be careful to play the melody note stronger than the harmony note.

In many of the arrangements, I move chords off the obvious counts to create more rhythmic interest. For example, in 4/4, I might chord on the "two" and "four" counts or the "two and three" rather than the more obvious "one and three" counts. See *Johnny Cope: arrangement #1* for a simple example of placing chords on counts other than "one and three." See **Fanny Power: arrangement with two-note chords* for an example of an arrangement of a tune that uses only two-note chords to create bass lines.

(4.) Three-note rolled chord

In this standard tool, we rapidly play three notes of the triad in the root, first or second inversions, while emphasizing the melody note as the last note in the sequence. Most players rely on "right-left-right" three-note chord patterns. This generally works just fine, but I like to give nearly equal time to left-right-left and right-left-right patterns. More important is to execute the three notes with exactly equal spacing and emphasis on the last (melody) note. My chief complaint is that people often play three-note chords a bit too aggressively. In fact, "punching" three-note chords prevents the creation of dynamics. I much prefer a light touch. (For an example of an arrangement that uses three-note chords almost exclusively, see **Southwind: three-note chords*). Again, I would almost never play an arrangement using only three-note chords, but an important skill to master is knowing all the possible three-note chords available to you in a piece.

(5.) Tremolos

We have no ability to sustain a note on the hammered dulcimer. While space is a good thing, sometimes we might want to suggest playing a

* *MB30441 "The Sandbridge Waltz and Slow Air Collection"*

longer note full value by playing a rapid succession of a single note or perhaps two different notes of a chord. I am most likely to use a tremolo for dotted quarter, half, or dotted half notes. Typically, I write the notes out as sixteenth notes (see measure #1 in **Ian Robertson* or measure #9 in **Bonny at Morn*). I try to shape tremolos dynamically in a variety of ways: start very lightly and gradually build through to the last note; or reverse the dynamic by starting big and fading out; or start quietly and build toward the middle of the tremolo, fading out at the end. Many other shapes are possible.

(6.) Hammered and bounced triplets

I typically write out a triplet which is hammered with separate strokes as an actual triplet while I indicate a "bounced" triplet as two grace notes followed by the melody note. For a bounced triplet, one hand plays two grace notes with a bounce of the hammer while the other hand plays the melody note. For example, measure #28 in the arrangement of *Tom Morrison's* begins with a bounced triplet and follows with a series of hammered triplets.

(7.) Valley rolls

A valley roll is a great way to play a chord. The right hand gently bounces from the right treble bridge to the bass bridge either playing a fifth, a fourth or a third. Immediately after the right hand has completely sounded, the left hand plays the melody note. In my playing of this technique, the right hand always precedes the left just slightly. While I could play the right and left at the same time, the technique loses its rhythmic feel and loses clarity when doing so. In my rendering of this technique, I use a single strike on the right treble bridge to generate a single bounce (two-notes). The second of these notes is moved quickly to the bass bridge. To create the movement to the bass bridge, I suggest having the stroke begin several inches from the left of the intended striking point on the right treble bridge. This little bit of a "backswing" provides momentum into the stroke. The motion is completed with a small follow-through past the note on the bass bridge. I represent the valley roll as two grace notes preceding the primary note.

The most common valley roll moves a fifth across from the right treble to the bass bridge. We can also move up a fourth or even up a third. Moving up a third from the right treble to bass bridge is a bit harder to execute because you have to jump over a note. I occasionally move from the bass bridge bouncing to the right treble bridge but I much prefer moving right treble to the bass bridge. It is quite possible to generate two bounces and play three notes with the right hand. I use this variant of the valley roll to play 7th chords. For example, to play a D7, I might strike an F♯ on the right treble bridge and bounce over and up to the bass bridge C and D. The left hand would play the melody note A on the right treble bridge, thus capturing all the notes of the D7.

For many years, most players have called this technique a "flam" but at the urging of Dan Landrum and others who hail from a percussion background, I've relinquished this term. Dan prefers "drag." I'm going with "valley roll" to suggest the movement of the right hand traveling through the "valley" between the right treble bridge and the bass bridge. Examples of valley rolls are plentiful. (See **The Down Home Waltz* for an annotated example.)

(8.) Arpeggio fills and color notes

Instruments such as a fiddle or flute are capable of sustaining a note to its full value. On the hammered dulcimer, we play a note and wait for the next one to come along! Again, space is a wonderful thing. But sometimes we may want to fill the space especially when faced with a dotted quarter note or with notes of longer duration. A common technique is to fill the space with quicker notes, most typically with eighth notes using notes of the chord. This is called an arpeggio fill. Thus, if we have a dotted quarter note, we might play the melody note followed by two eighth notes that are in the chord. With a half note, we could play a melody note followed by three fill notes. The order with which one plays the notes in the fill is arbitrary.

It is a lovely technique that is relatively easy to master, but I have a couple of cautions. First, once folks learn the technique, it is very tempting to use it all the time and "overfill," leaving no space in the tune. This is a judgment call and a question of taste, but I am a believer in keeping space and resisting the urge to fill every space just because we can. Perhaps it is helpful to think of ourselves as wind players

* *MB30441 "The Sandbridge Waltz and Slow Air Collection"*

who have to take breaths. My second caution is that there is a tendency to play fills a bit too aggressively. In general, I prefer that my fills are played lightly. I often float through fills and barely hit some of the notes. In fact, many musicians in other genres and on other instruments use a technique called ghosting, where notes are intentionally dropped, but our ears tend to fill them in. I ghost (leave out) many of the fill notes frequently, even when I have written them down. (More on ghosting later!!)

The arpeggio fill need not only use the notes in the chord. Notes that reside in between the notes of a chord can provide "color" to the arpeggio fill. There are many examples of this technique in this volume. (See **The Down Home Waltz* for examples of fills.)

(9.) Drones or pivot notes

When there are a series of quarter notes in a measure, an easy "fill" technique is to insert an eighth note "drone." The drone is a note of the chord played either above or below the melody. The drone or pivot note should be played quieter than the melody notes. I sometimes use an idea which I call the "double drone," where both hands play a drone note. (See the B part of **Polska: arranging ideas* for various uses of droning).

(10.) Melodic runs

This is a relatively simple concept where we "run" through a piece of a scale. Melodic runs can be used to replace arpeggios, to connect chords in a piece of music, or to fill space. There are countless examples of runs in this volume. The simplest melodic run entails playing a scale, starting either at the root of the chord and moving to the five of the chord, or conversely, starting at the five of the chord and moving to the one (e.g. a D chord run could be "D-E-F♯-G-A" or "A-G-F♯-E-D"). (See **Coleman's March: arrangement #2* for examples of melodic runs.) Runs can skip notes in the scale or borrow from notes outside of the scale as in a chromatic run. Melodic runs can also be used to replace arpeggios in tunes. (See measure #6 in **Forvantan: arrangement #1*.) An advantage of melodic runs, unlike arpeggio fills, is that they are "directional" and can be used to connect chords to go from one note in a melody to another by traveling through a chord or scale. Combining melodic runs with arpeggio fills can provide even more interest.

* *MB30441 "The Sandbridge Waltz and Slow Air Collection"*

(11.) Ghost notes

It is likely that I originally started playing "ghost" or "implied" notes on the hammered dulcimer because I heard fiddlers use this technique and I use it myself when fiddling. The idea is simply to not play one or more melody notes as a rhythmic device to give the music some space to breathe. Our ears tend to fill in these missing notes. This is a simple idea but can be a difficult one to grasp as not all melody notes are created equal. Most tunes have a skeleton of critical notes that must be played to represent the tune. Some musicians refer to the skeleton as "corners" or "anchors" of the tune. This suggests that there are other notes that may be dropped or altered. And that is where the fun begins.

Some tunes are highly structured melodically, but many tunes have notes that are not essential to adequately represent the tune. How does one determine which notes are needed and which can be altered or dropped? This is partly achieved through experimentation and partly through experience. There are two primary ways that I use ghost notes. First, I drop out disposable notes to give the tune space. The disposable notes tend to occur especially on the counts of "and" in a piece of music. Pickup notes are also easily dispensable. The second use of ghosting is to drop out notes on the primary counts that are seemingly important to the melody. This is a much harder idea to master. This second usage is a purely rhythmic device. It is used especially in Québécois fiddling. I use it frequently in Québécois tunes but I seldom notate the idea. (See measure 14 in *Carnaval* and measure 21 in *Reel du Nord*).

(12.) Note replacement

Expanding on the concept that certain notes may be dropped out of a melody, I often replace melody notes that are less critical to the integrity of the tune with harmony notes or bass line notes. This is an extremely powerful tool that I use frequently, especially to create ascending and descending bass lines, and to bring out the chord progression. There are countless examples in this book. (See the A part of *Cuckoo's Nest: arranging ideas*.)

(13.) Replacing phrases with brief harmony passages

In some ways, it is surprising that this idea should work at all. But it does, if used for just a brief passage in the music. Look at measures 15 and 28 of *Shenandoah Falls: variations*, where I jump briefly to a harmony line before returning to the melody. Somehow your ears still hear the original line. Typically, I match exactly the rhythm of the melody.

(14.) Chord theory and chord substitutions

There is a vast supply of potential chords at our disposal to replace a major chord: minor, major and minor 7ths, dominant sevenths, diminished sevenths, and so on. We can use our ears to find these, but knowing chord theory really helps our search. This is such a big area that it is not possible for me to present an adequate discussion of finding chord substitutions and how to develop chord progressions. Suffice it to say that I use a wide variety of chord substitutions sometimes even in very straightforward tunes such as **Southwind* and *St. Anne's Reel*. Perhaps a quick primer on chord formation will be useful. If you are feeling fuzzy on your chord knowledge, I encourage you to study chord theory further.

The formula for building chords is super simple; we simply count 1-3-5 from each note in the major scale. There are seven unique notes in a major scale so there are exactly seven "triads" (chords with three notes) that can be formed in a major key, each chord being formed from each note in the scale and counting 1-3-5. There are a couple of types of triads but by far the most important are *major* and *minor* chords. The three major chords are built on the first, fourth and fifth notes of the scale. On the hammered dulcimer, they are conveniently color coded as your markers! These are often called the I, IV and V chords. *Minor* chords are built on the second, third and sixth notes of the scale (often called ii, iii, vi chords). It is vital to learn these chords in each of the big dulcimer keys. Just for the record, the chord built on the seventh note of the scale is diminished. It is rarely used; you can ignore it for the most part, but you should know of its existence in case it makes an appearance.

A chord that you should absolutely know is called the *dominant seventh* chord (e.g. A7, D7, G7). At a minimum, I would know the dominant seventh chords that exist in the most important keys. The dominant seventh chord is formed by counting 1-3-5-7 from the *fifth* note of the scale. The dominant seventh chord is the most important chord of tension and ultimately movement. The chord that almost always follows a dominant seventh chord is down a *fifth*. For example, A7 moves down (or resolves) to D, D7 to G, and G7 to C.

Other seventh chords that are next in importance include the following (1.) the *major seventh chord*. This is a major chord that has a major third (two full steps) added to it. It is a chord of color and has a warm fuzzy quality (if you are old enough, think Chicago's "Color my World"). There is much confusion as to the difference between a major seventh and a dominant seventh, but the functions of these two chords are quite different. The notes of the chord are the same except that the seventh is lowered a half step for the dominant seventh chord. Thus the last note is different. As an example, an A major seventh typically appears as AMaj7 (or just AM7) and includes the notes A C♯ E G♯. A dominant seventh appears as A7 (and uses A C♯ E G). (2.) The minor seventh chord is a minor chord with a minor third (one and a half steps) built on top. By adding the seventh, we "color" the chord. Alternately, a minor seventh can be used as a chord of movement much like a dominant seventh but its push to move down a fifth is considerably weaker. Both major and minor sevenths are often used to create interesting bass lines.

A *diminished seventh chord* is much less commonly used, but can provide significant tension and interest. I use them sparingly but am always on the look-out for a spot to put them in. (See measure #74 in the C part of **Kevin Keegan's* and measure #12 of **Caspian Lake*.) I find these chords very exciting when they work!

A *suspension* is another type of chord that can add tension. A typical suspension involves replacing the third in a chord with the fourth. A "Dsus4" (or D suspended fourth) is played with D-G-A instead of D-F♯-A. A Dsus4 may precede a D chord.

Secondary dominants. A secondary dominant, in brief, is a dominant seventh chord that does not belong in the key (i.e. it borrows one or more notes from outside the scale) and utilizes the circle of fifths movement of chords to strengthen a progression. The chord does not formally exist in the key because it

* *MB30441 "The Sandbridge Waltz and Slow Air Collection"*

must employ at least one alteration of the original scale. In **The Tennessee Waltz*, I use a secondary dominant to move from a D chord to G chord by introducing a D7. The D7 strengthens the movement from the original D (I) to G (IV) chord. The note that causes the movement and is not in the key of D is the C natural. In this case, the D7 is often called the "five of the four chord." A DMaj7 chord is used prior to the D7 to create a chromatic descending baseline (D, C#, C, B). I use a couple of secondary dominants in sequence when moving from the B7 to E7 to A7 and eventually back to D. The B7 and E7 are both secondary dominants utilizing circle of fifths movement. One of my favorite examples of the use of secondary dominants is the B part of **The Down Home Waltz*.

My harmonization of **Southwind* presents a simple example of using major and minor chords to spruce up the tune. The tune easily could be played, and often is, with only major chords. Especially after playing it in hundreds (or thousands!?) of jams over the years, I have enjoyed using chord substitutions. I like to say that I am on a mission called "The Southwind Improvement Project" or SIP for short! I am not sure if I have improved it, but it sure is fun to shake things up with these alternate chords. I substitute in some minor chords, add in a suspension now and again, along with a very occasional use of a *secondary dominant* to strengthen the chord movement (the B7 moving to Em). I wouldn't use the B7 on my first pass of the tune, but just using it now and again can be a nice change of pace.

If any significant chunk of this discussion didn't make sense to you, I recommend learning about these chords, as they can be much fun and are super important in many types of music. You may not like all my choices, but I hope you will keep an open mind and try them! I am a big believer in understanding theory. At a minimum, you should know the chords formed in each of the big keys that you are mostly likely to play on the hammered dulcimer. Nearly equally important is to know how the most common modes (Dorian, Aeolian, Mixolydian) are formed, where they lay out on the dulcimer, and what chords are most likely to occur in each of these modes. It is simply too much material to cover in this book, but I expect to publish a book of music theory and backup for the hammered dulcimer – stay tuned!

(15.) Swing

In the written transcriptions for many types of tunes (fiddle tunes, waltzes), the eighth notes are evenly spaced. But, true to the traditions from which the tunes hail, we often add "swing." The amount of swing to add is up to the individual player and is often tune-specific and a subjective choice. Some tunes sound better with more and some with less swing. An easy way to think of swing is to slightly delay the count of "and" when counting "ONE and TWO and THREE and FOUR and". Writing out the tunes with a dotted rhythm would significantly overstate the swing and unnecessarily complicate the transcriptions. It is best to hear the tunes played to fully grasp how much to swing the tunes.

(16.) Accent shifts

To create surprises and greater interest in the phrasing of the music, a common technique is to move accents away from obvious counts. For example, when playing dance tunes in 4/4, we naturally feel the counts of "one" and "three". That is where most folks will tap and feel the rhythm. It is common practice among fiddlers to shift, at a minimum, to the "two" and "four" counts. Further accent shifts move to the counts of "and." In some of the transcriptions, I add accent marks to suggest moving accents away from the obvious counts. (See *Willafjord, Sail Away Ladies, *The Clock Waltz*.)

(17.) Additional rhythm ideas

I frequently include simple syncopations (see measure #17 in *Lonesome John*) and many more elaborate techniques to shift accents and create rhythmic interest. *Anticipations* are another commonly used variation in rhythm. Broadly defined, we anticipate a note when we arrive at the note earlier than it is expected or written. Typically, we might pull a note from the "one" count of a measure into the "four" count of the preceding measure. It is best understood when heard or written (see measure #18 of *Lonesome John*).

Another effective idea is to play three notes in one hand against two notes in the other – or alternately

* *MB30441 "The Sandbridge Waltz and Slow Air Collection"*

four against three. A common method to execute this idea is for one hand to play a constant rhythm while the other hand does not (see measures #29-31 in *The Silver and Gold Two Step* and the second B part in *Cuckoo's Nest: arranging ideas*).

Many rhythm ideas are largely unique to certain types or styles of tunes. For example, there is a moveable accent pattern common in Québécois (French Canadian) music that is much fun. (See measure #21 in *Carnaval: arranging ideas* and measures #11-12 in *Frenchie's: arranging ideas*.) But I will sometimes borrow the idea and use it in other styles of music as well.

There are some tunes that I included because they are almost exclusively focused on establishing a groove and exploiting rhythm ideas, and of course I like playing them. (See *Snowdrops and Sail Away Ladies*.) In many tunes, I will insert an accent shift pattern that is a central defining idea in rags. Thus, I call it, not surprisingly, a *rag rhythm*. (See its use in multiple measures in *Snowdrops*, *Lonesome John* and *Sail Away Ladies*.) Since swing, groove and rhythm are so vital to fiddle tunes, most of the fiddle tunes in this volume include techniques that exploit rhythm. (Some examples include *Carnaval*, *Frenchie's*, *The Silver and Gold Two-Step*, *Sail Away Ladies*, *Snow Drop*, and *Lonesome John*.)

(18.) Borrowing from backup

I can't begin to tackle the vast subject of backup here. In quite a number of the transcriptions, I have included suggested backup ideas. Backup is perhaps my favorite area of exploration in music because it can be so creative, largely operating in the spheres of rhythm and chords. One of the great fringe benefits of working out a range of backup ideas is that living in the chords and the rhythm of the tune greatly informs the playing of the lead, especially in improvisation. For example, there are many *vamps* that I use when playing backup. One of the nice benefits of learning a backup is that I often borrow from my backup ideas and vamps to incorporate them into the tune. I sometimes replace the melody using an entire measure of what was essentially a backup or a vamp. This is tricky business, but it is much fun!

(19.) Dynamics

To keep the writing as simple as possible, I chose not to include any dynamic markings. But dynamics are hugely important to me and warrant some discussion. While I recognize it is generally necessary to first get the mechanics of playing a tune and executing the many techniques available in these transcriptions, I recommend first mastering the melody simply, and focus on shaping the piece dynamically before adding embellishments. A tune such as *Washington's Hornpipe* can be quite beautifully played with no embellishments.

Perhaps the bigger question concerns where or how to find dynamics. The common response that "you just have to feel it" is probably not all that helpful. While "feeling" or emotion is certainly vital to creating dynamics, we can create a *dynamic* line by carefully examining both the *melodic line* and *harmony line* or *bass line* in the music. For example, a slowly ascending line in the melody may suggest a crescendo (or decrescendo). Alternately, a repeated melodic section might have a falling or rising bass line which can be exploited to build and diminish in volume. A repeating note or phrase might suggest a dynamic "echo." Or perhaps an echo phrasing might be explored in two measure phrases. Even if you are at first not inspired to find dynamics through the emotion of the piece, there is an endless supply of ideas suggested by examining both the melody and the bass line.

Interestingly, I find that the act of practicing dynamics often results in finding the emotion of the piece which in turn substantially increases your ability to find and express dynamics. Ultimately, I strive to vary my dynamics and keep exploring new ways to play a piece. I did not indicate any dynamic markings and have left that up to you to decide what sounds best.

(20.) Combining, varying ideas and improvisation

You will see many examples where I have combined ideas in a single measure. Some examples include: combining a valley roll with a fill; inserting a valley roll "inside" a three-note chord; or combining a melodic run with an arpeggio fill. And of course, throughout a piece, I often vary my playing by pulling in many ideas from the tool chest. This brings me to improvisation, another topic which is way too big to address here. In performance, many of my "arrangements" are in part or sometimes almost completely improvised. In the sections above, I have identified many ideas that one can incorporate to create spontaneous arrangements on the fly. But there is more and this gets a bit philosophical. I like to think that I truly know a piece of music when I can hear and see simultaneously the melody, the chord progression (and chord substitutions), bass line(s), harmony, backup, and the anchors of the tune. This is clearly a lot of information to keep in your head at once. I try to practice all the elements of the puzzle (i.e. practice the melody, a couple of backups, a harmony, variations, and counter melody). In so doing, I strive to connect all of those pieces to see the big picture of a piece of music and fully understand it. It is not for everyone but it works for me.

I hope you enjoy the tunes!

Are You Sleeping Maggie

Scotland: Arranged by © Ken Kolodner

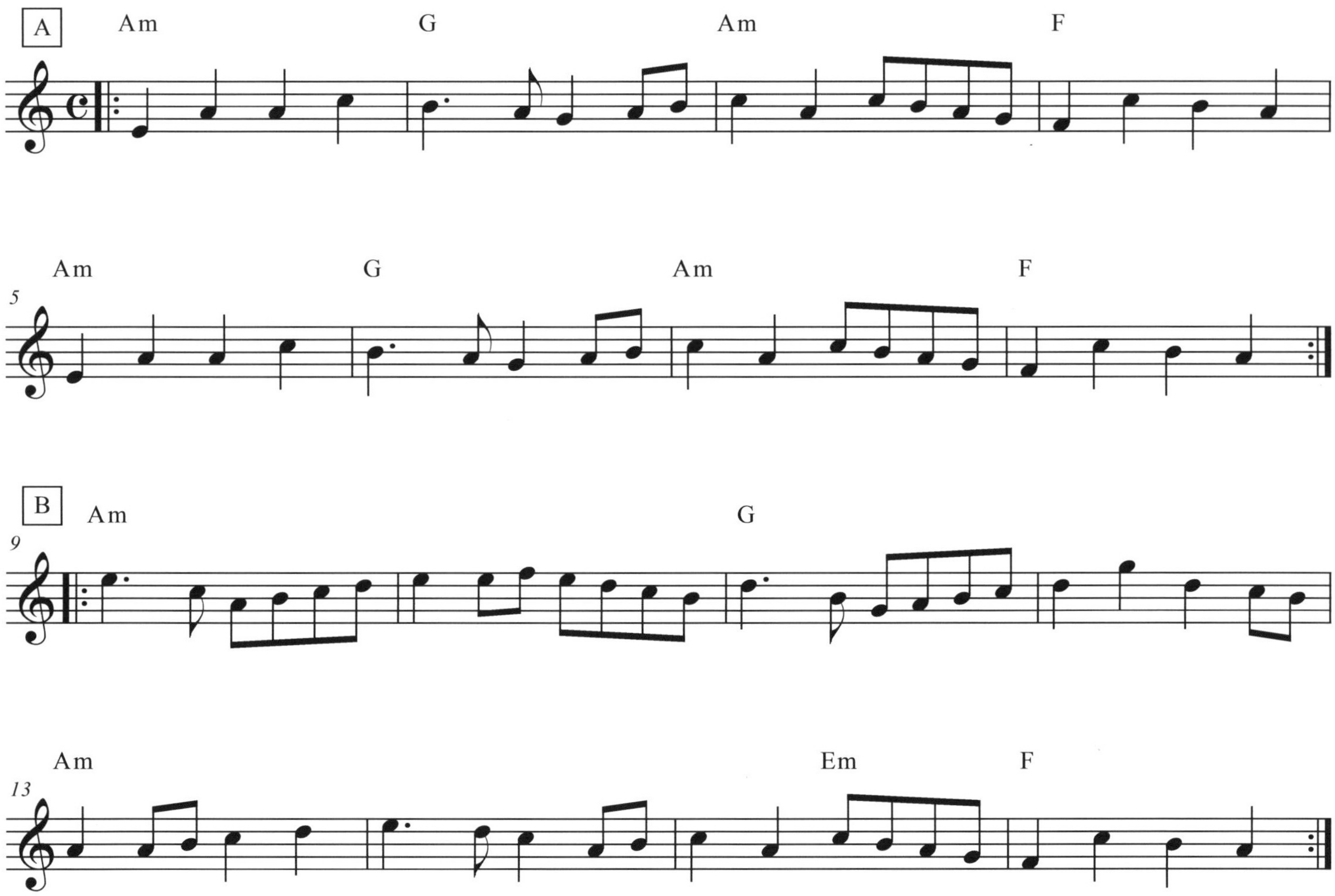

Are You Sleeping Maggie: arrangement

Scotland: Arranged by © Ken Kolodner

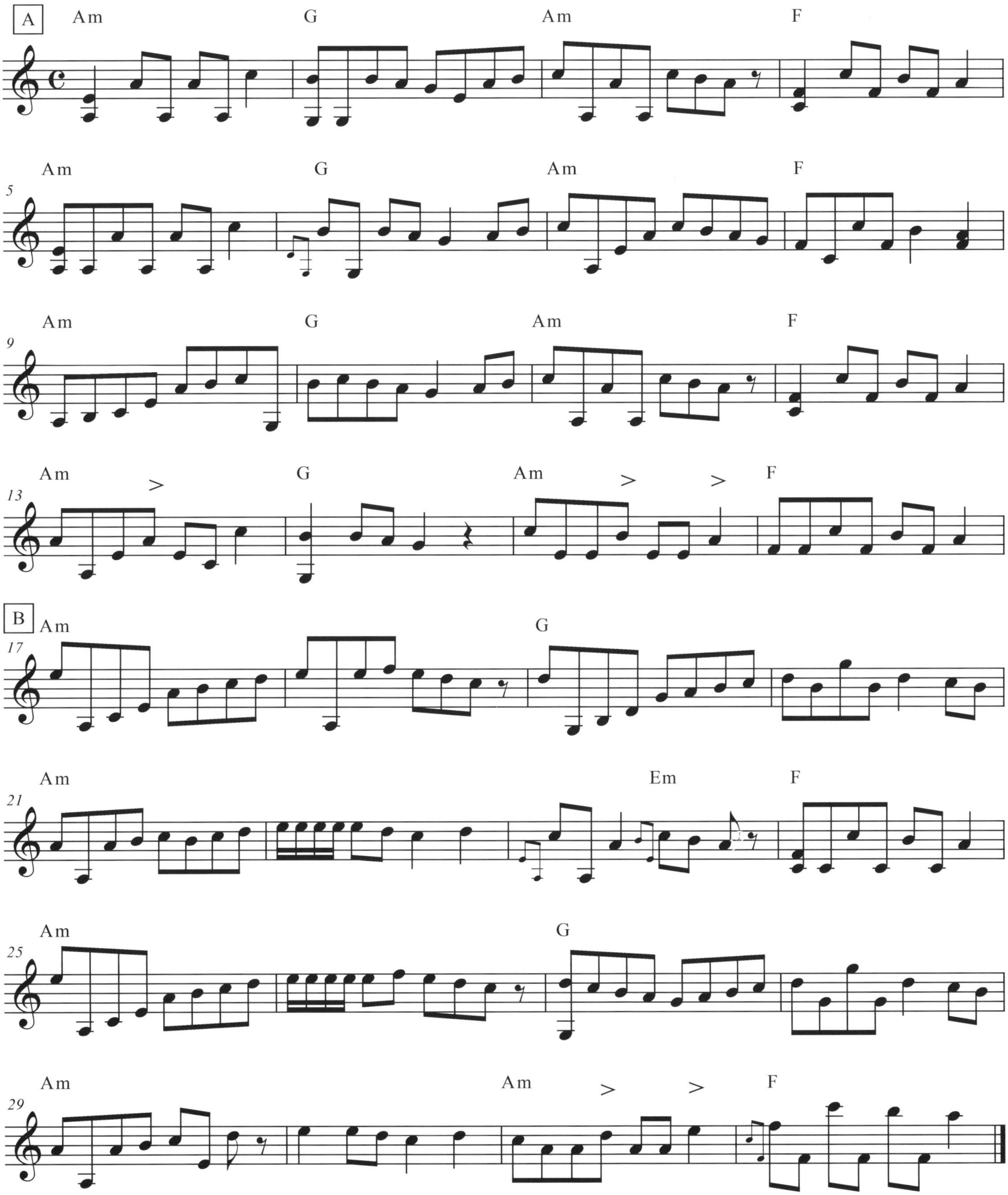

Beaumont Rag

Originally in F

U.S.: Arranged by © Ken Kolodner

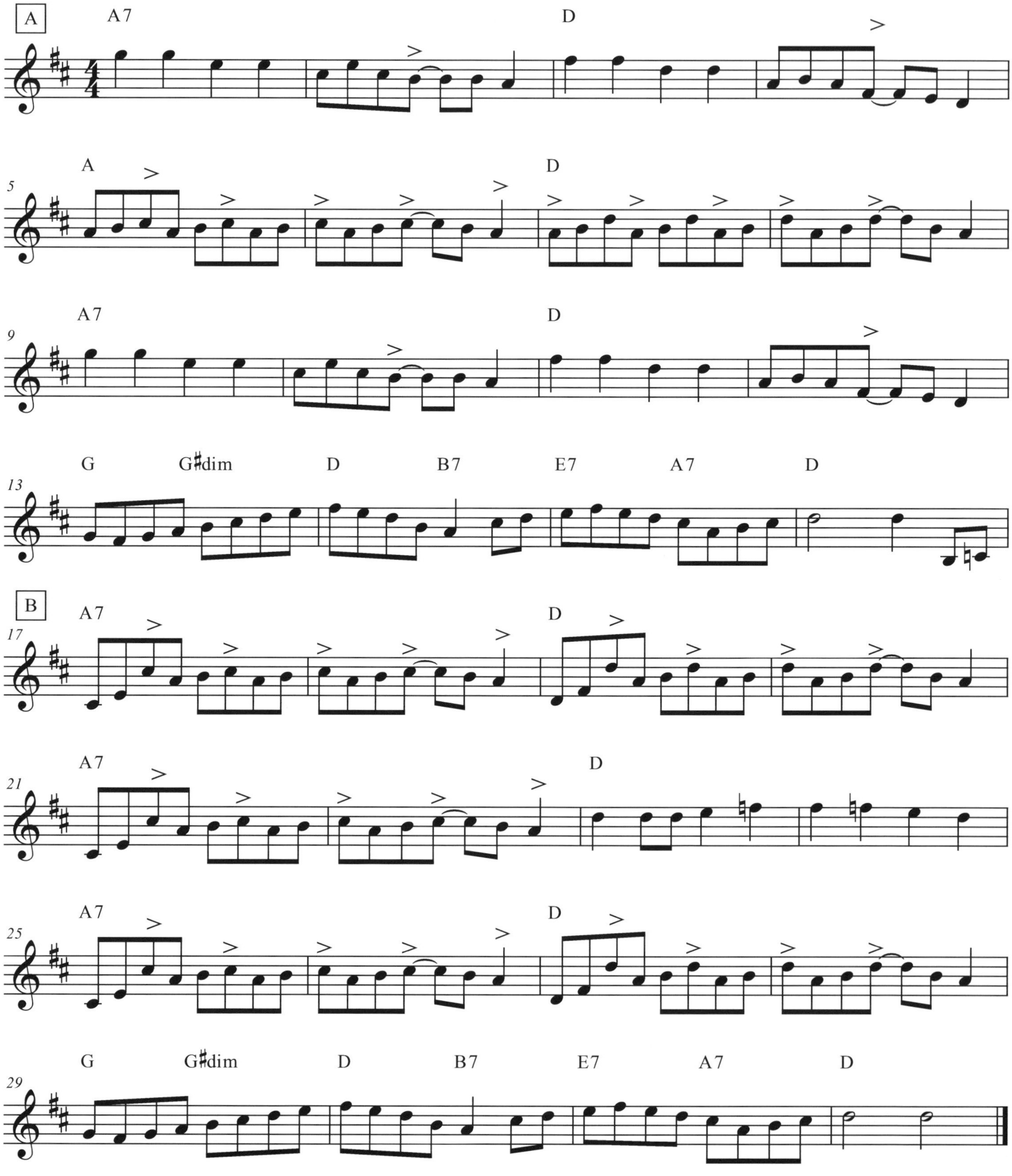

Beaumont Rag: arranging ideas

Originally in F

U.S.: Arranged by © Ken Kolodner

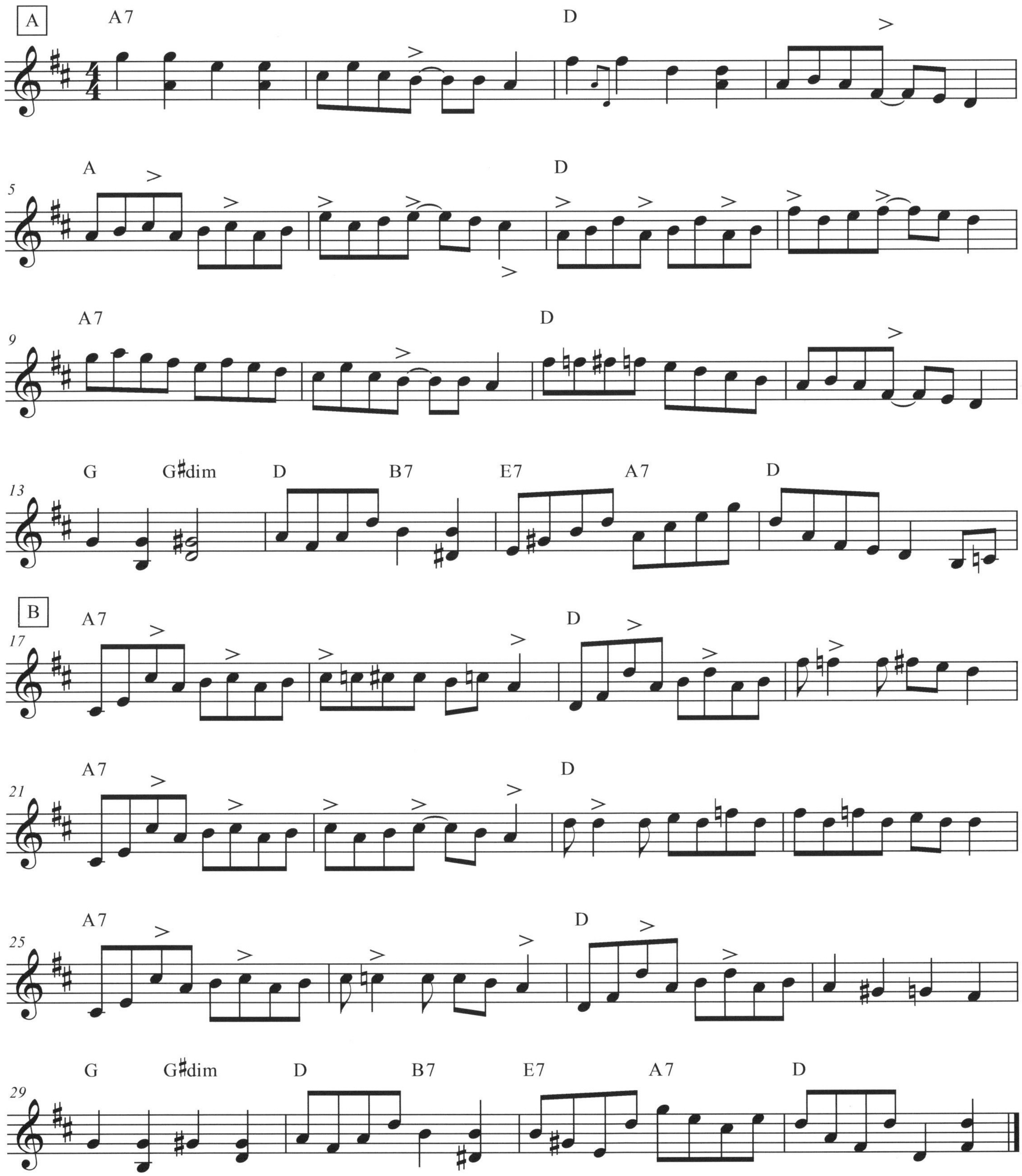

Big Scioty with accompaniment

Recorded on Brad and Ken Kolodner's "Otter Creek" (2011)

U.S.: Arranged by © Ken Kolodner

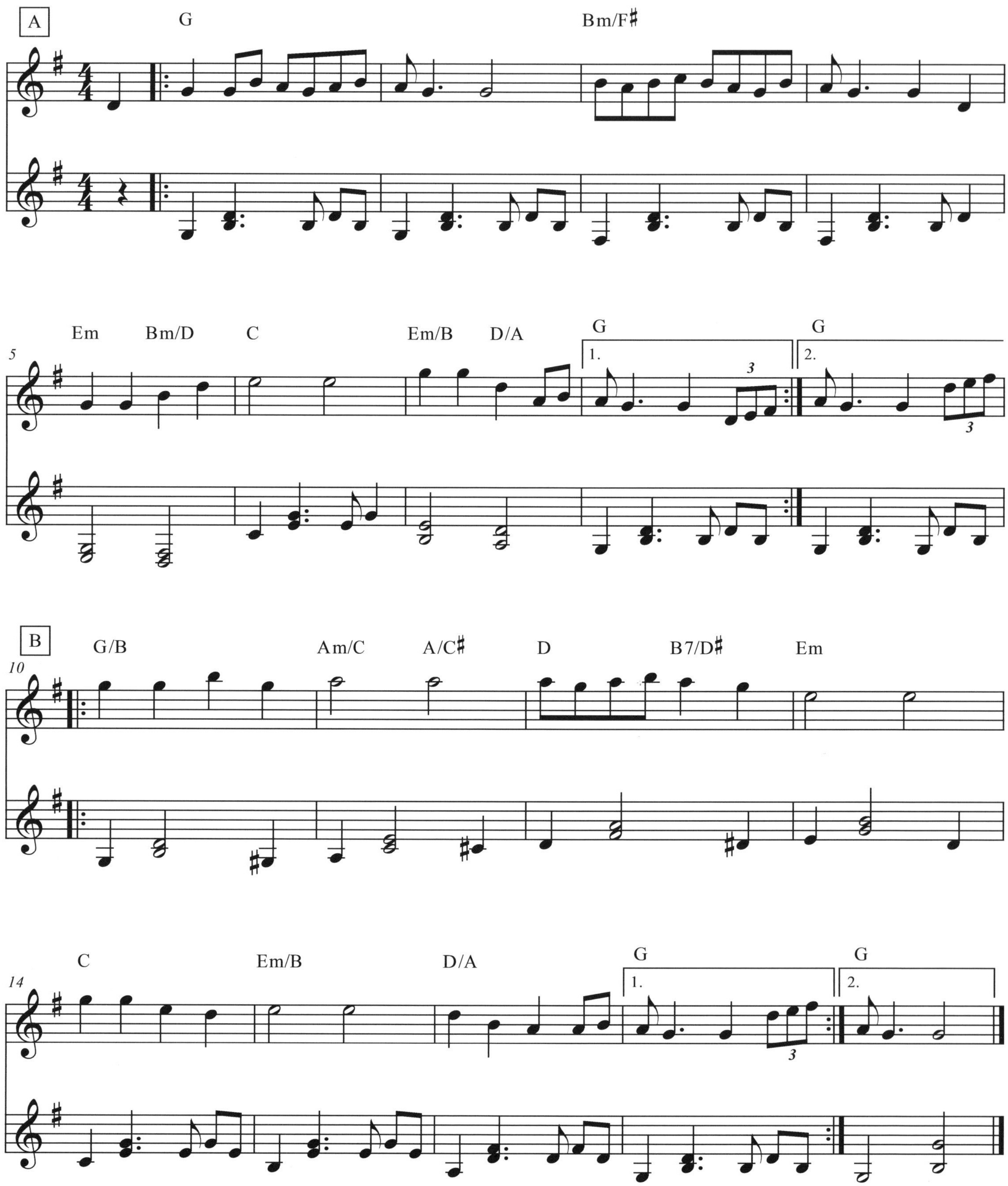

This chord progression is definitely not what is commonly played. But it is a lot of fun.

Big Scioty: arranging ideas

Recorded on Brad and Ken Kolodner's "Otter Creek" (2011)

U.S.: Arranged by © Ken Kolodner

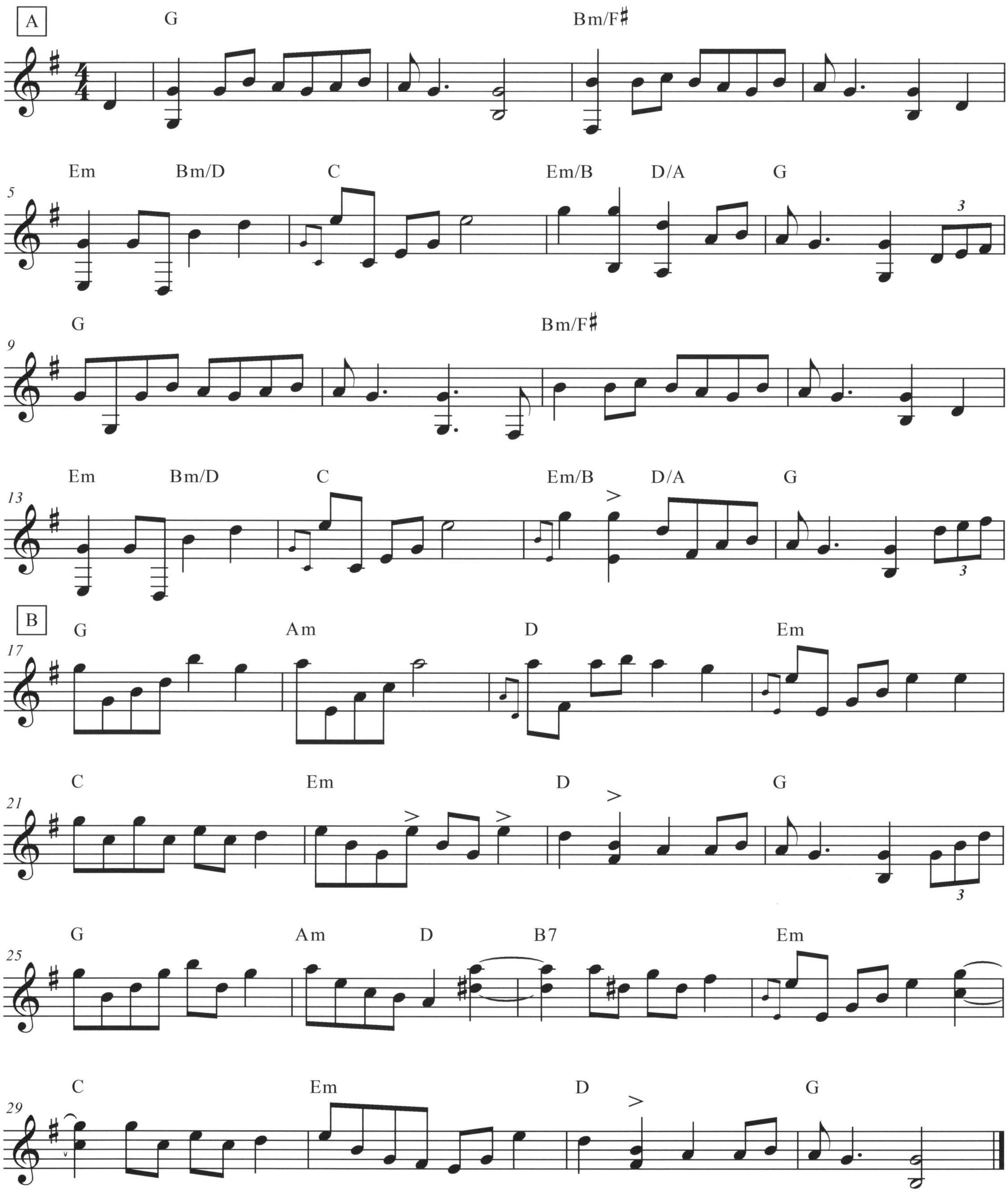

Bill Cheatham

Recorded on Helicon's "Helicon" (1987) with Ken Kolodner, Chris Norman, Robin Bullock

U.S.: Arranged by © Ken Kolodner

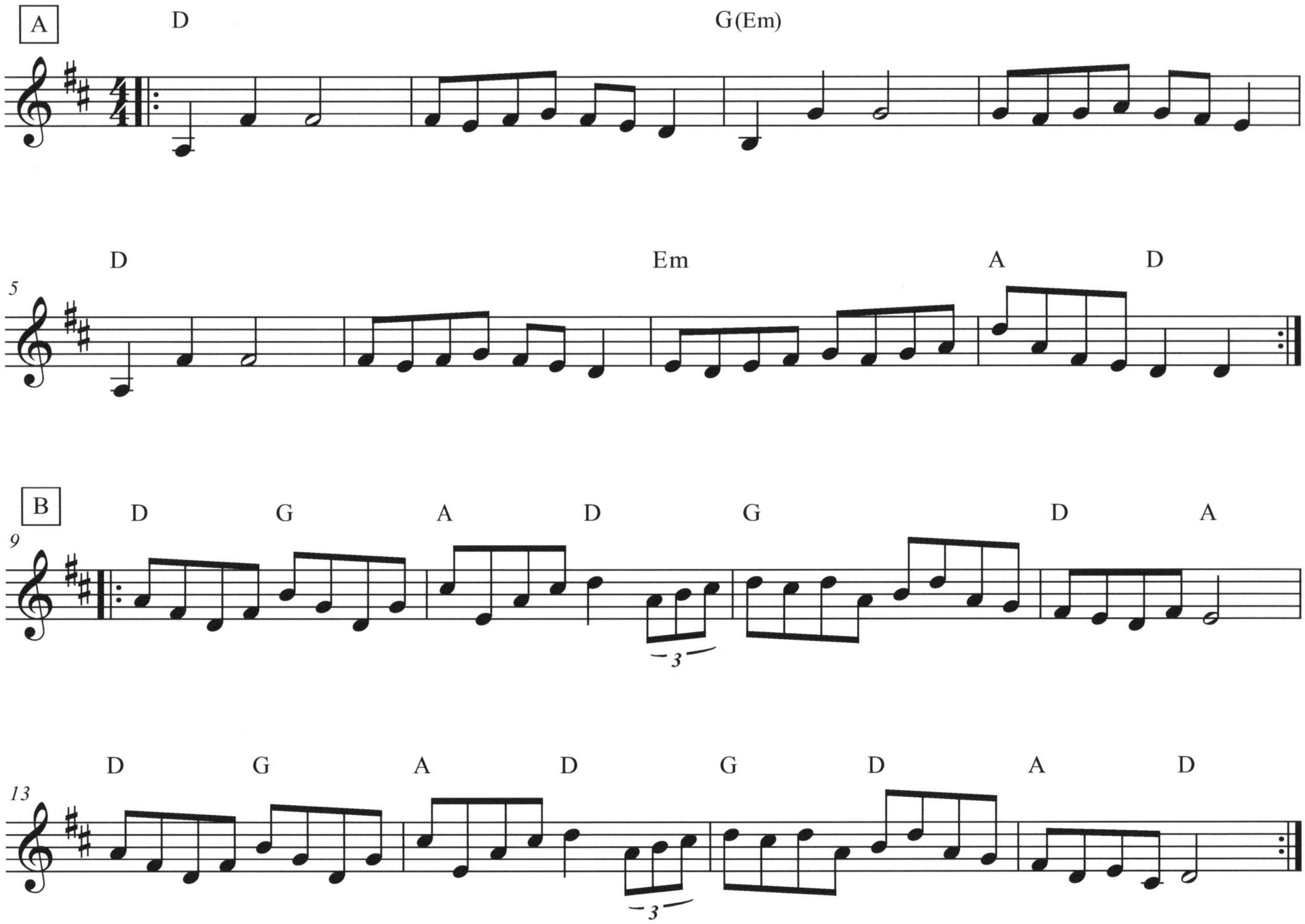

Bill Cheatham: arranging ideas

Recorded on Helicon's "Helicon" (1987) with
Ken Kolodner, Chris Norman and Robin Bullock

U.S.: Arranged by © Ken Kolodner

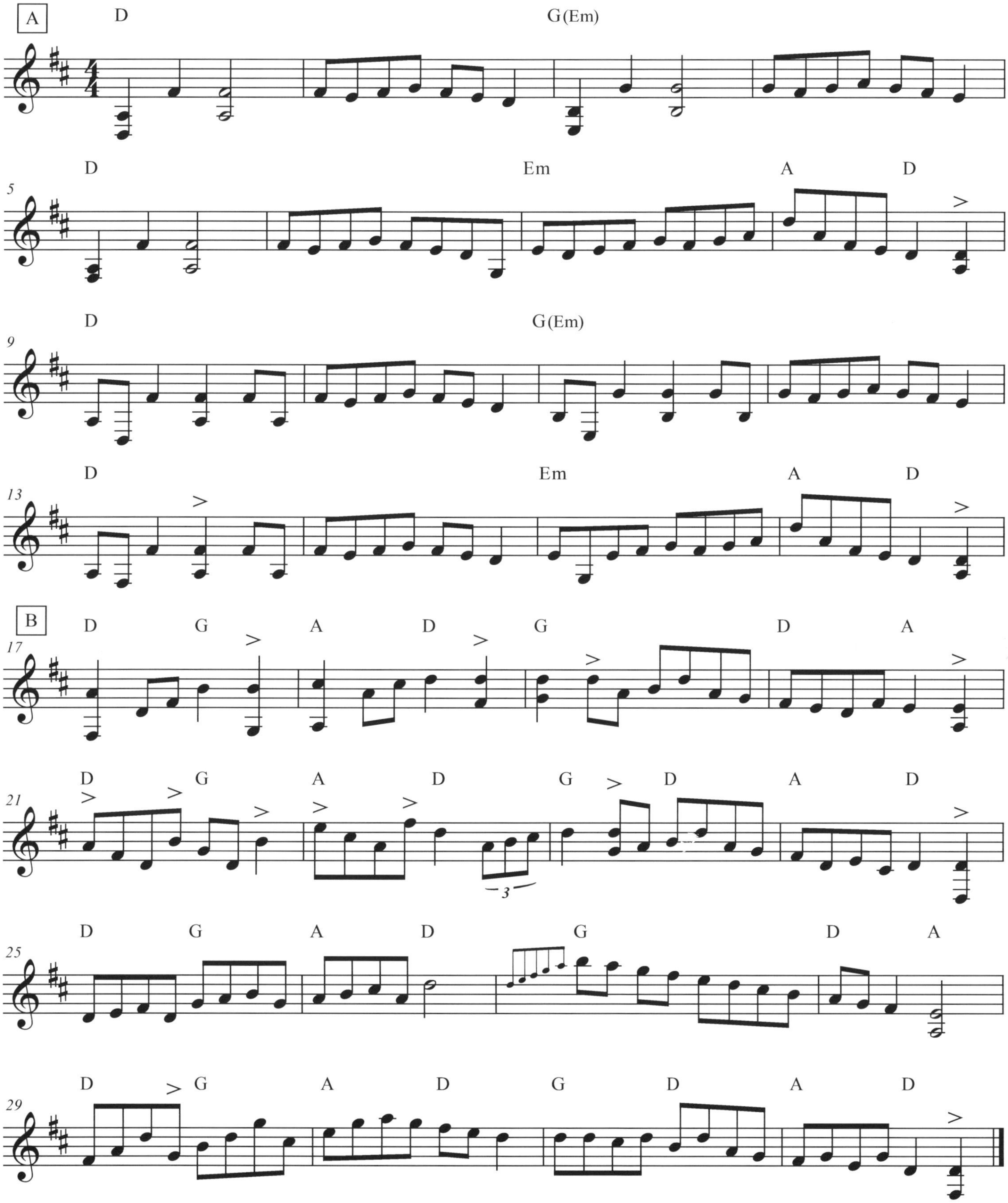

Billy in the Lowground: melody, accompaniment

Recorded on Brad and Ken Kolodner's "Skipping Rocks" (2013)

U.S.: Arranged by © Ken Kolodner

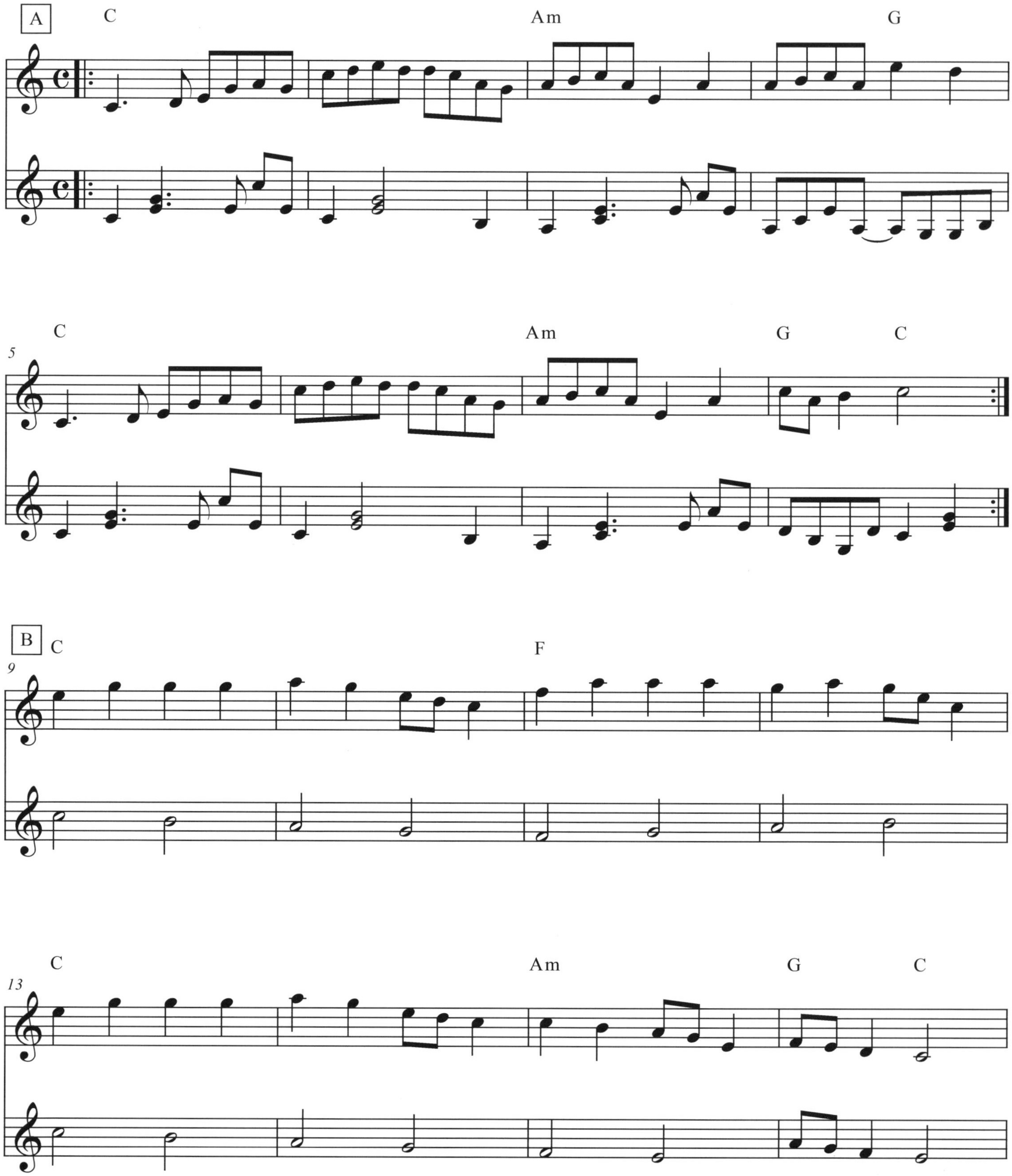

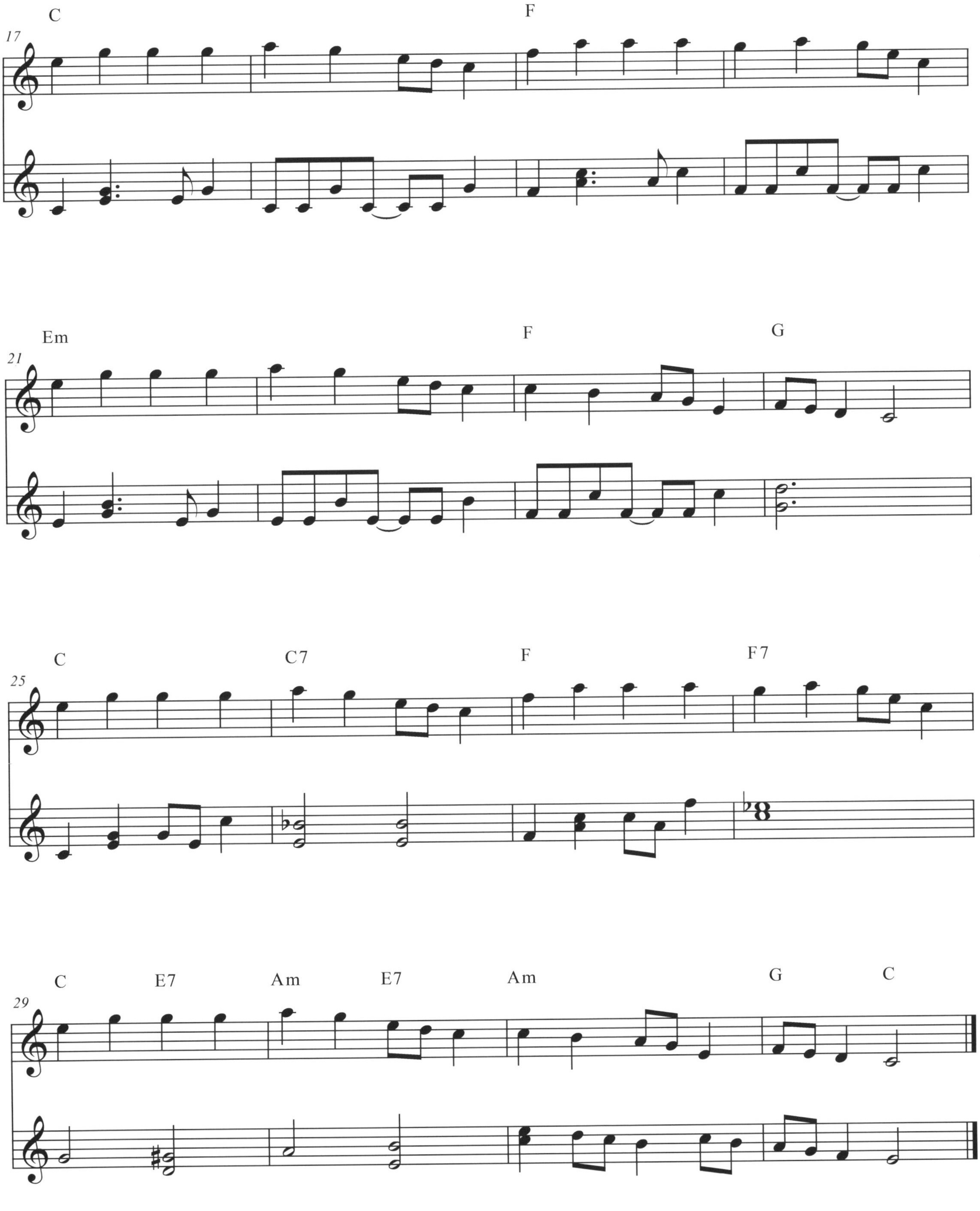

I have repeated the B part three times to accommodate three alternate chord progressions.

Billy in the Lowground: variations

Recorded on Brad and Ken Kolodner's "Skipping Rocks" (2013)

U.S.: Arranged by © Ken Kolodner

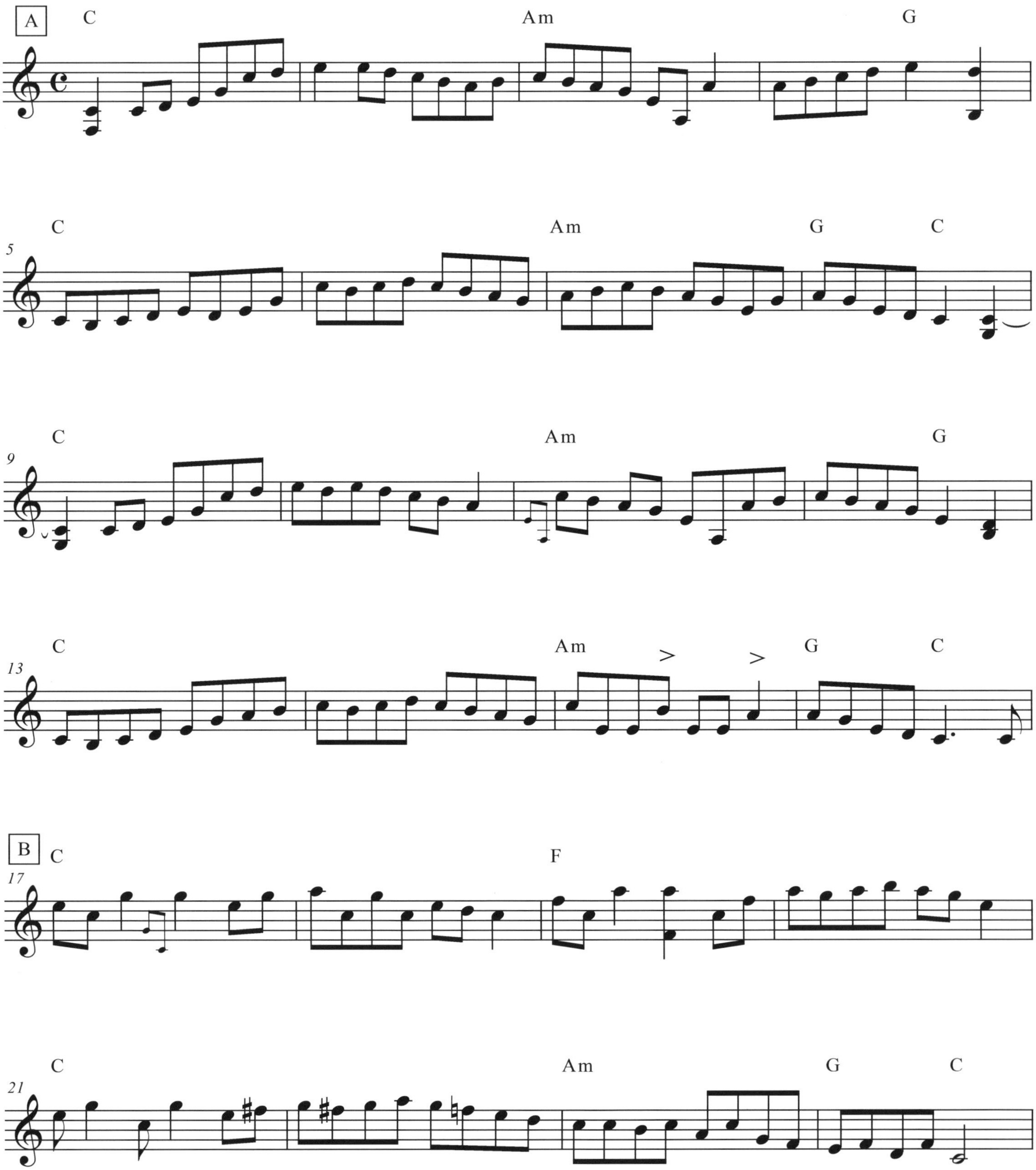

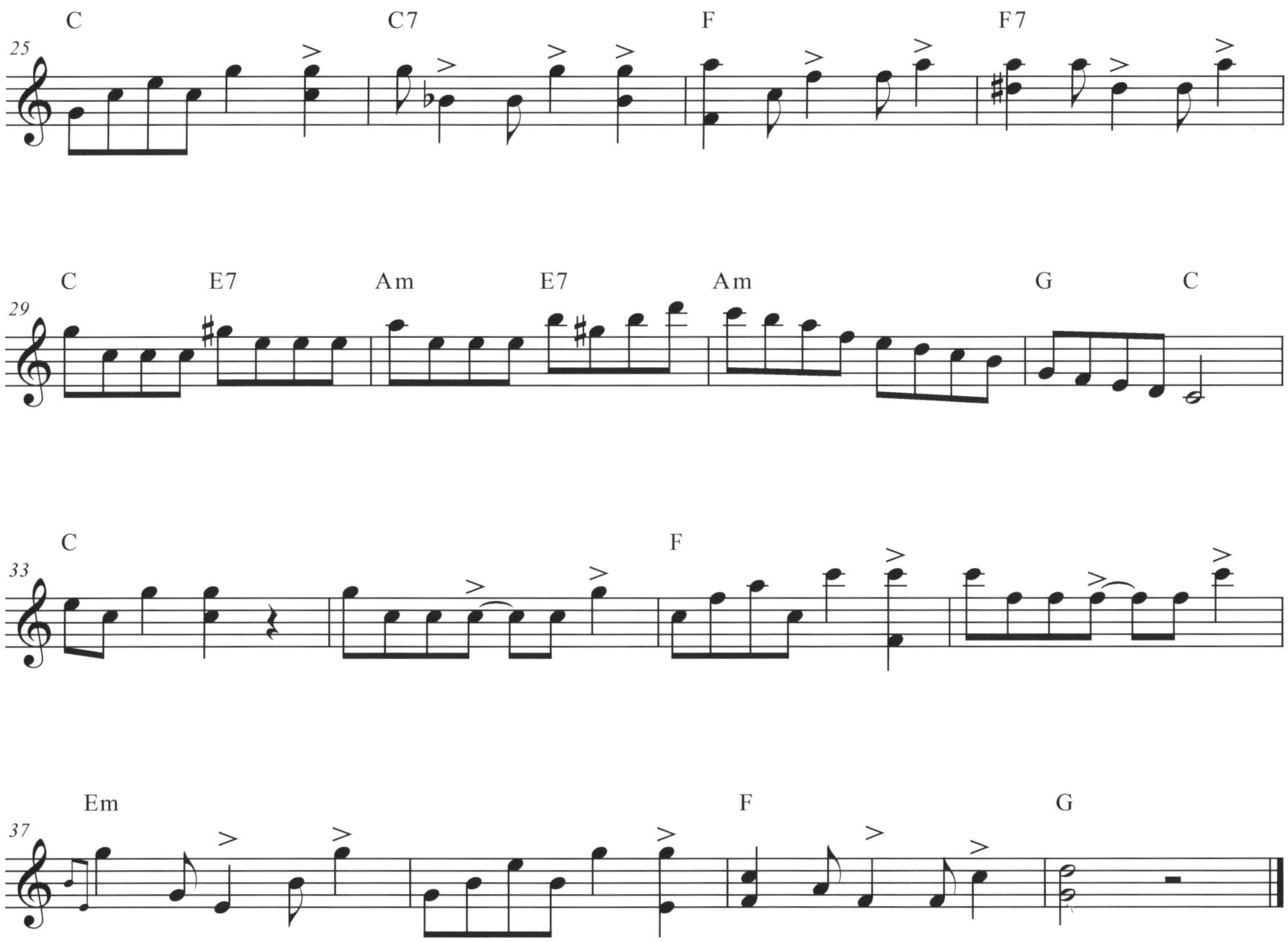

This is admittedly an unusual take on this standard in Bluegrass and Old-Time circles. Most notably are the chord substitutions in the B part. I have repeated the B part a third time to accommodate the three alternate chord progressions. The third B part ending on the G chord is not resolved and should only be used when playing through the tune once more. Keep an open mind!

The Black Nag

England: Arranged by © Ken Kolodner

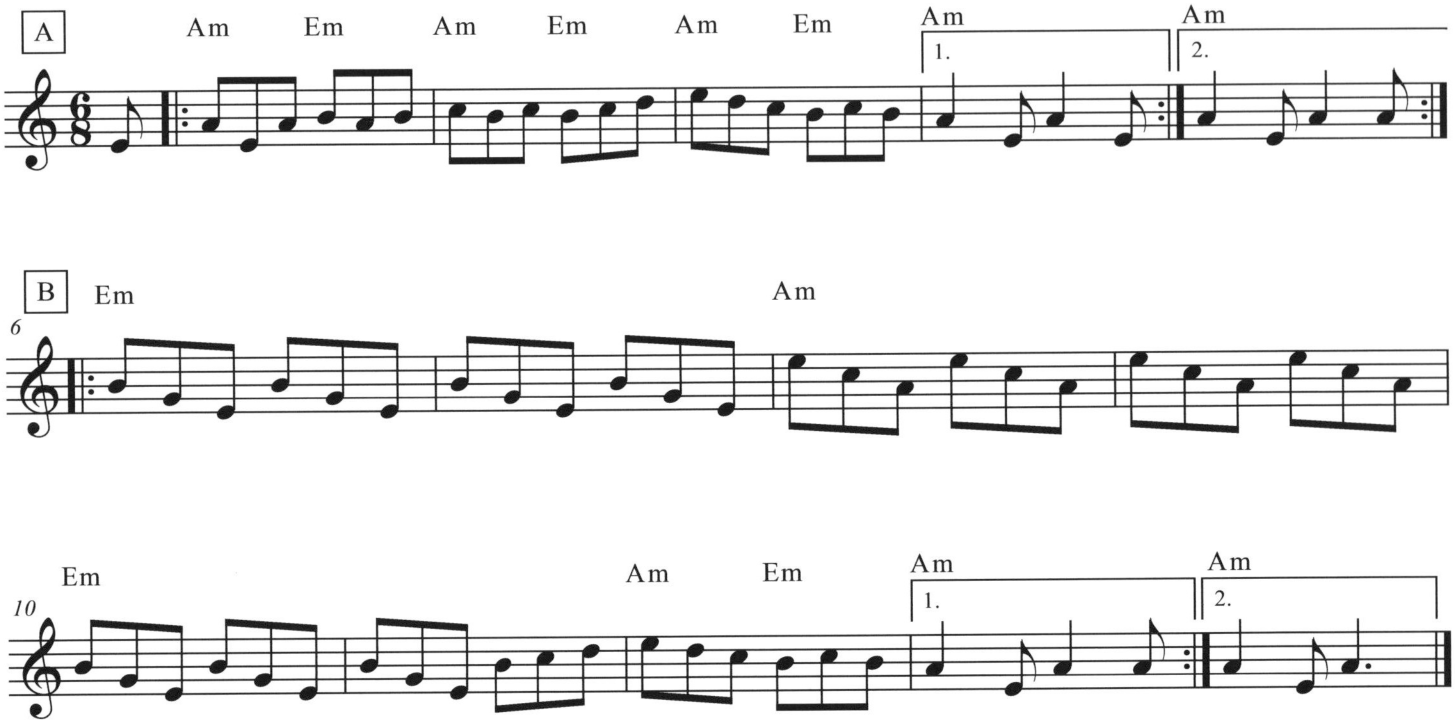

Try starting with the right hand and alternate. Play the entire tune on the right treble bridge. You may also be able to play the entire tune one octave up on the left treble bridge and play the entire tune on your bass bridge.

The Black Nag: variations

England: Arranged by © Ken Kolodner

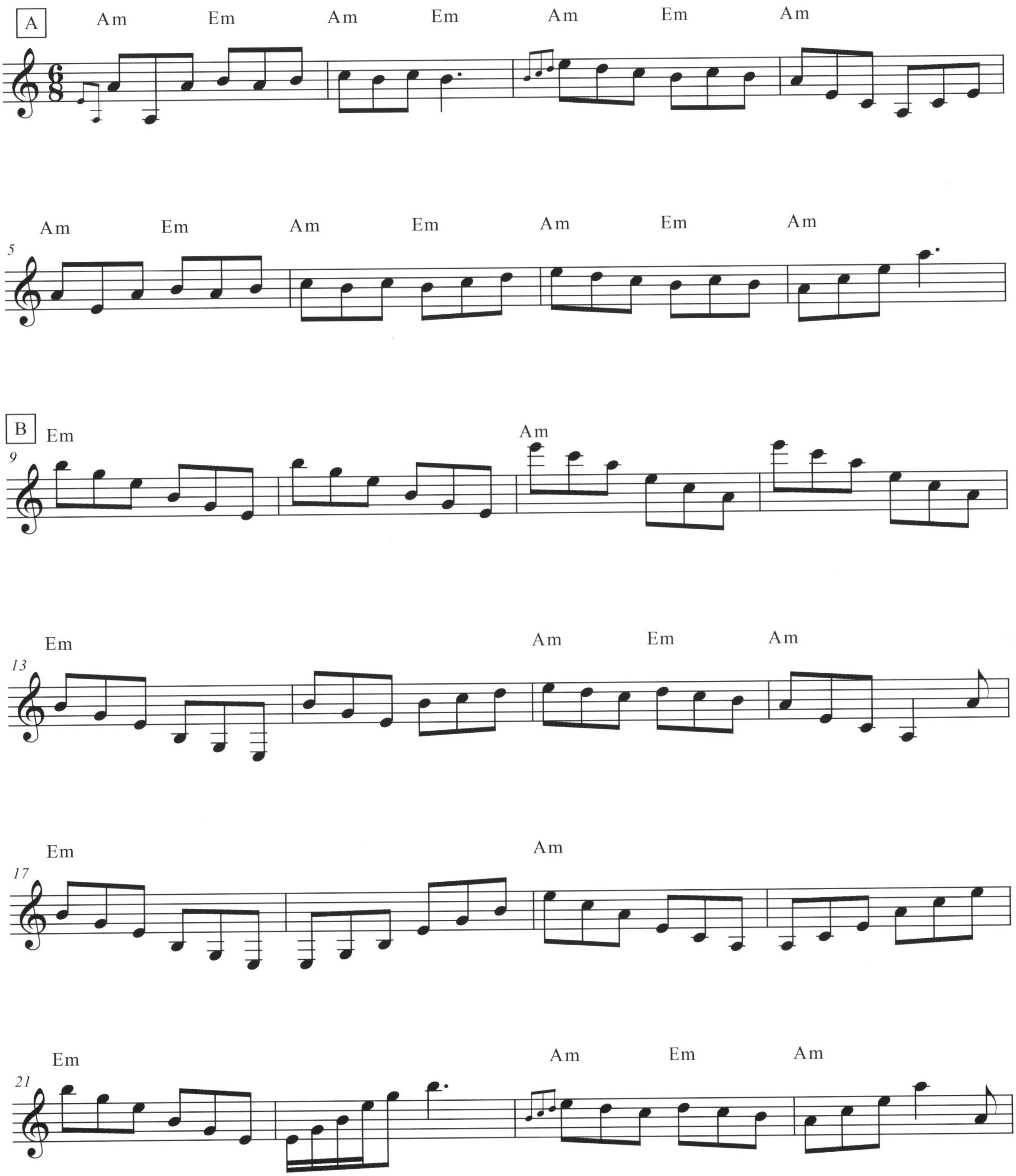

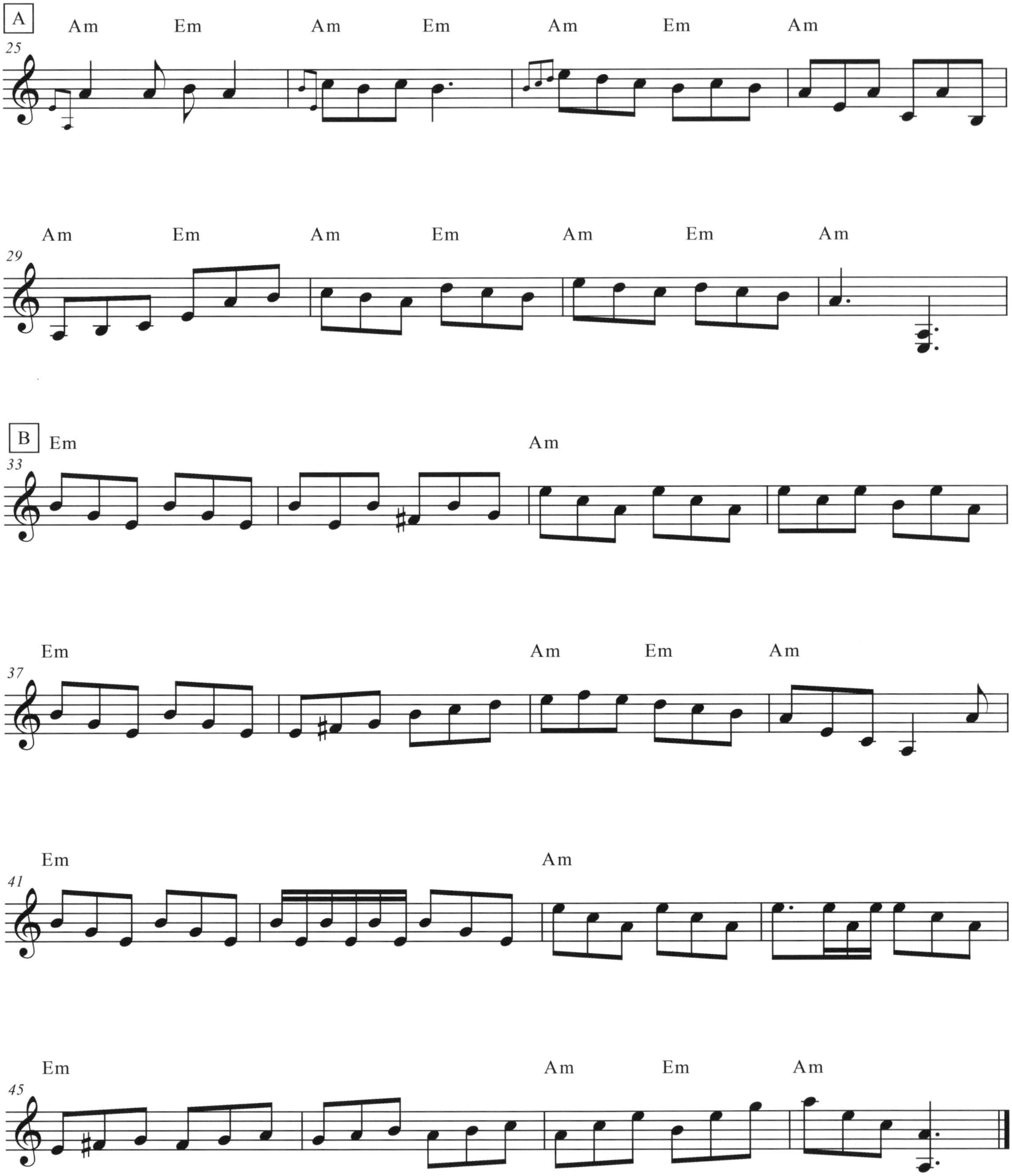
A
Am Em Am Em Am Em Am
25
Am Em Am Em Am Em Am
29
B
Em Am
33
Em Am Em Am
37
Em Am
41
Em Am Em Am
45

Carnaval ("Beatrice")

Recorded on Ken Kolodner and Elke Baker's "Out of the Wood" (2011)

Quebec: Arranged by © Ken Kolodner

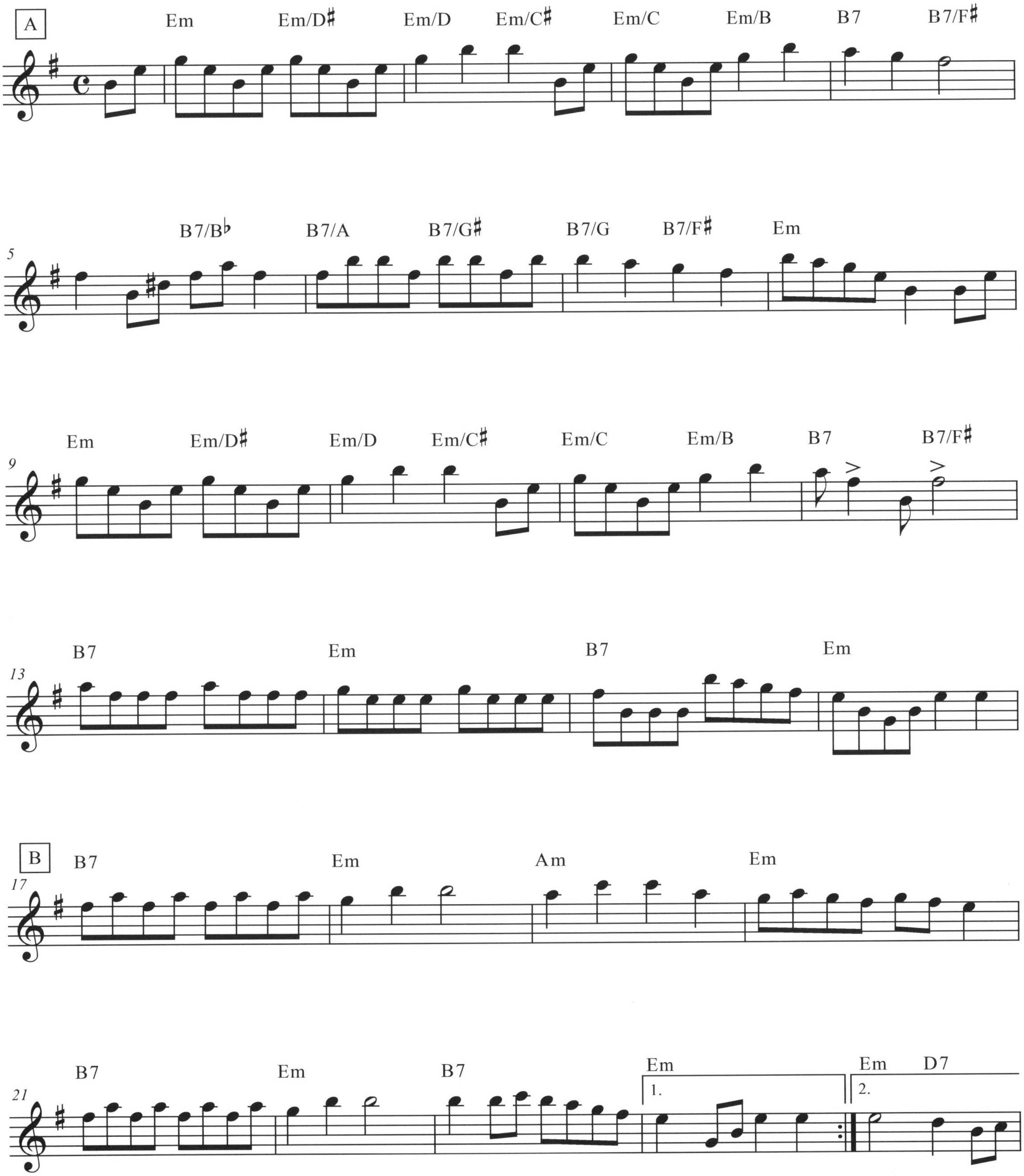

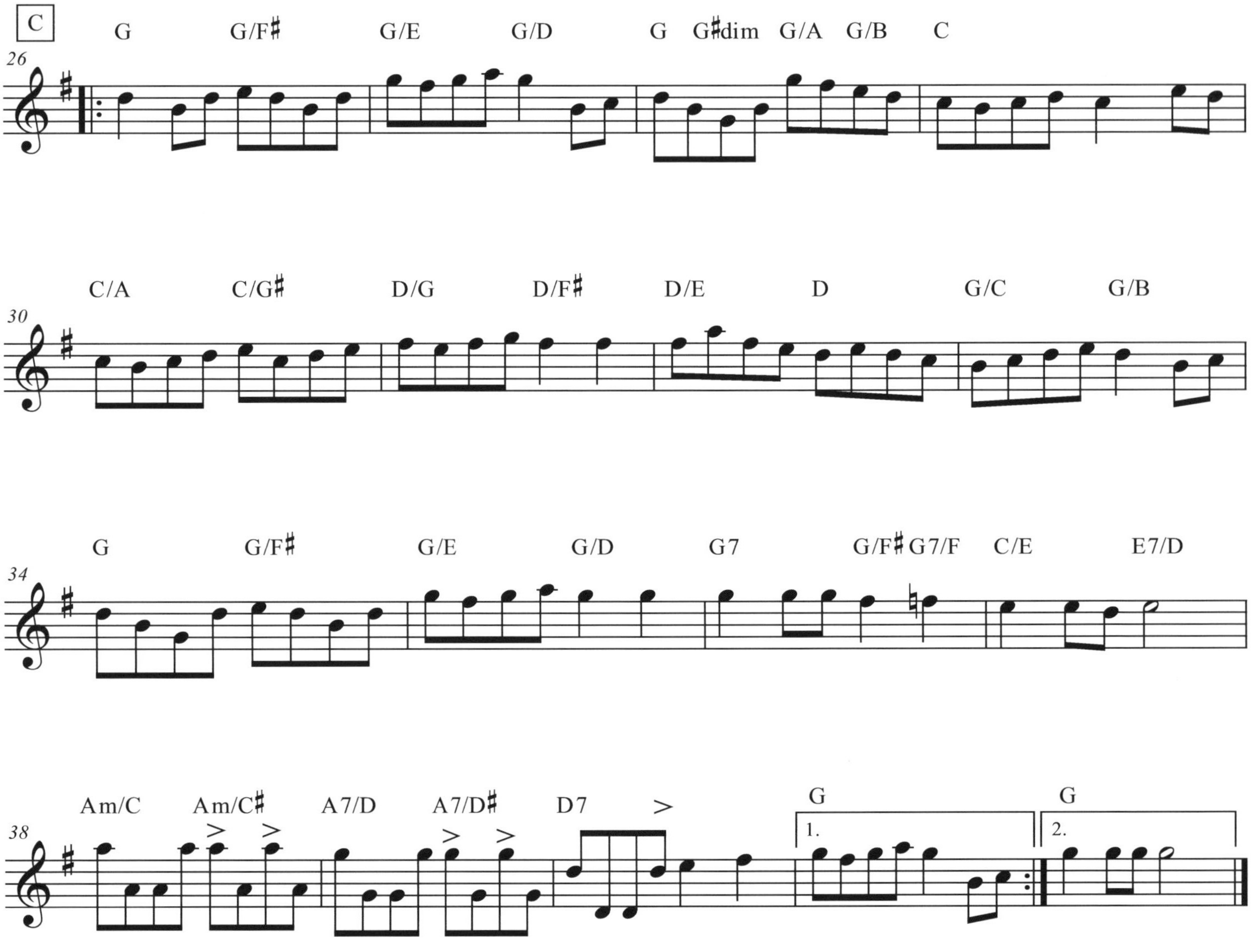
C
G G/F♯ G/E G/D G G♯dim G/A G/B C
C/A C/G♯ D/G D/F♯ D/E D G/C G/B
G G/F♯ G/E G/D G7 G/F♯ G7/F C/E E7/D
Am/C Am/C♯ A7/D A7/D♯ D7 G G
1.
2.

Carnaval ("Beatrice"): variations and accompaniment

Recorded on Ken Kolodner and Elke Baker's "Out of the Wood" (2011) with Eric Eid-Reiner

Quebec: Arranged by © Ken Kolodner

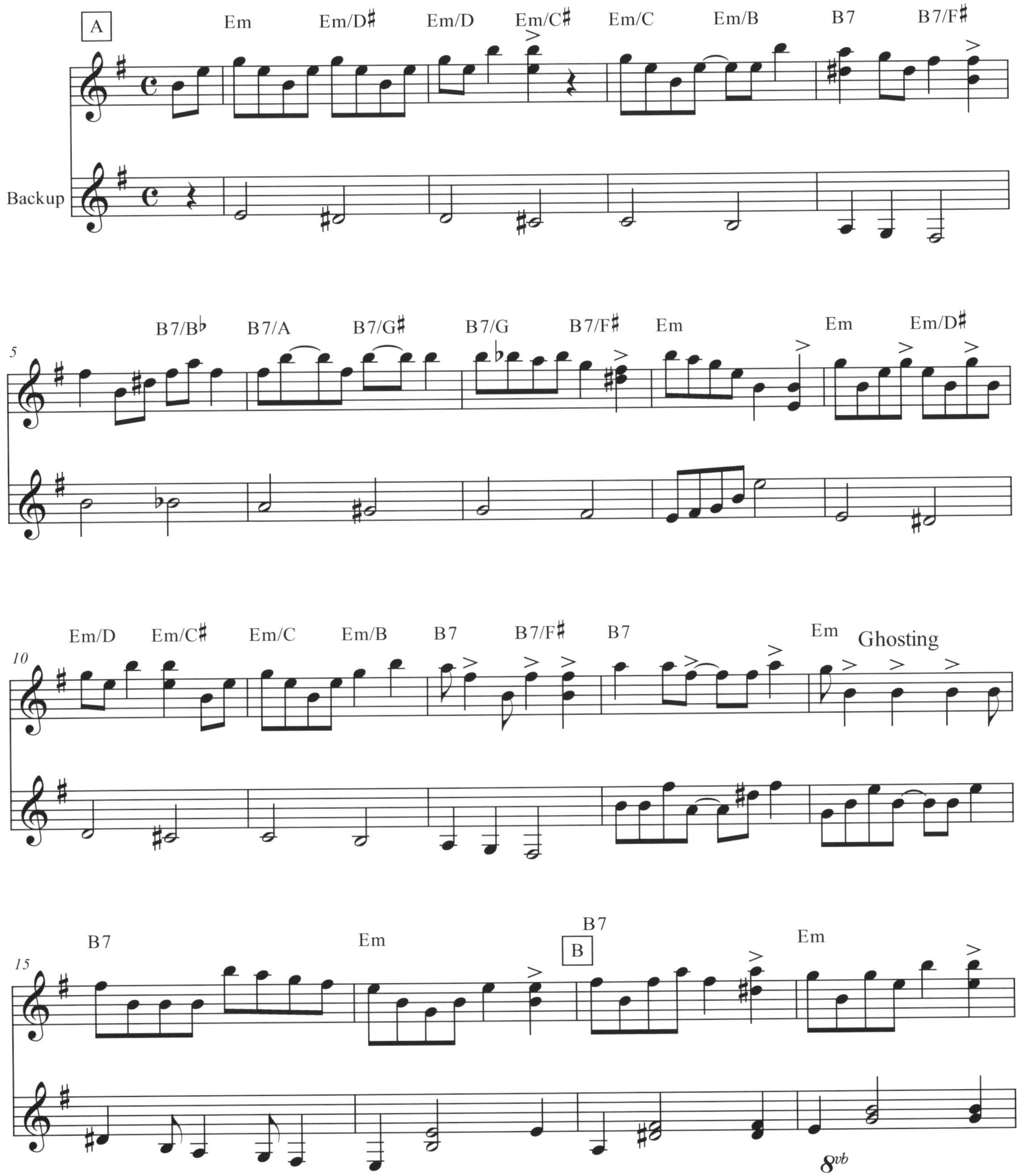

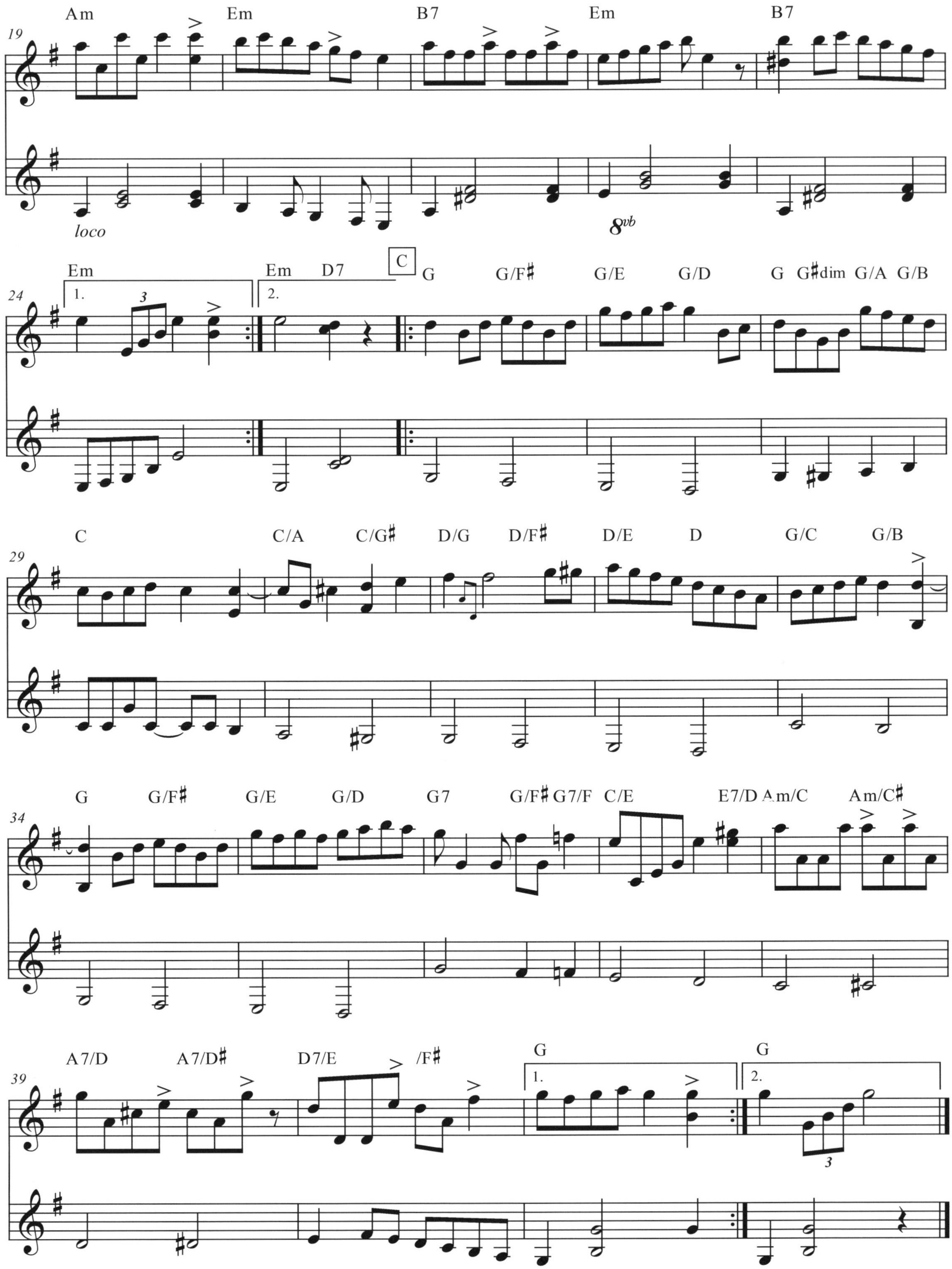
Am
Em
B7
Em
B7
loco
8vb
Em
1.
Em D7
2.
C
G
G/F♯
G/E
G/D
G G♯dim G/A G/B
C
C/A
C/G♯
D/G
D/F♯
D/E
D
G/C
G/B
G
G/F♯
G/E
G/D
G7
G/F♯ G7/F
C/E
E7/D Am/C
Am/C♯
A7/D
A7/D♯
D7/E
/F♯
G
1.
G
2.

Cuckoo's Nest: melody and accompaniment

Recorded on Ken Kolodner's "Walking Stones" (1997, re-released 2006) with Laura Risk & Robin Bullock and on "Hammered Dulcimer Arrangements: Reels Volume II" (2005)

Ireland/Scotland/U.S.: Arranged by © Ken Kolodner

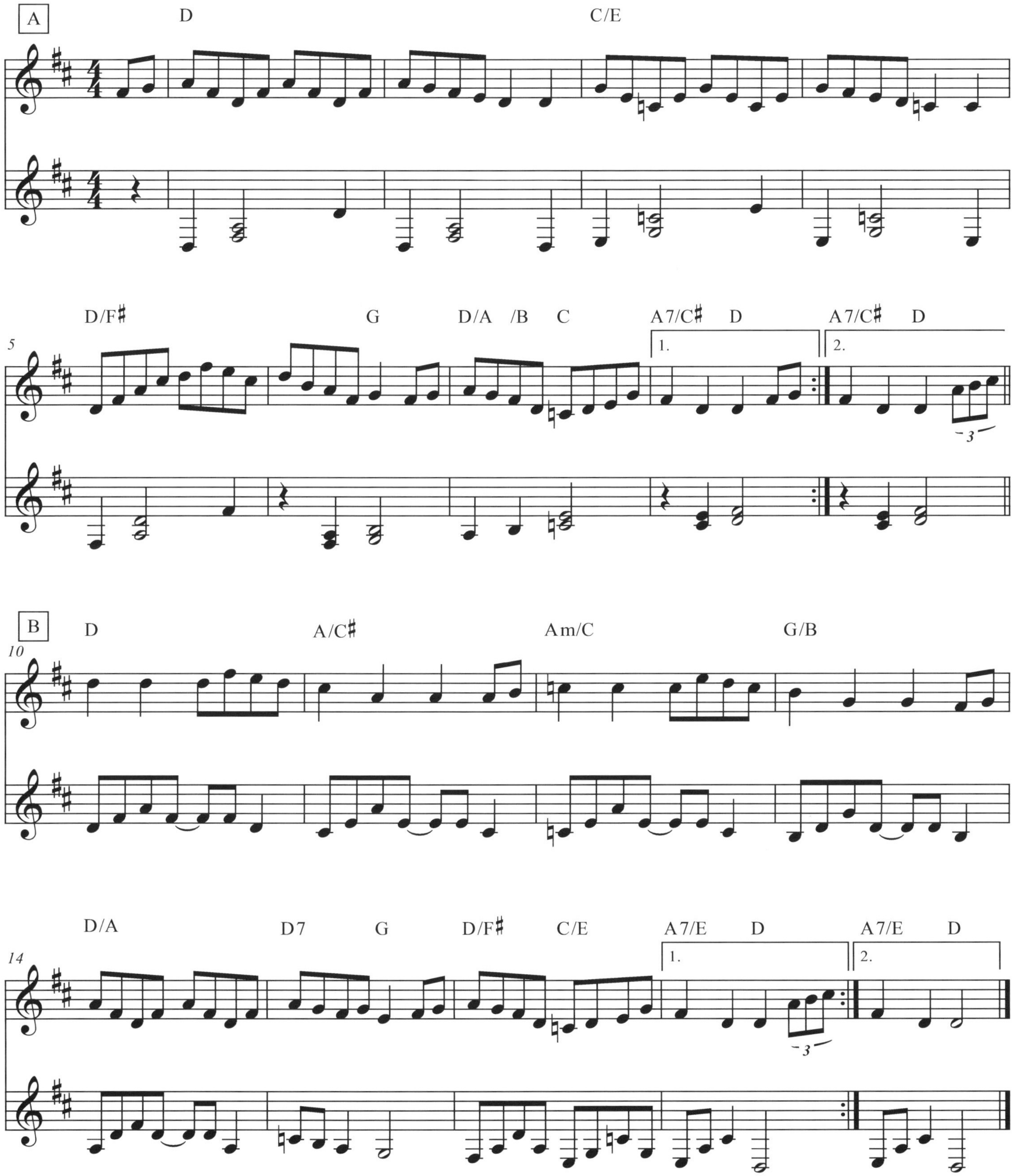

Cuckoo's Nest: arranging ideas

Recorded on Ken Kolodner's "Walking Stones" (1997, re-released 2006) with Laura Risk & Robin Bullock and on "Hammered Dulcimer Arrangements: Reels Volume II" (2005)

Ireland/Scotland/U.S.: Arranged by © Ken Kolodner

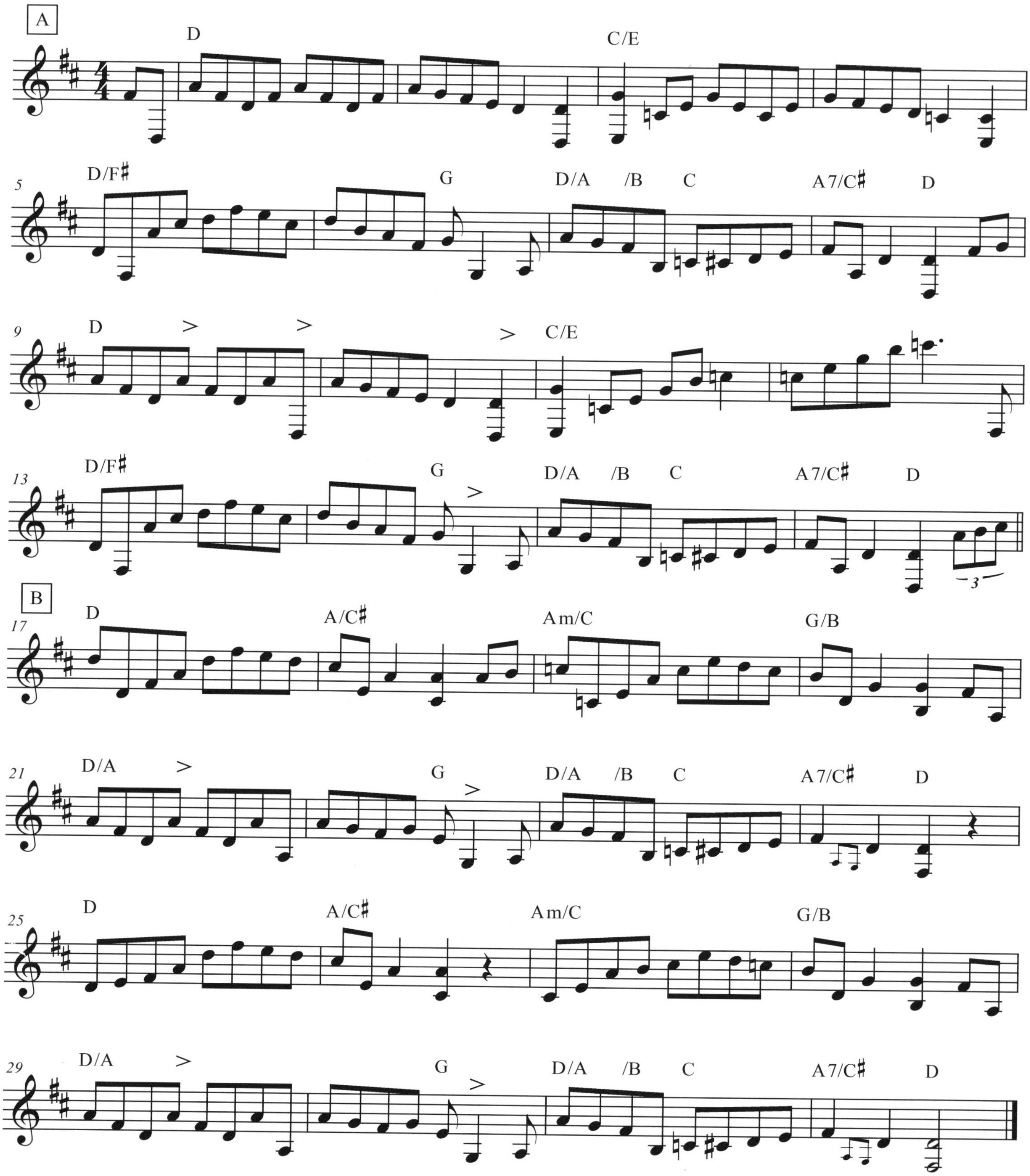

The bass line in the B part can continue to descend through the entire line or it can be reversed to rise, for example, as is presented at the end of the part.

Cumberland Gap

U.S.: Arranged by © Ken Kolodner

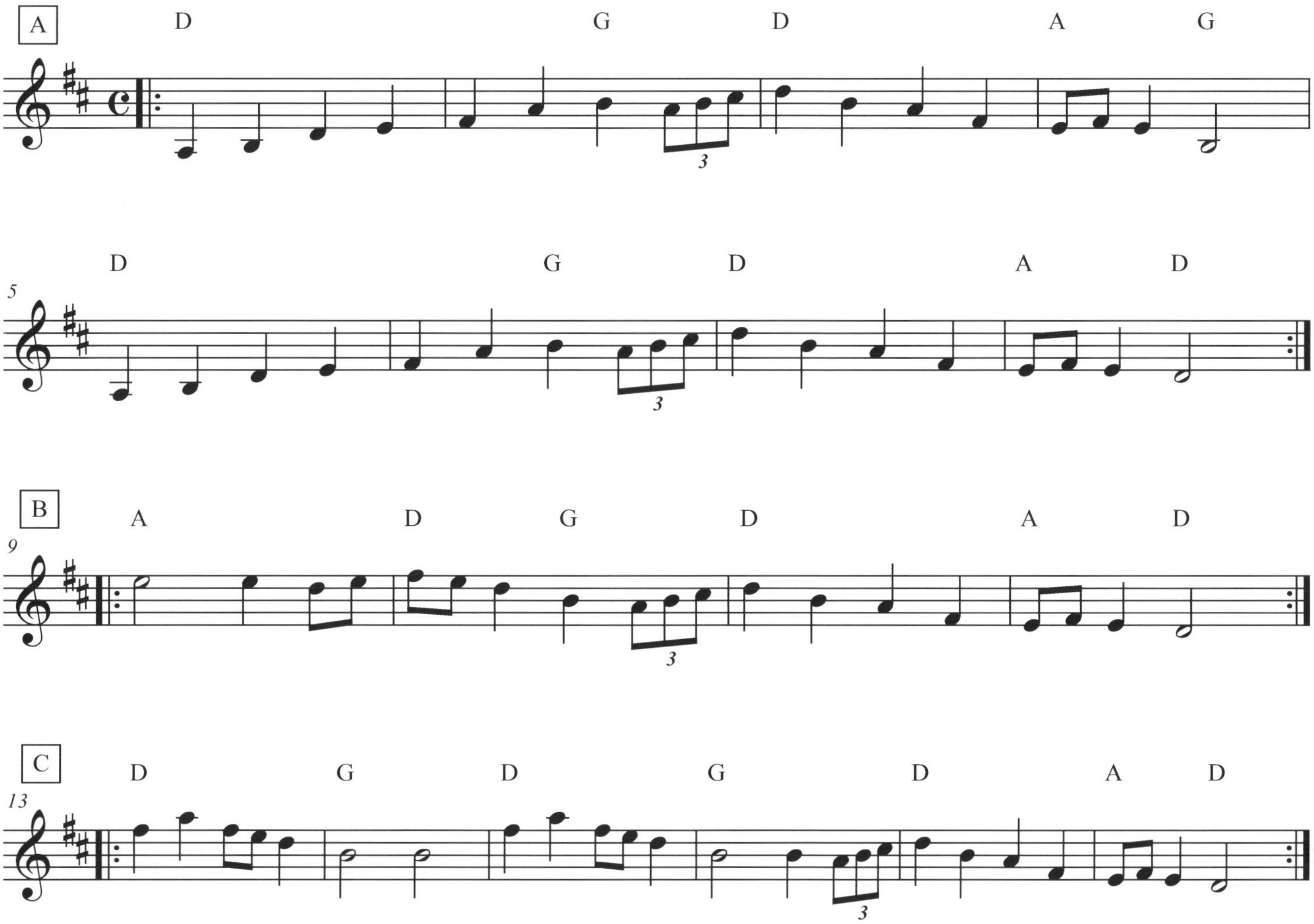

This fiddle tune is a standard in old-time circles.

Cumberland Gap: arrangement #1

U.S.: Arranged by © Ken Kolodner

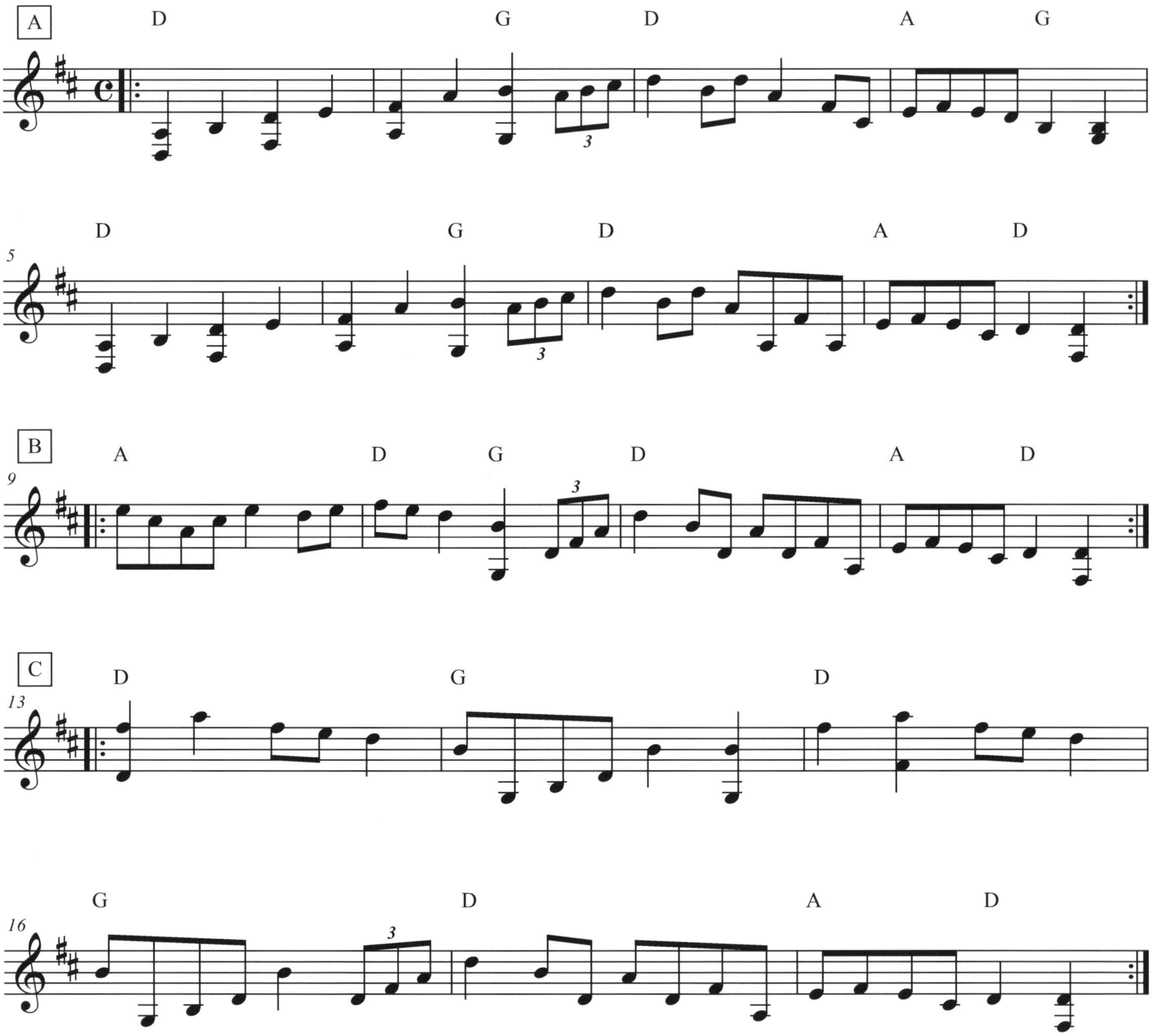

This is intended as a relatively straightforward arrangement.

Cumberland Gap: arranging ideas

U.S.: Arranged by © Ken Kolodner

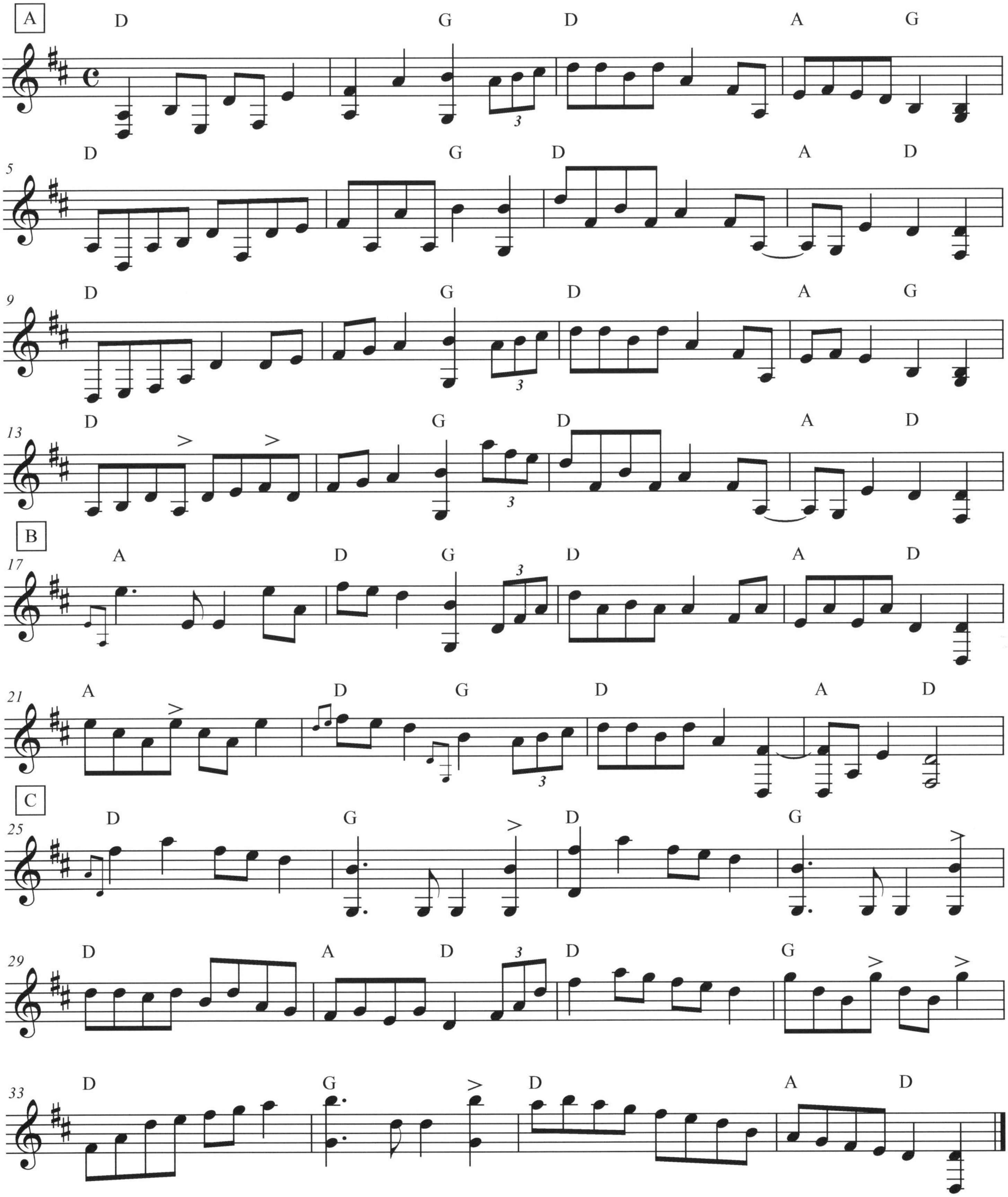

East Tennessee Blues

U.S.: Arranged by © Ken Kolodner

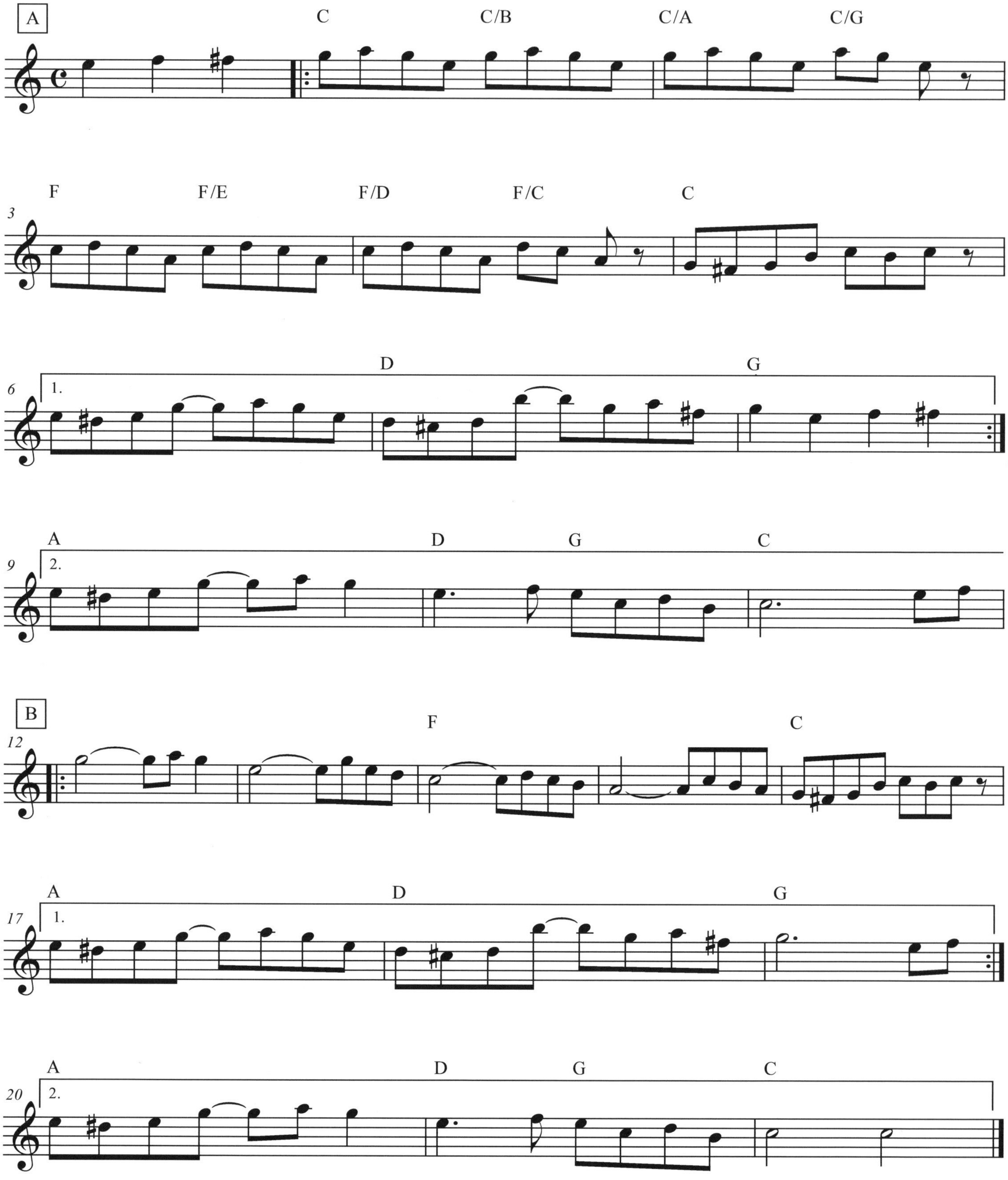

East Tennessee Blues: arrangement #1

U.S.: Arranged by © Ken Kolodner

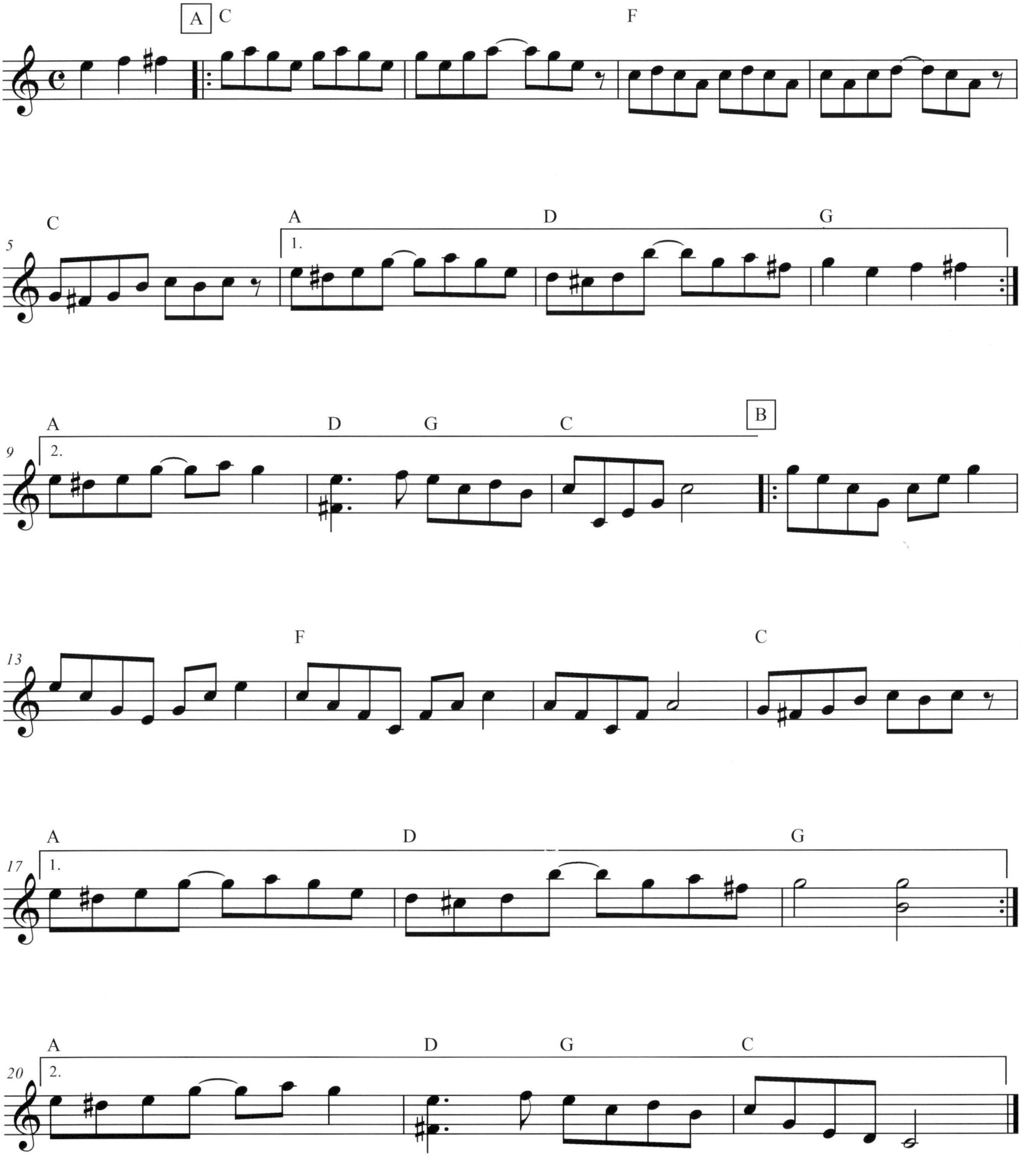

East Tennessee Blues: arrangement #2

U.S.: Arranged by © Ken Kolodner

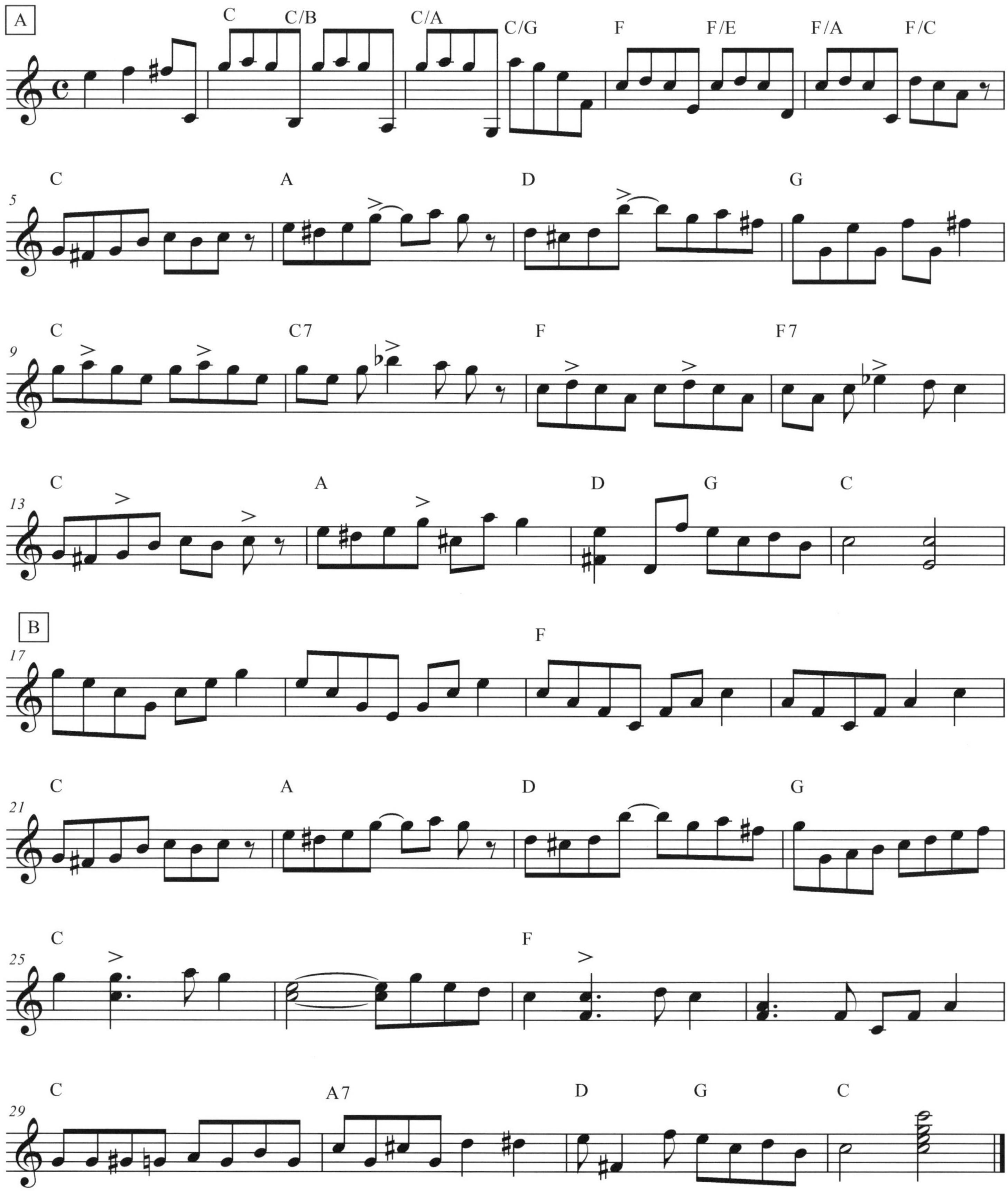

Eagan's Polka

Ireland: Arranged by © Ken Kolodner

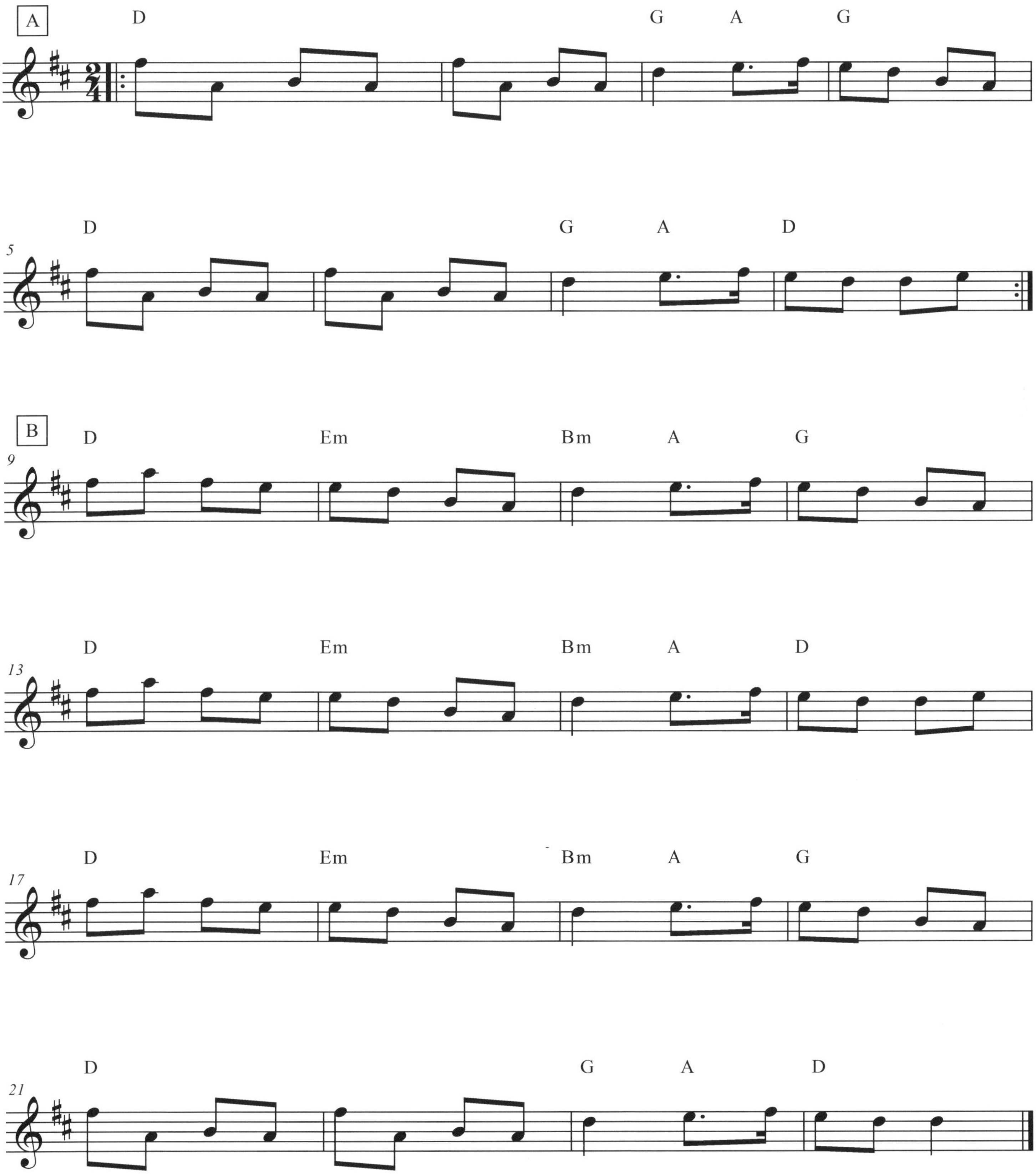

Eagan's Polka: arrangement #1

Ireland: Arranged by © Ken Kolodner

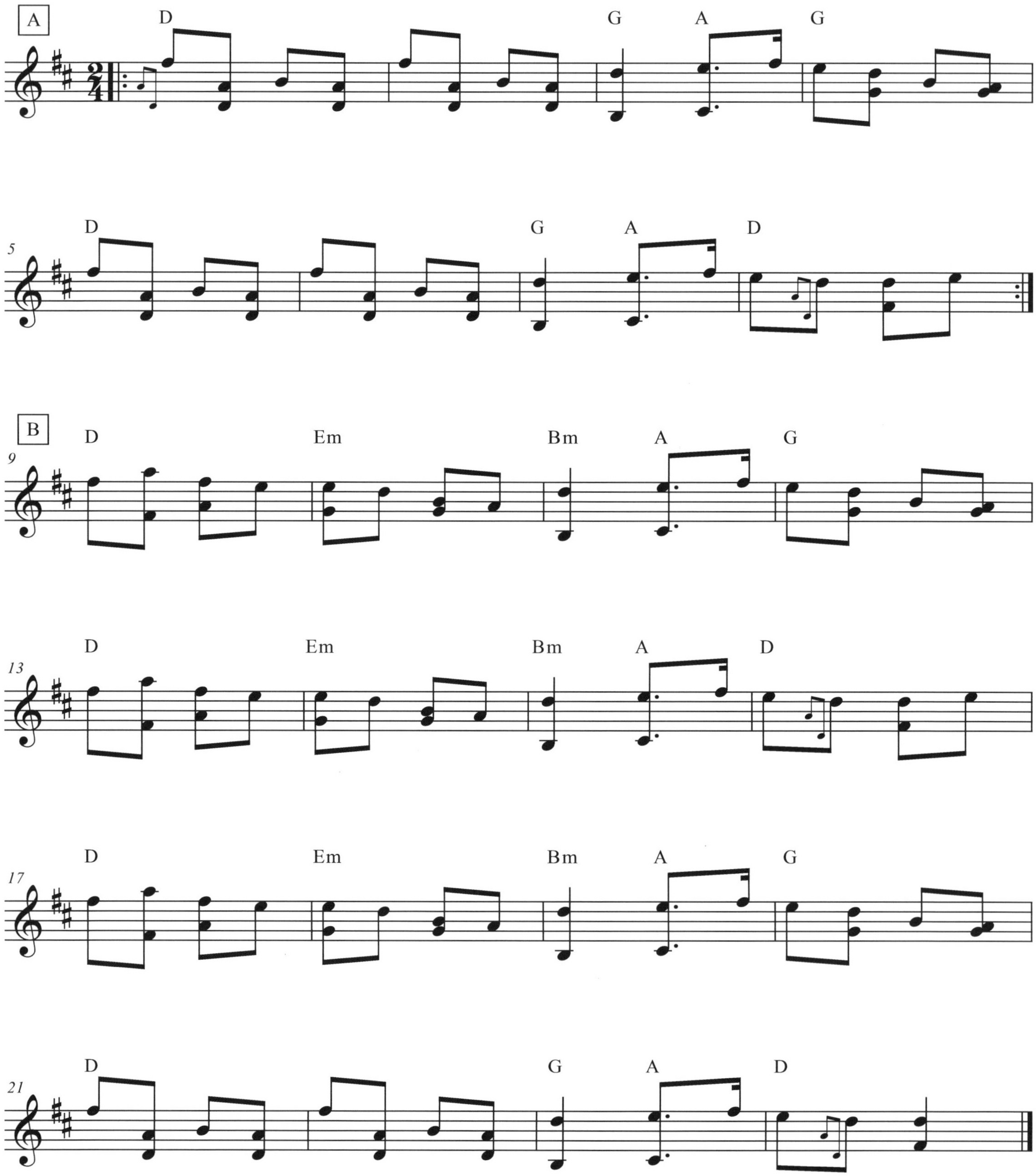

Fly Around My Pretty Little Miss

U.S.: Arranged by © Ken Kolodner

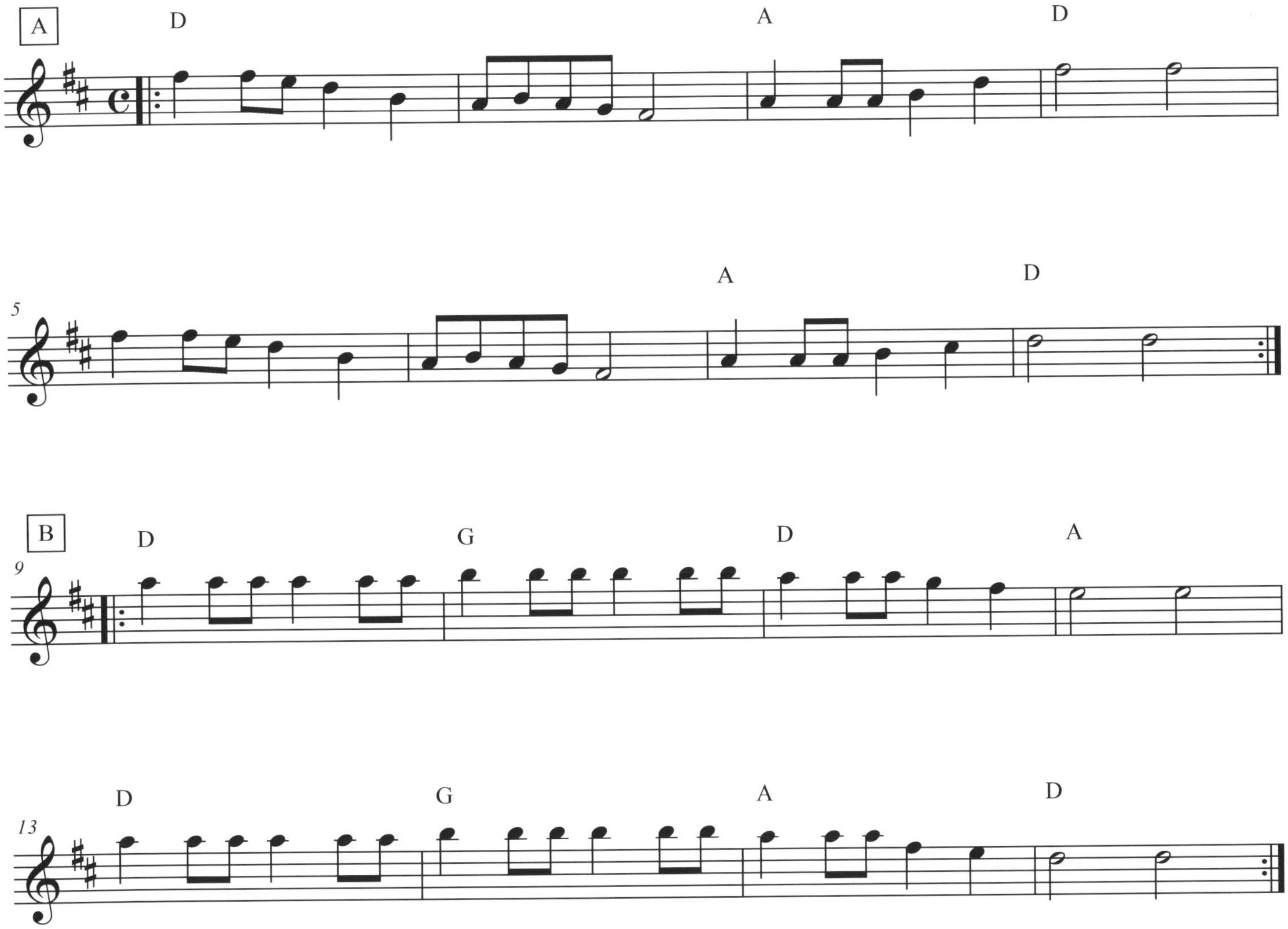

Fly Around My Pretty Little Miss: arrangement #1

U.S.: Arranged by © Ken Kolodner

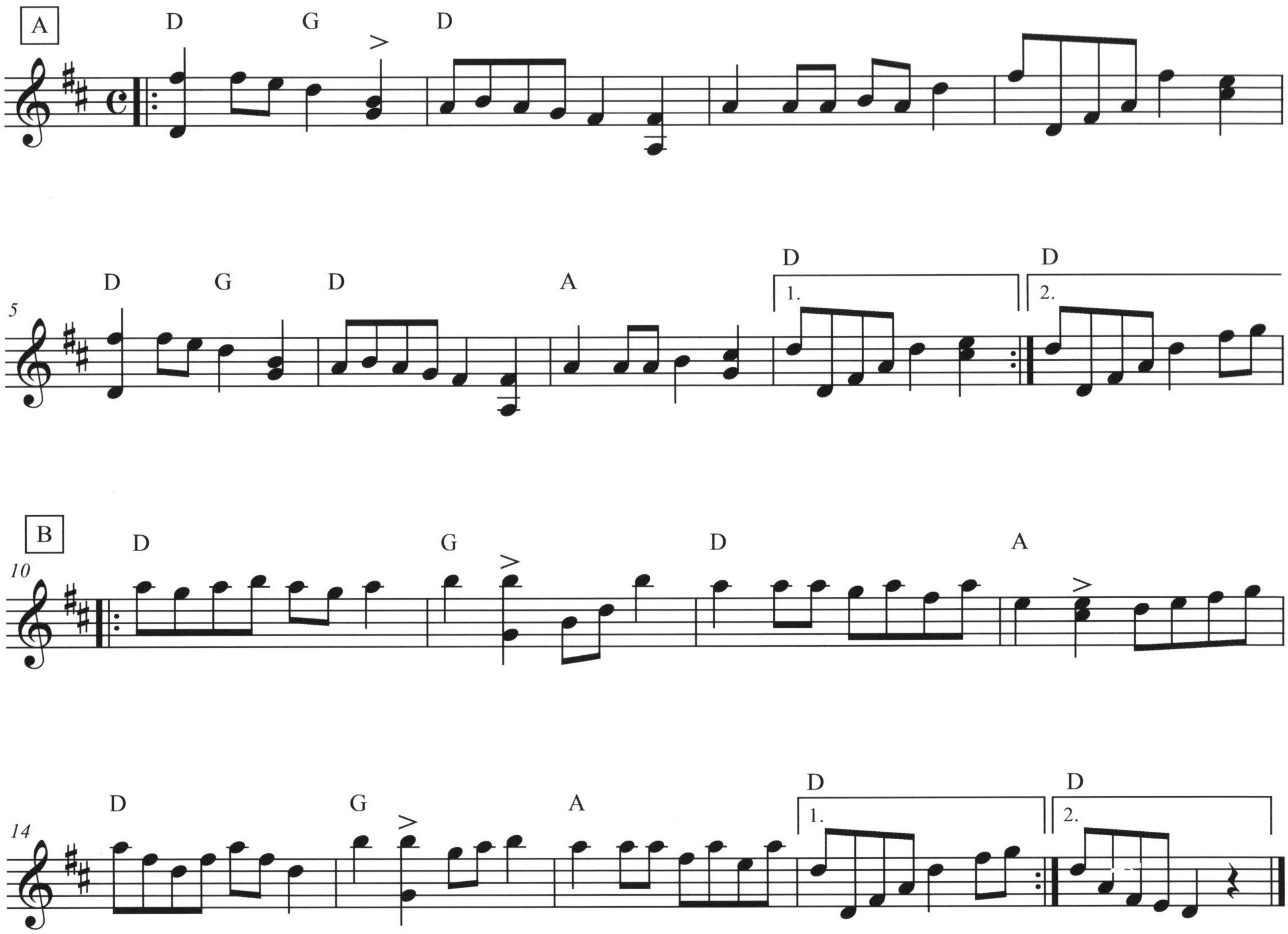

The G chord in measure 1 and 5 is highly optional.

Fly Around My Pretty Little Miss: variations

U.S.: Arranged by © Ken Kolodner

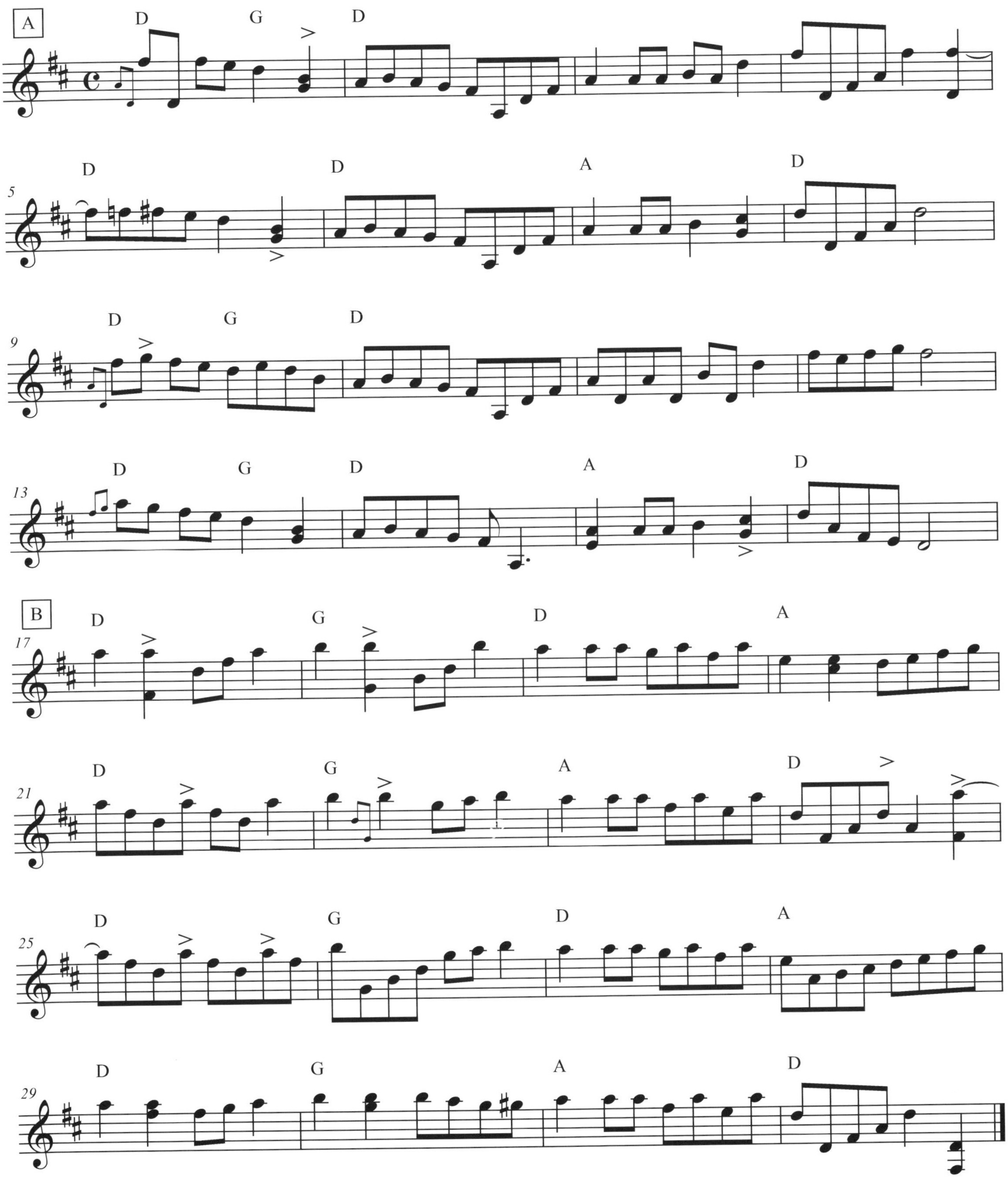

Frenchie's Reel: melody, harmony and accompaniment

Recorded on Mark Grobner and Ken Kolodner's "SunRise" (2011)

Originally in B♭

Ward Allen and Mel Lavigne: Arranged by © Ken Kolodner

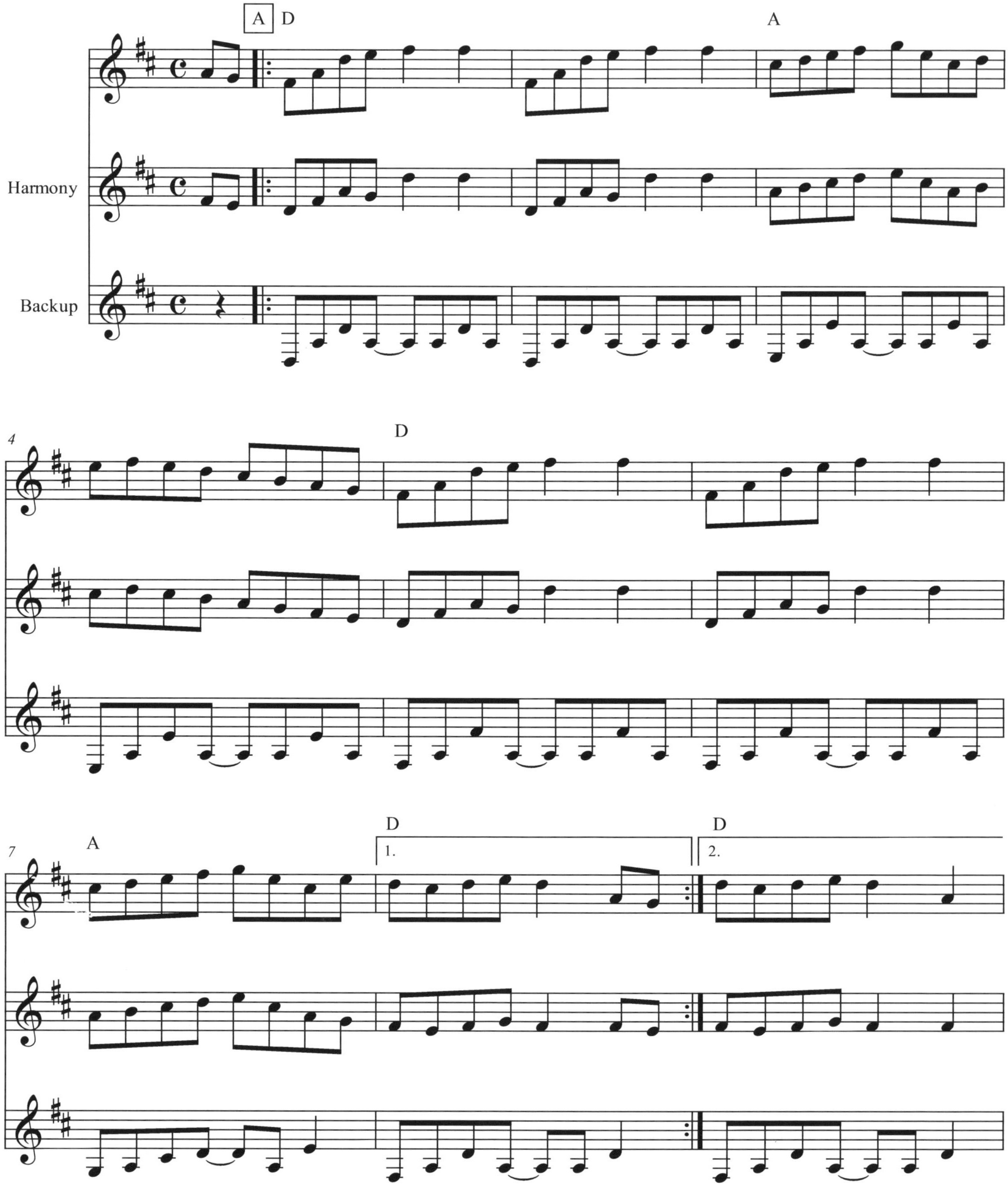

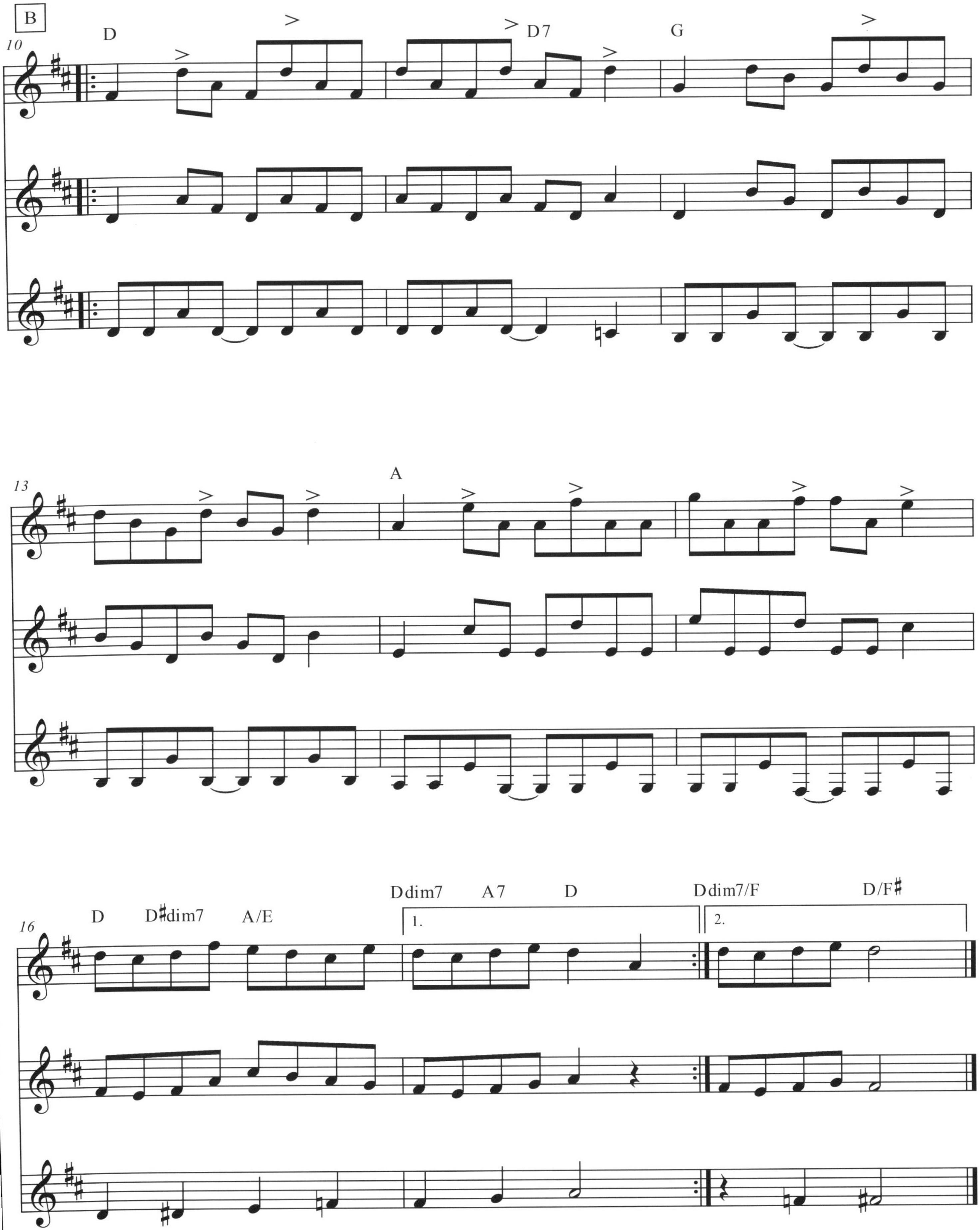
B
10
D
D7
G
13
A
16
D
D♯dim7
A/E
Ddim7
A7
D
1.
Ddim7/F
D/F♯
2.

Frenchie's Reel: arranging ideas

Recorded on Mark Grobner and Ken Kolodner's "SunRise" (2011)

Originally in B♭

Ward Allen and Mel Lavigne: Arranged by © Ken Kolodner

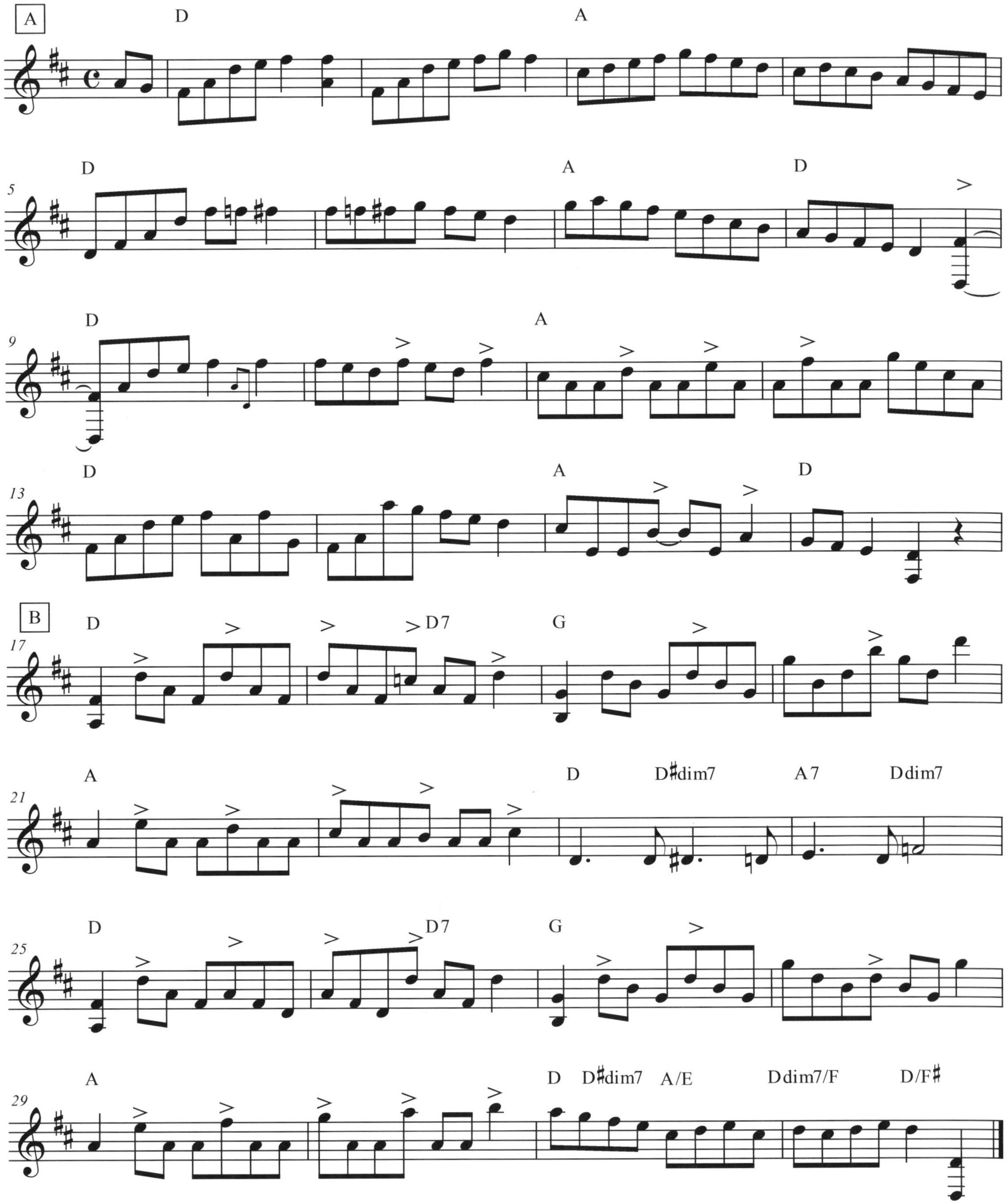

Galway Hornpipe

Recorded on Greenfire's (Ken Kolodner and Laura Risk) "Roof for the Rain" (2001)
with Joseph Sobel and Keith Murphy

Ireland: Arranged by © Ken Kolodner

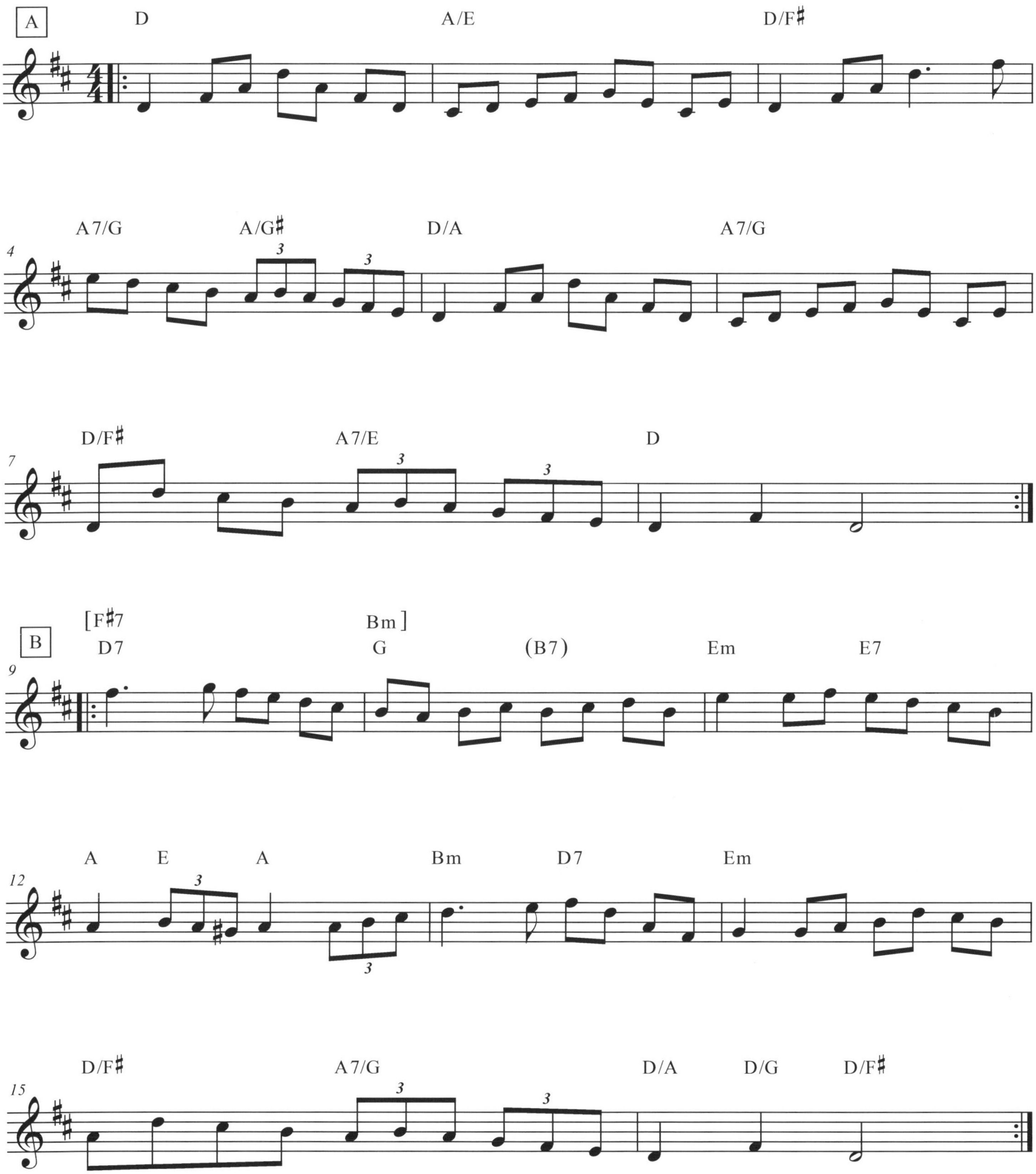

Galway Hornpipe: arranging ideas

Recorded on Greenfire's (Ken Kolodner and Laura Risk) "Roof for the Rain" (2001)

Ireland: Arranged by © Ken Kolodner

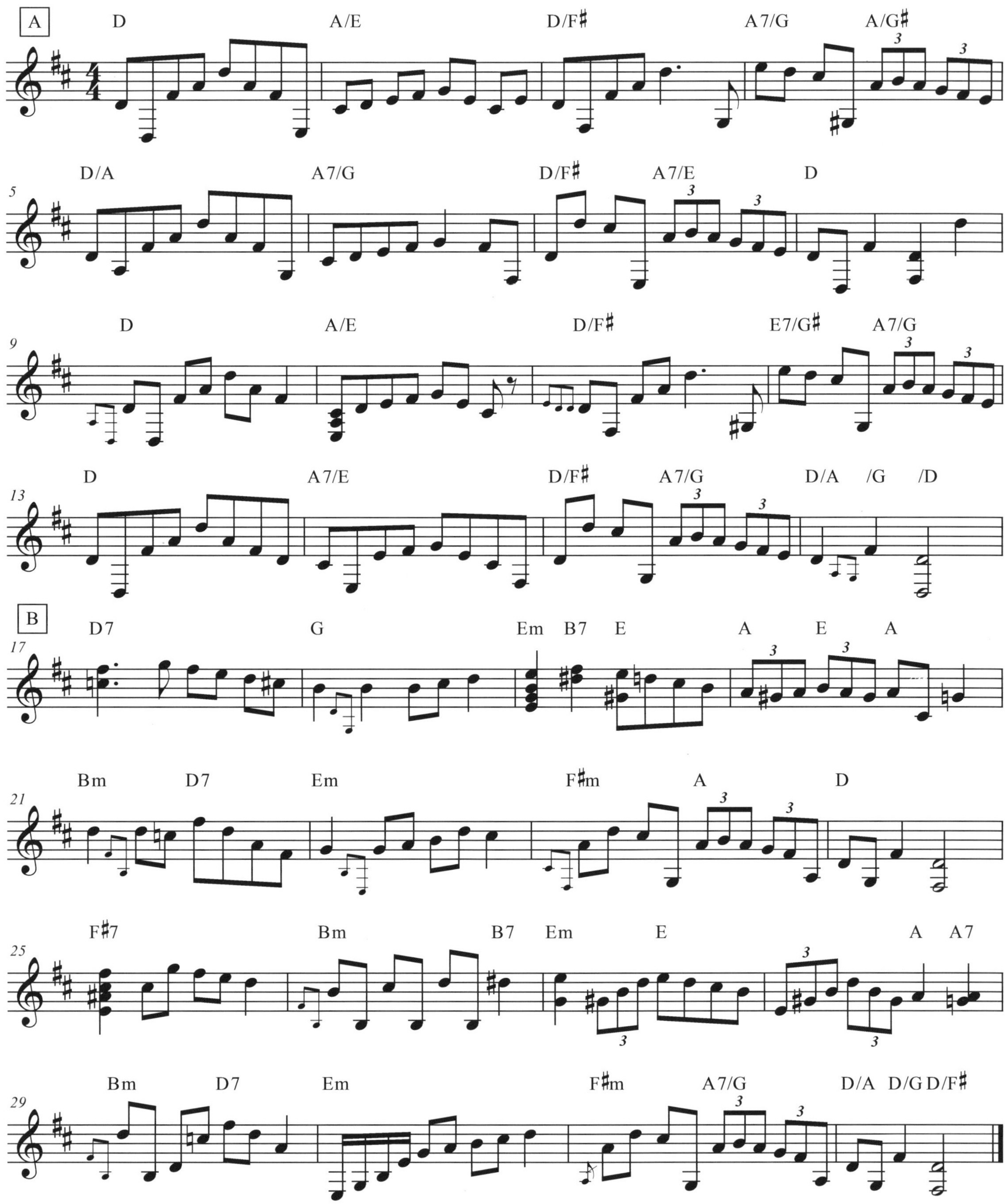

Grub Springs

Recorded on Ken and Brad Kolodner's "Skipping Rocks" (2013)

U.S.: Arranged by © Ken Kolodner

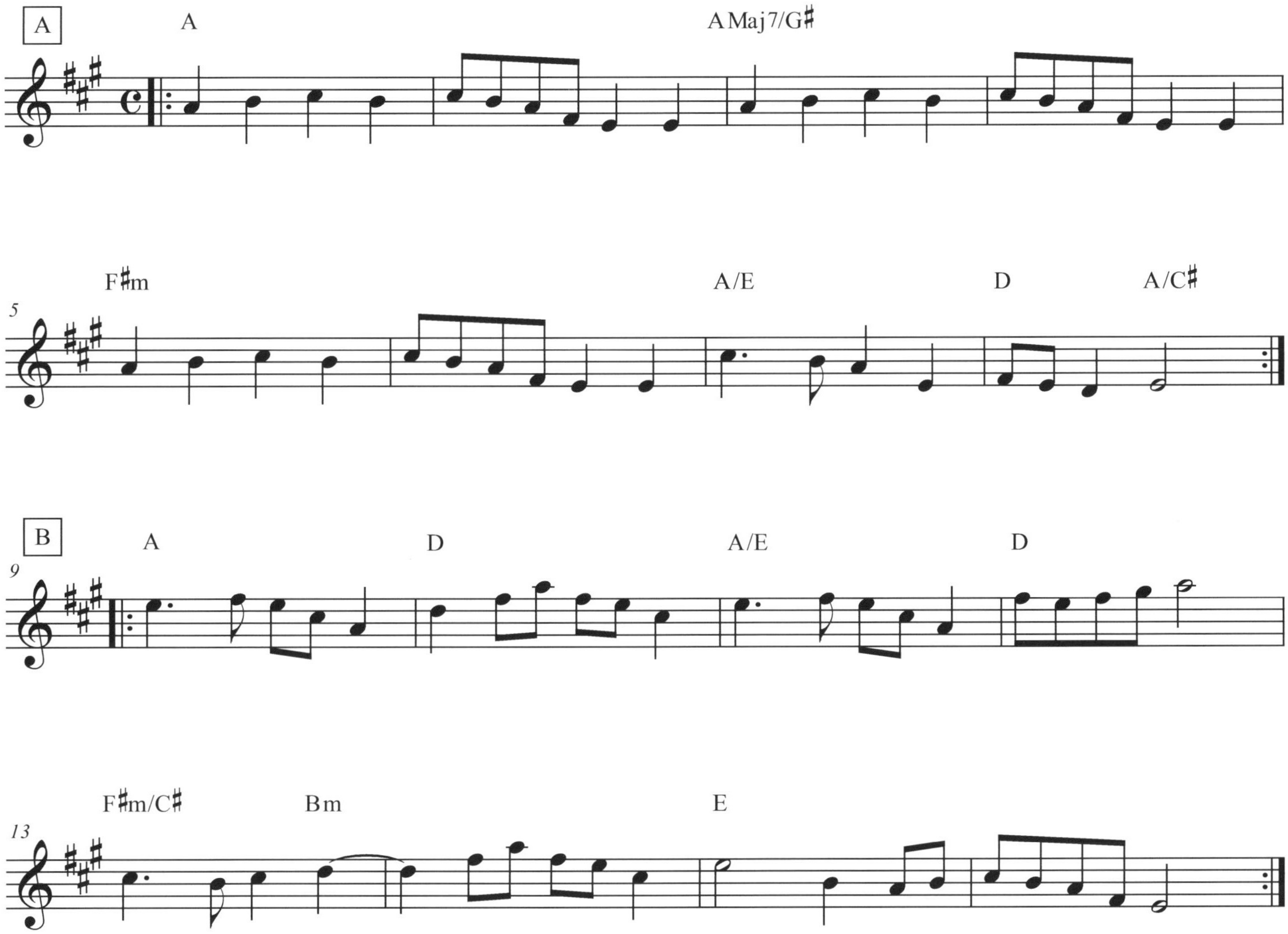

Be warned that I have suggested a chord progression that is decidely not standard (surprise!) and dramatically changes the feeling of this tune. "Traditional" old-time players would not necessarily appreciate the descending bass line in the A part and would likely avoid the minor chord substitutions. In most jams, I stick to major chords but I much prefer these chords!

Grub Springs: arrangement #1

Recorded on Ken and Brad Kolodner's "Skipping Rocks" (2013)

U.S.: Arranged by © Ken Kolodner

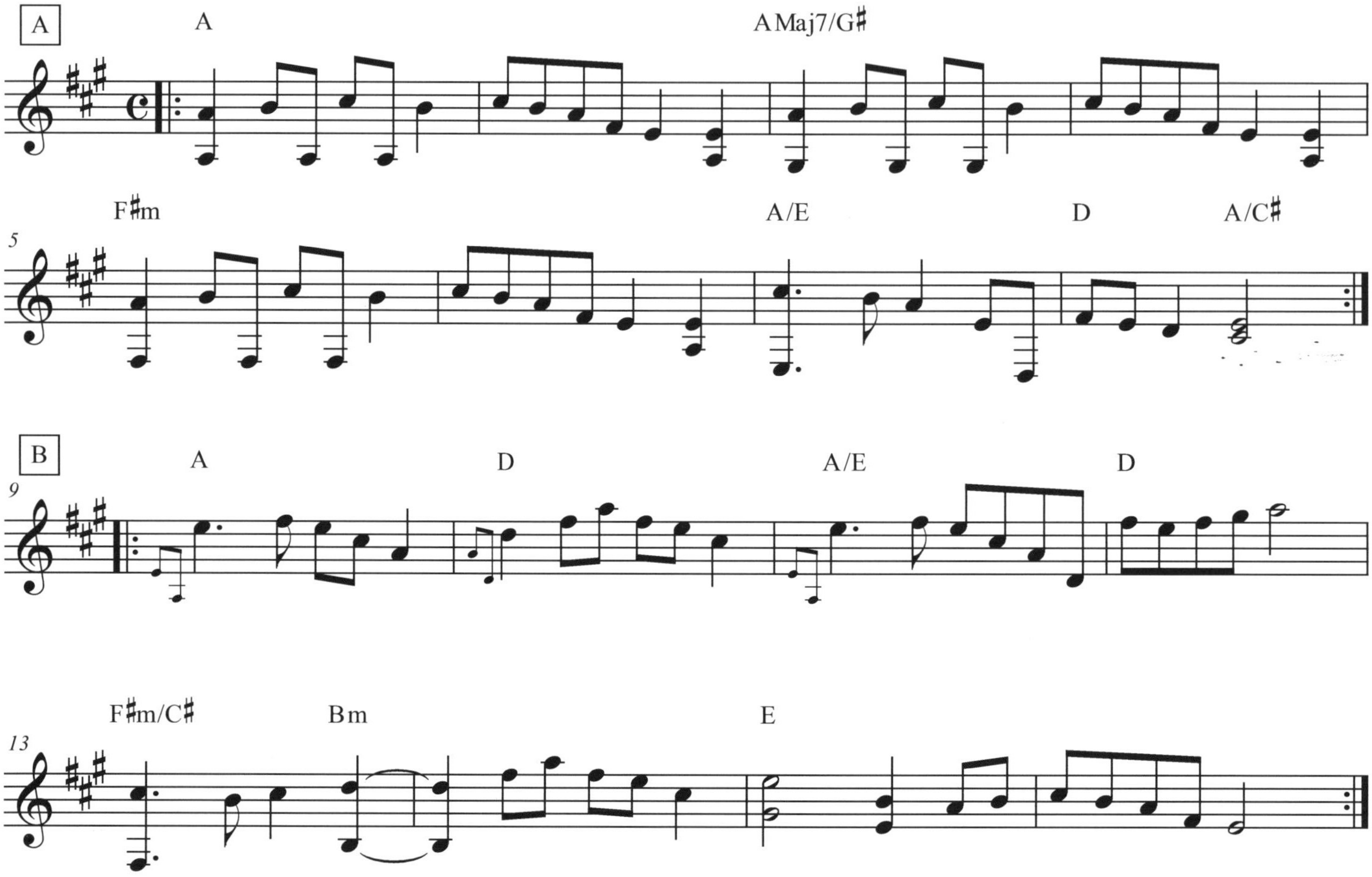

Yes, I like ending "Grub Springs" un-resolved on the "five" chord of E!

Grub Springs: more arranging ideas

Recorded on Ken and Brad Kolodner's "Skipping Rocks" (2013)

U.S.: Arranged by © Ken Kolodner

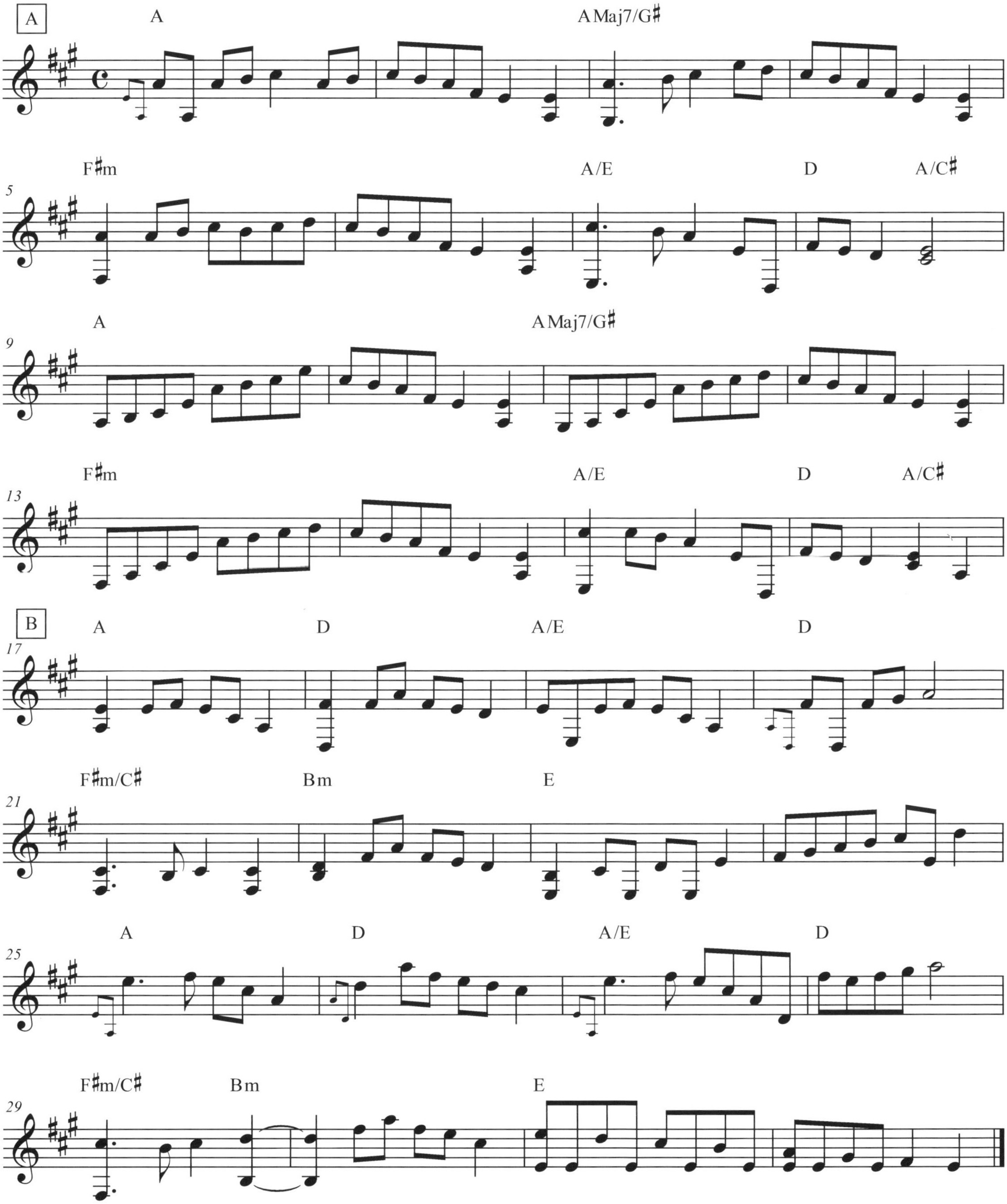

John Brown's March

Recorded on Ken and Brad Kolodner's "Skipping Rocks" (2013)

U.S.: Arranged by © Ken Kolodner

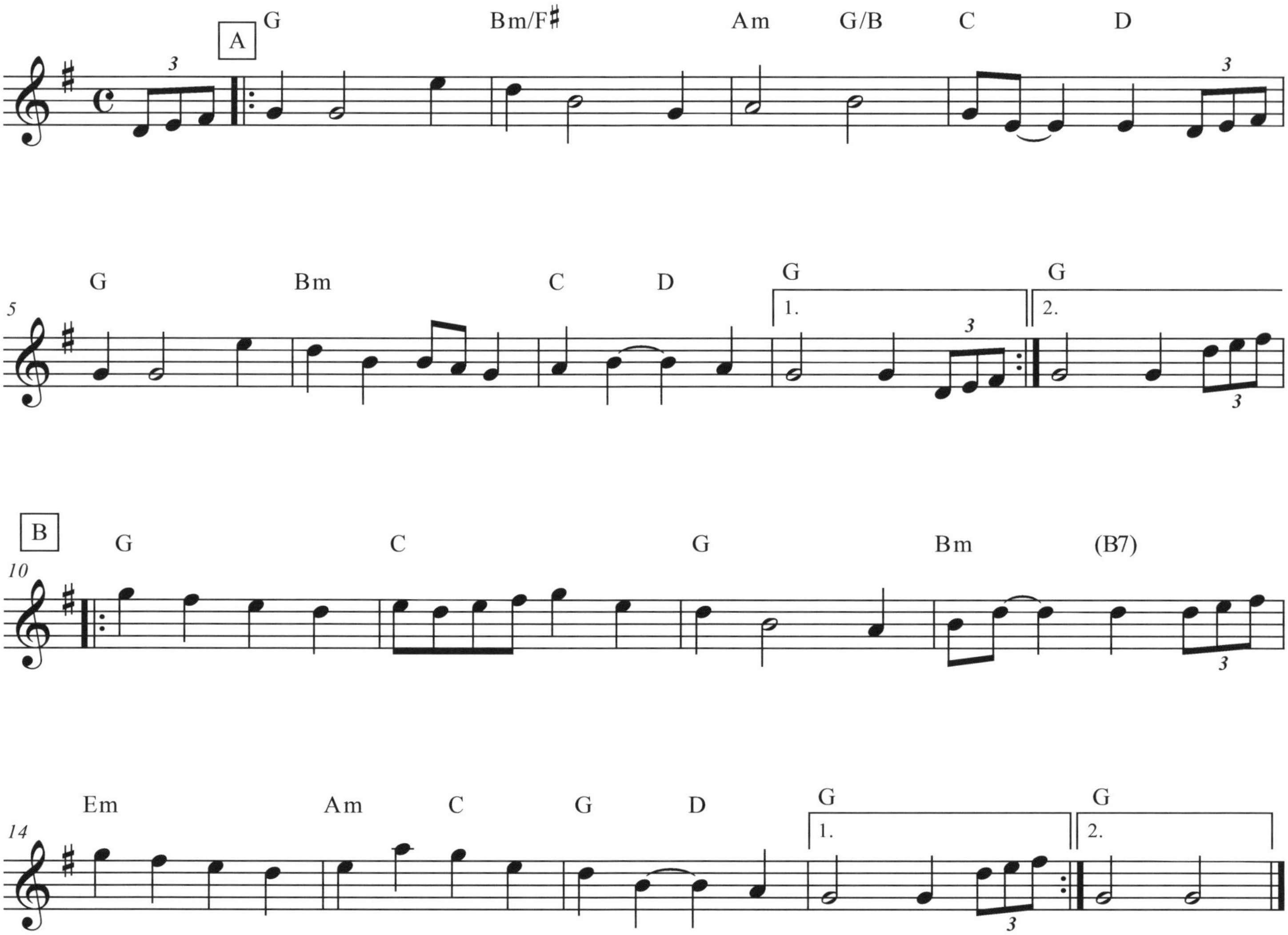

John Brown's March: arranging ideas

Recorded on Ken and Brad Kolodner's "Skipping Rocks" (2013)

U.S.: Arranged by © Ken Kolodner

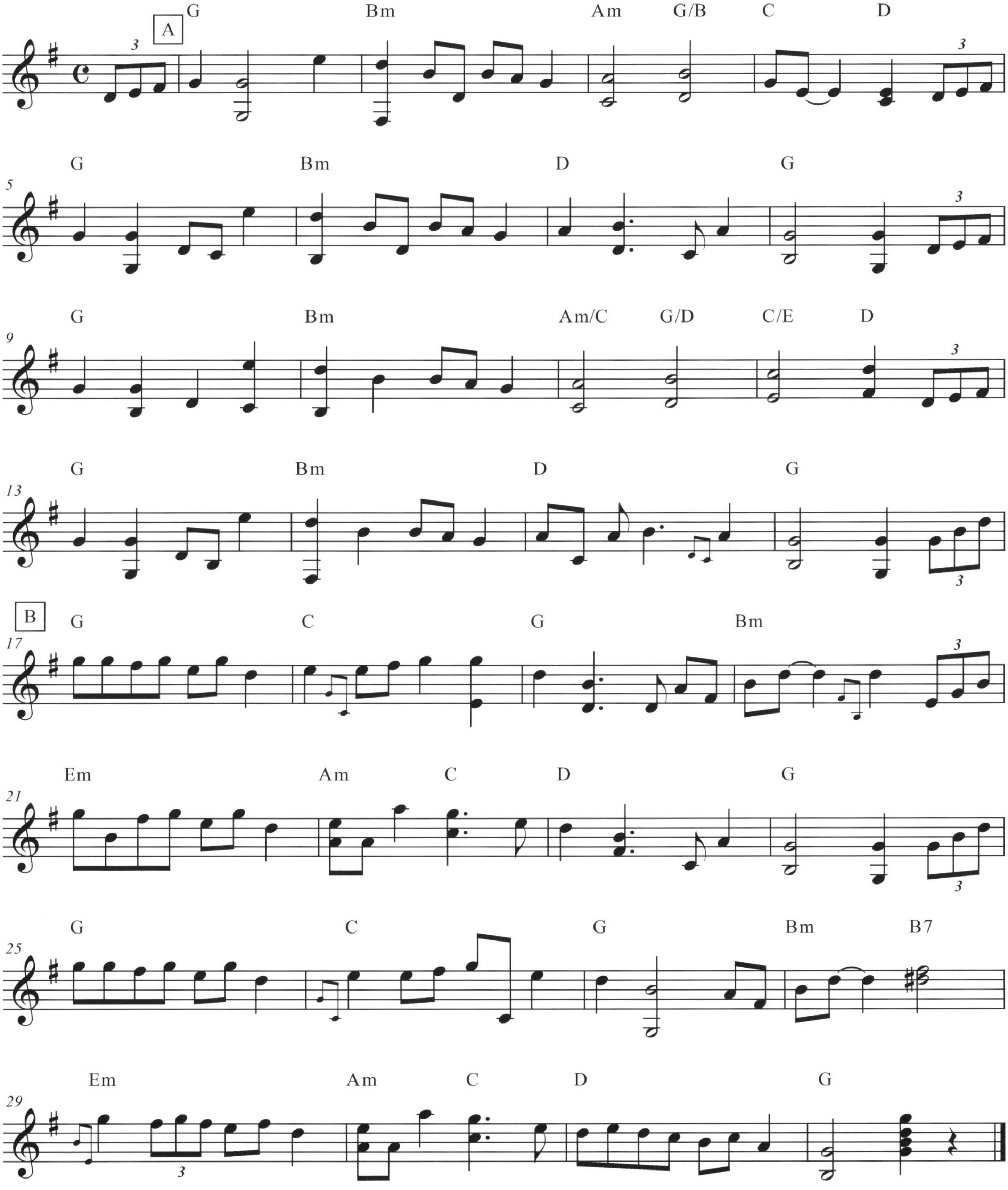

Johnny Cope: melody with harmony

Recorded on Mark Grobner and Ken Kolodner's "SunRise" (2011)

Swing eighth notes

U.S.: Arranged by © Ken Kolodner

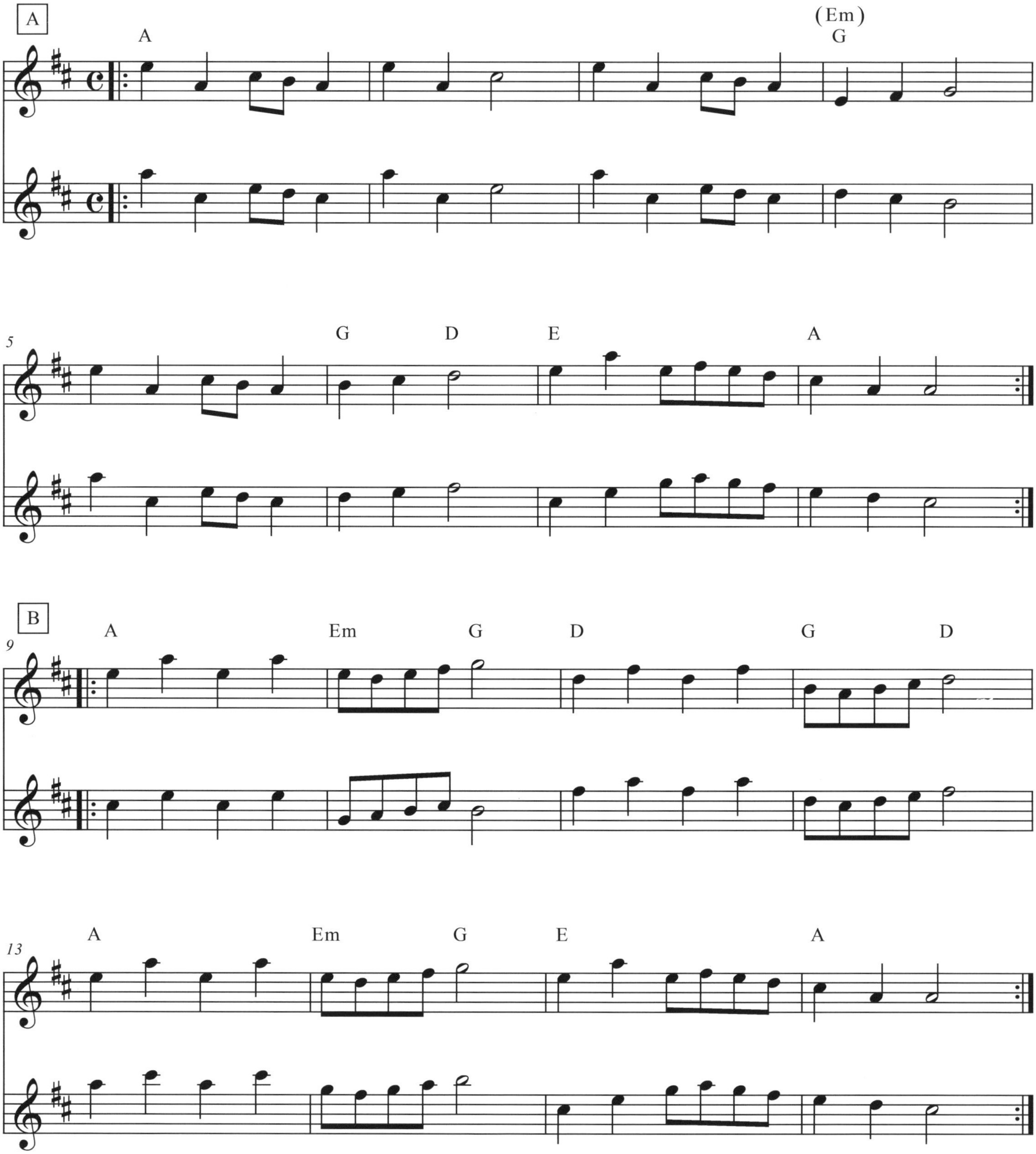

Optional chords include: D in measure 6, Em in measure 10 and 13, and D in measure 12. A G chord may also sub for the E major chord. This tune is probably unrelated to the Scottish tune by the same name.

Johnny Cope: arrangement #1

Recorded on Mark Grobner and Ken Kolodner's "SunRise" (2011)

Swing eighth notes and shift accents!!

U.S. (possibly originally Scotland): Arranged by © Ken Kolodner

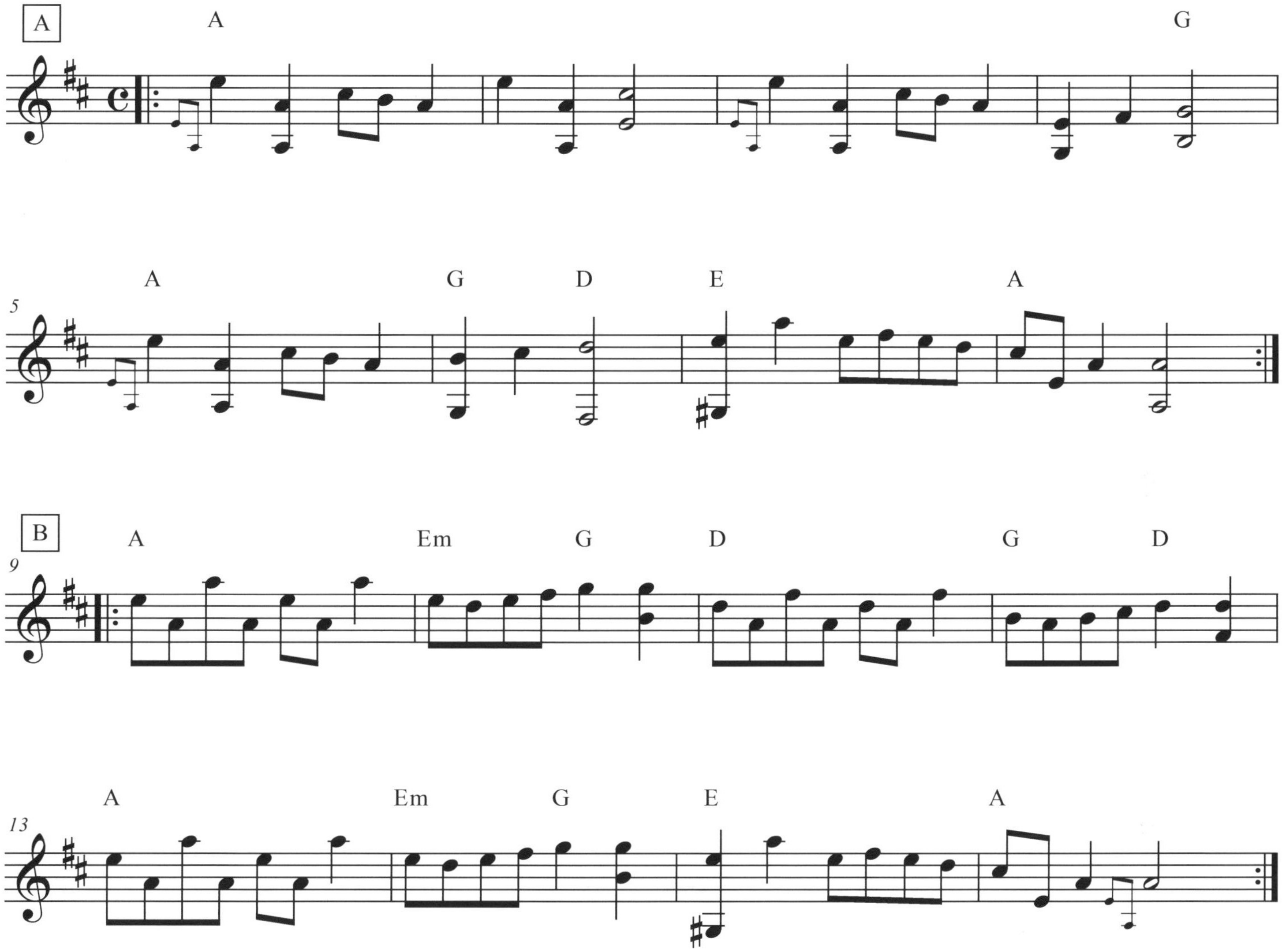

Johnny Cope: variations

Recorded on Mark Grobner and Ken Kolodner's "SunRise" (2011)

Swing eighth notes and shift accents.

U.S.: Arranged by © Ken Kolodner

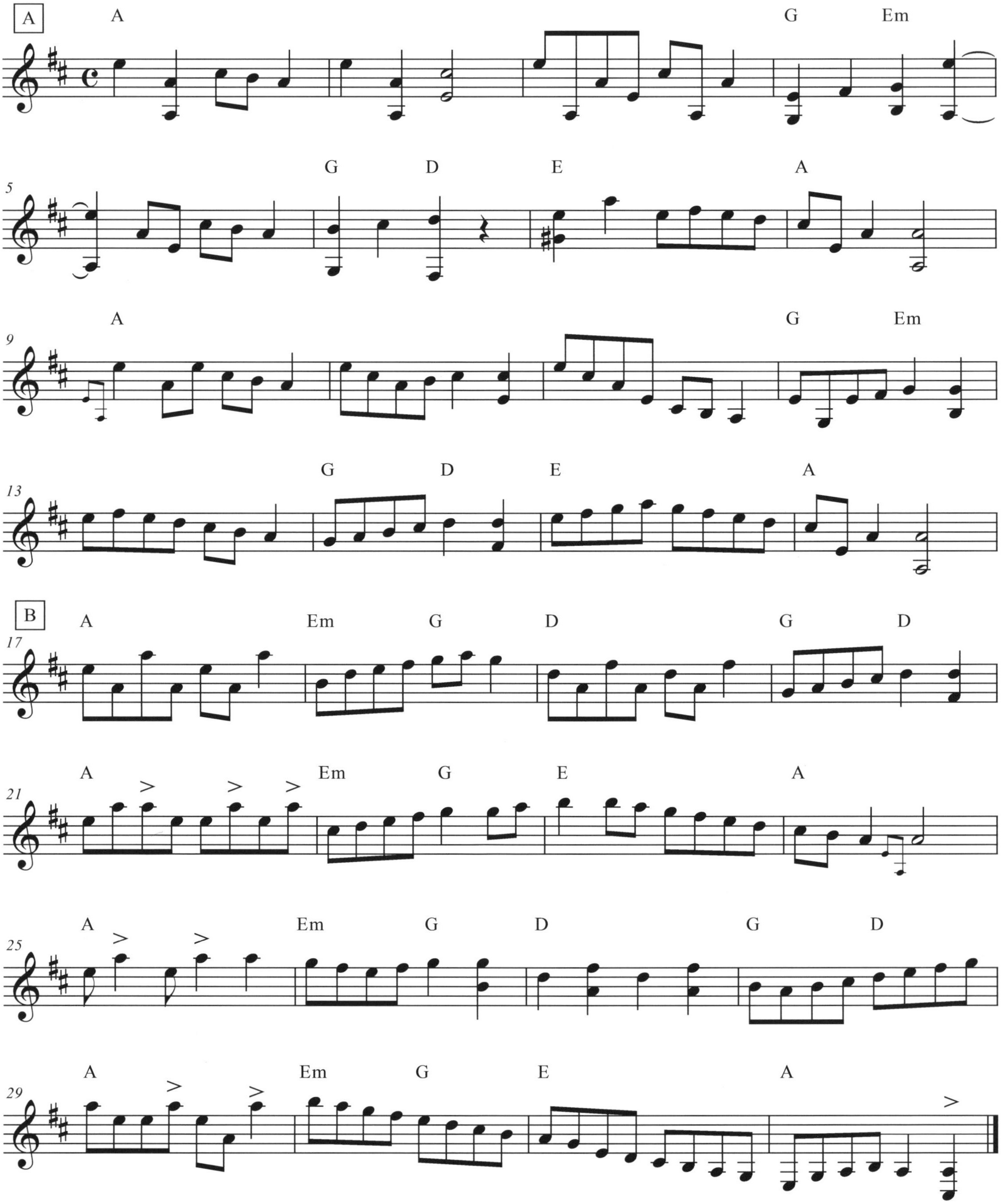

Kitchen Girl

U.S.: Arranged by © Ken Kolodner

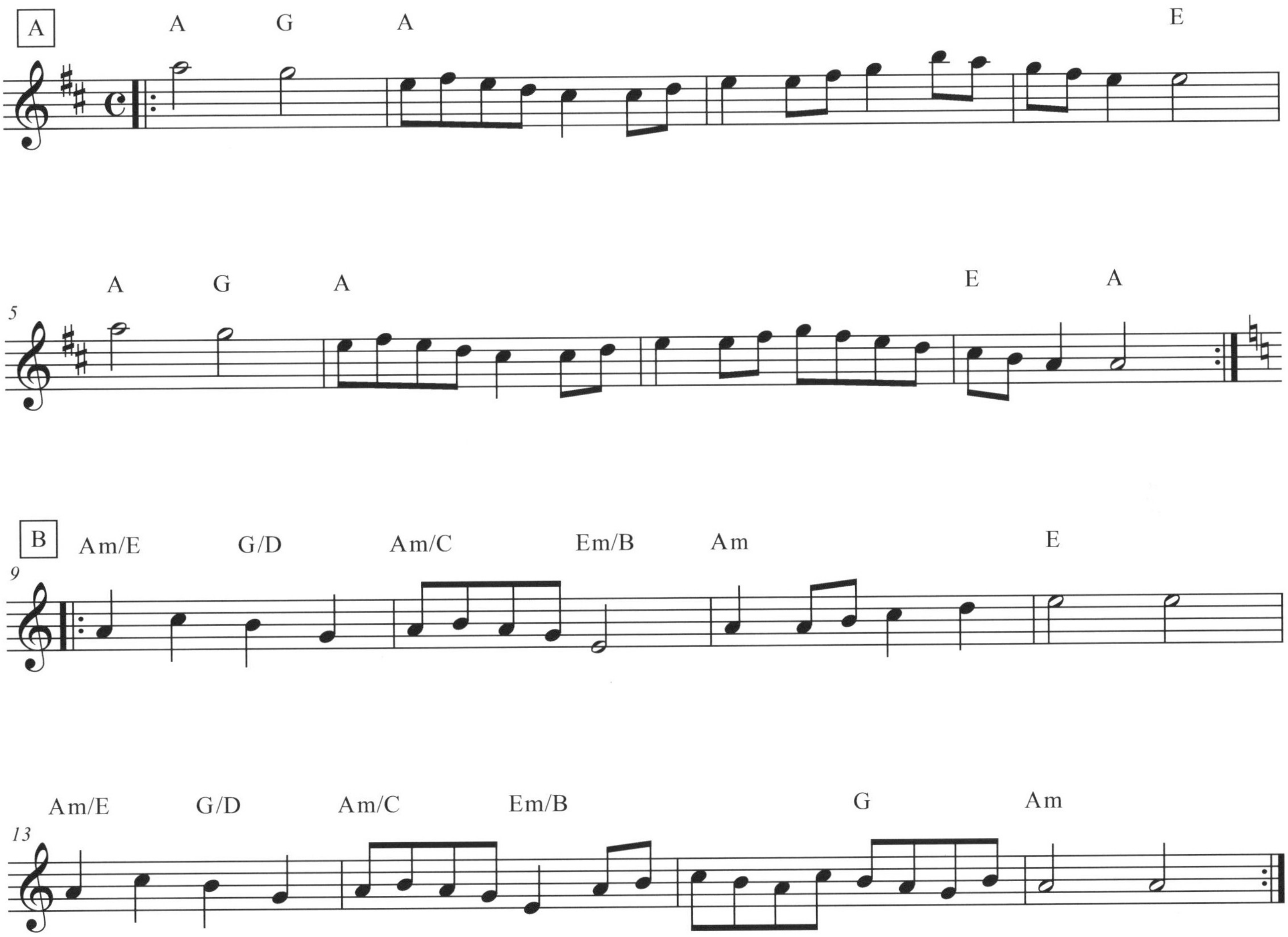

Kitchen Girl: arrangement #1

U.S.: Arranged by © Ken Kolodner

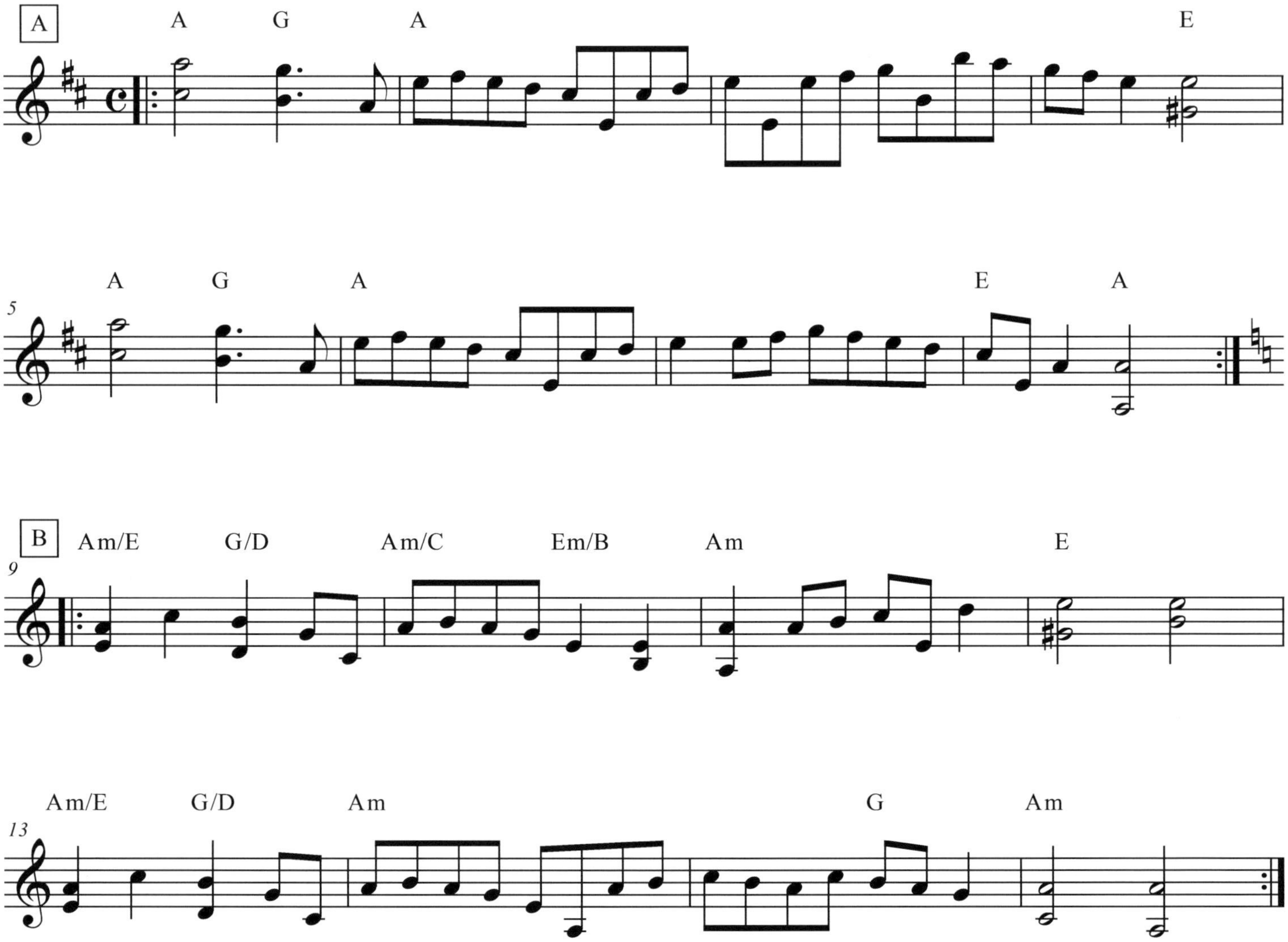

Kitchen Girl: more arranging ideas

U.S.: Arranged by © Ken Kolodner

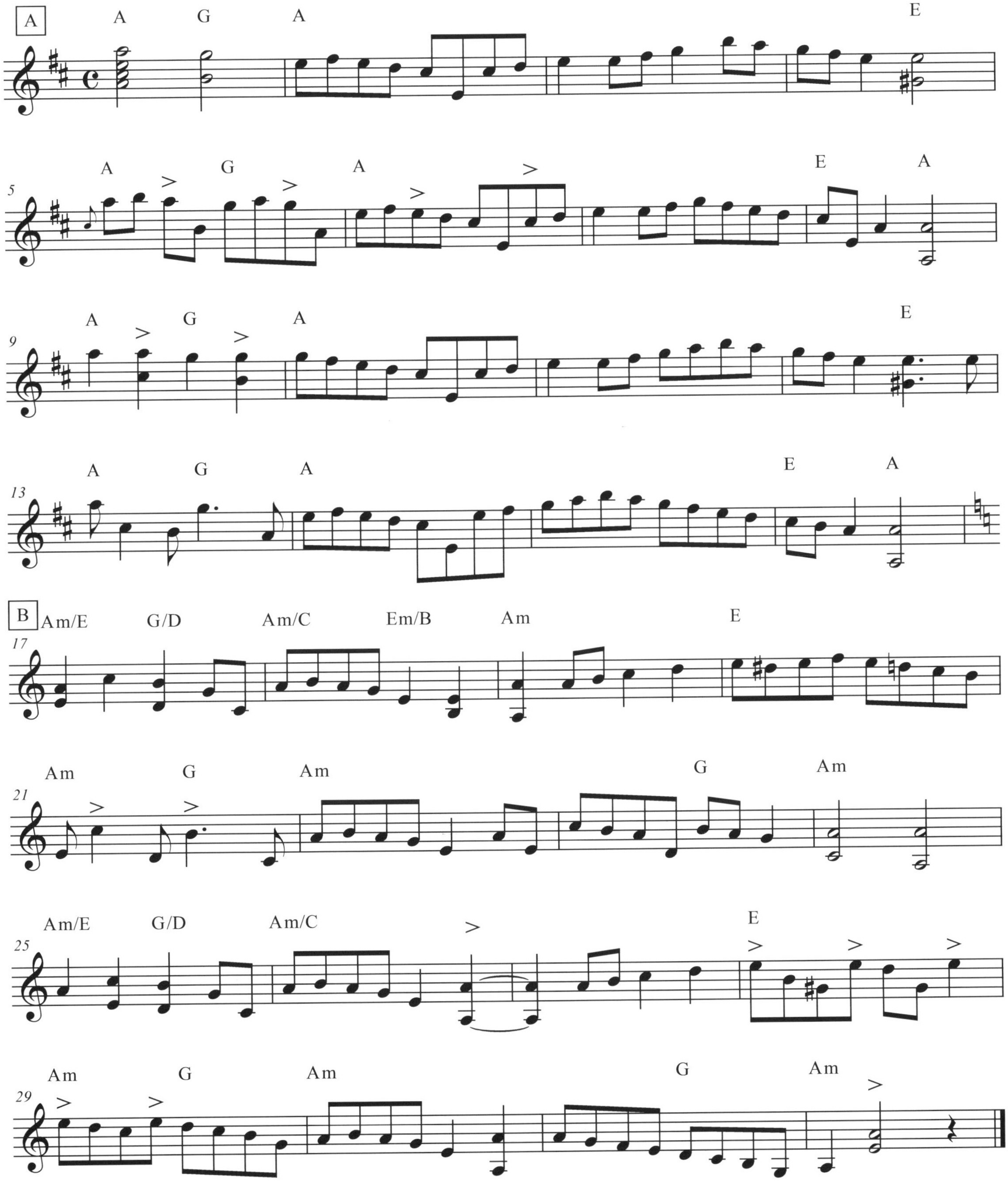

Lad O'Bierne's: with harmony

Recorded on Ken Kolodner's "Walking Stones" (1997, re-released 2006)
with Laura Risk and Robin Bullock

Ireland: Arranged by © Ken Kolodner

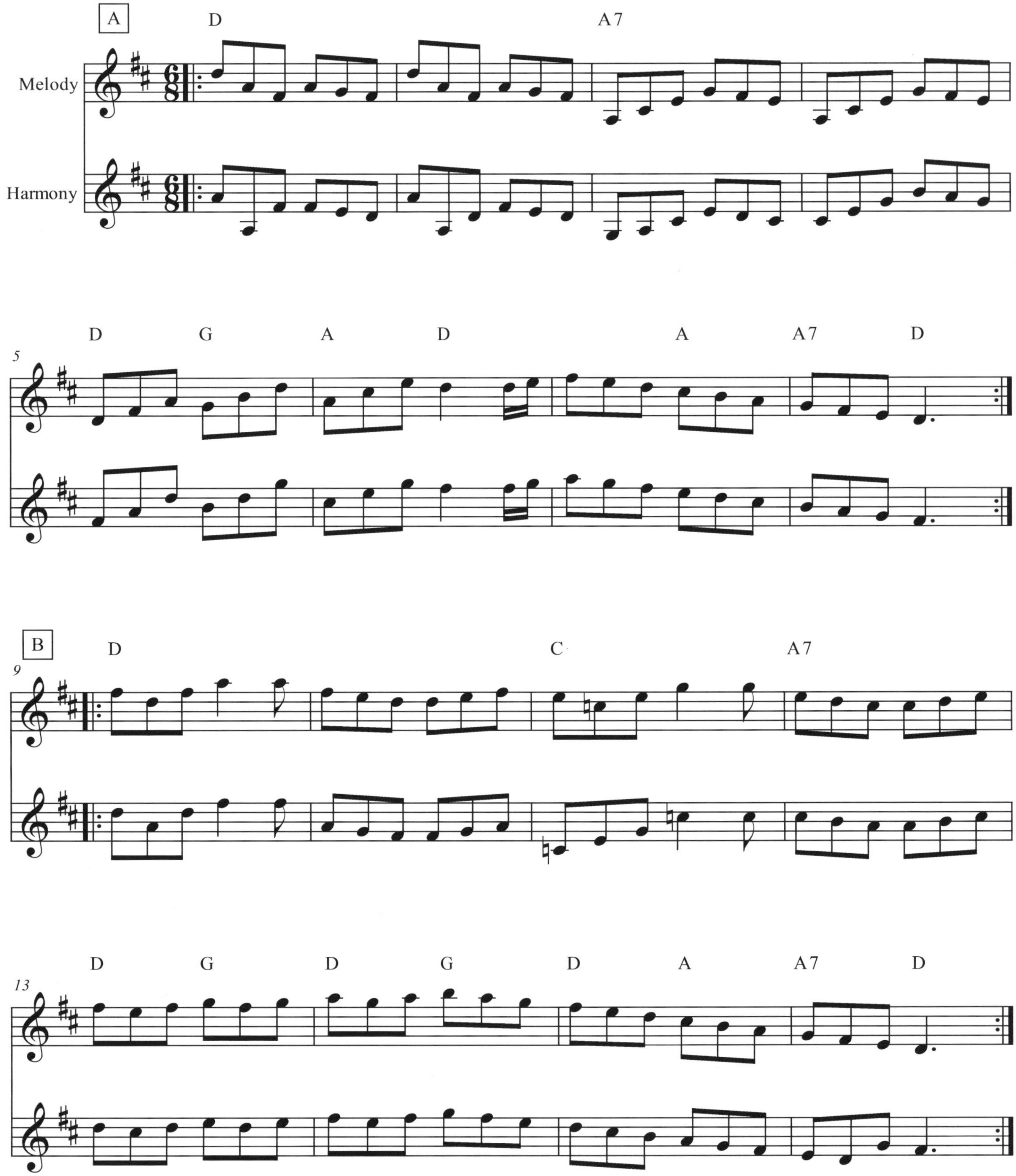

Lad O'Bierne's: arranging ideas

Recorded on Ken Kolodner's "Walking Stones" (1997, re-released in 2006)
with Laura Risk and Robin Bullock

Ireland: Arranged by © Ken Kolodner

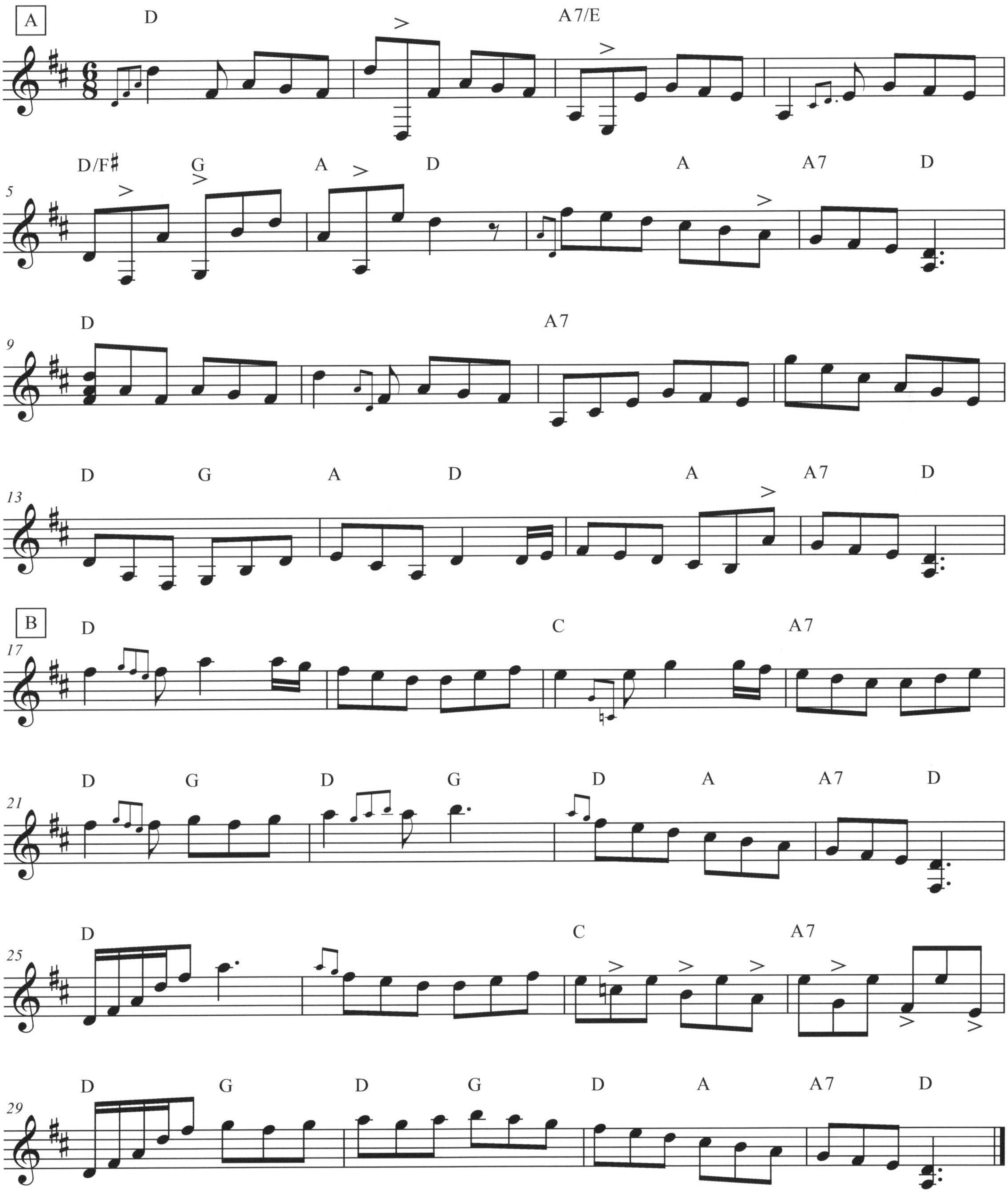

Lonesome John with accompaniment

Recorded on Ken and Brad Kolodner's "Otter Creek" (2011)

U.S.: Arranged by © Ken Kolodner

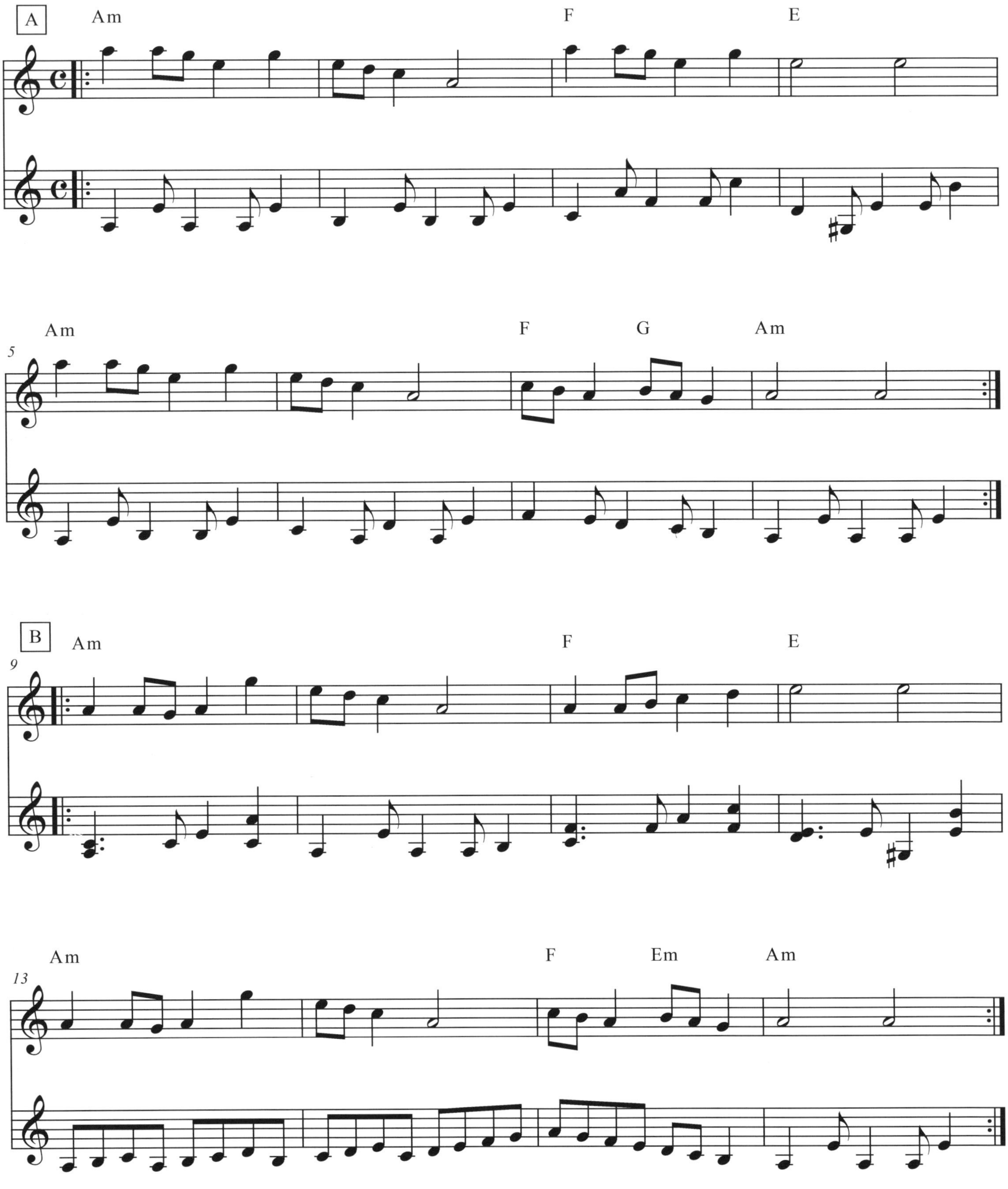

Lonesome John: arranging ideas

Recorded on Ken and Brad Kolodner's "Otter Creek" (2011)

U.S.: Arranged by © Ken Kolodner

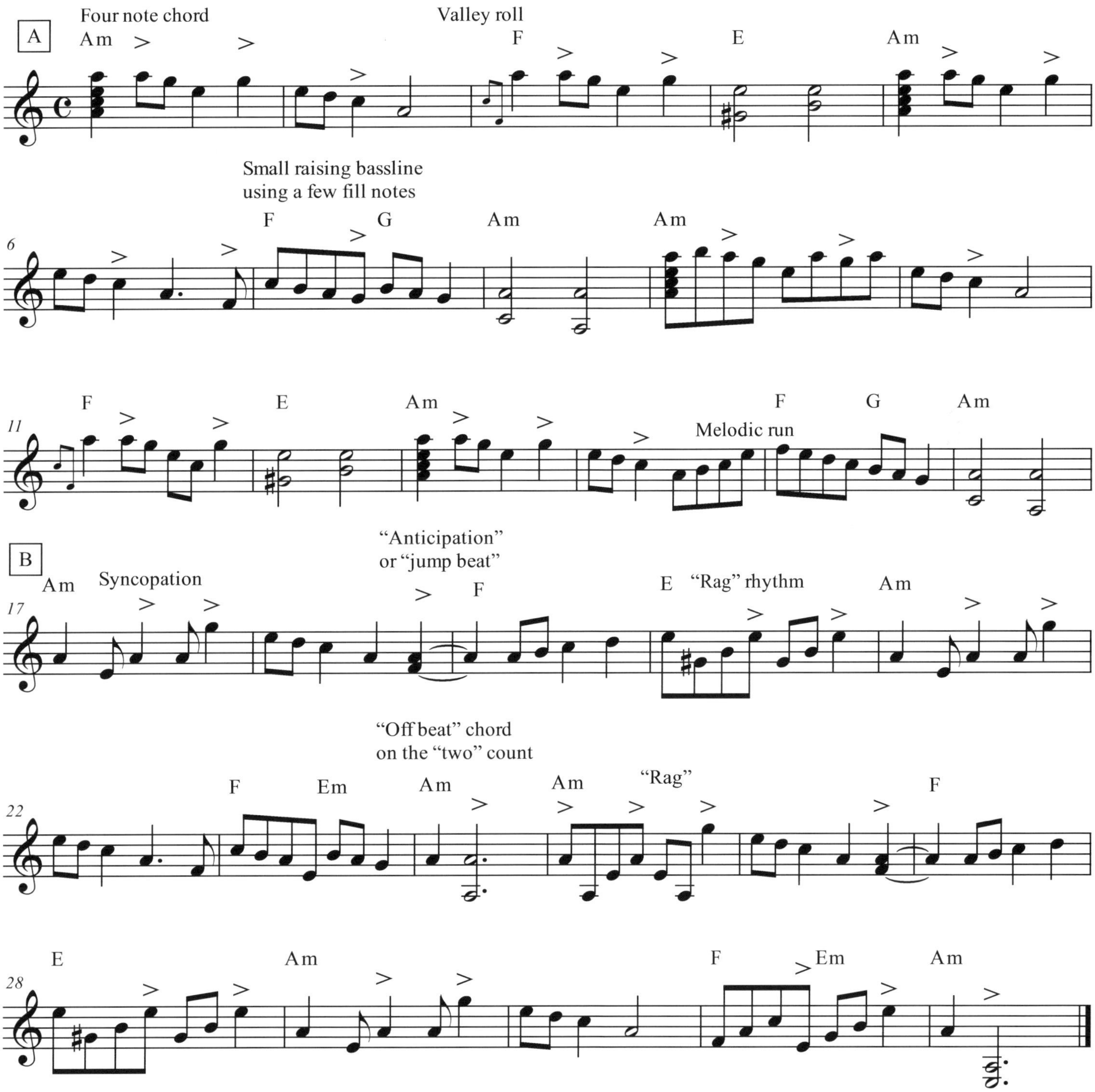

Swing the eighth notes and accent the "2" and "4" counts at least periodically. I have placed lots of accent marks on the "2" and "4" counts as a possible guide. Otherwise assume that the "1" and possibly the "3" counts are accented. The whole tune and most of the arranging ideas fit well in the lower octave. Shifting octaves is a relatively easy way to expand your arrangement after you have it thoroughly in the upper octave. I prefer this tune at a modest tempo--sort of a slow fiddle tune speed.

Missouri: melody with vamp accompaniment

Mike Dappert: Arranged by © Ken Kolodner

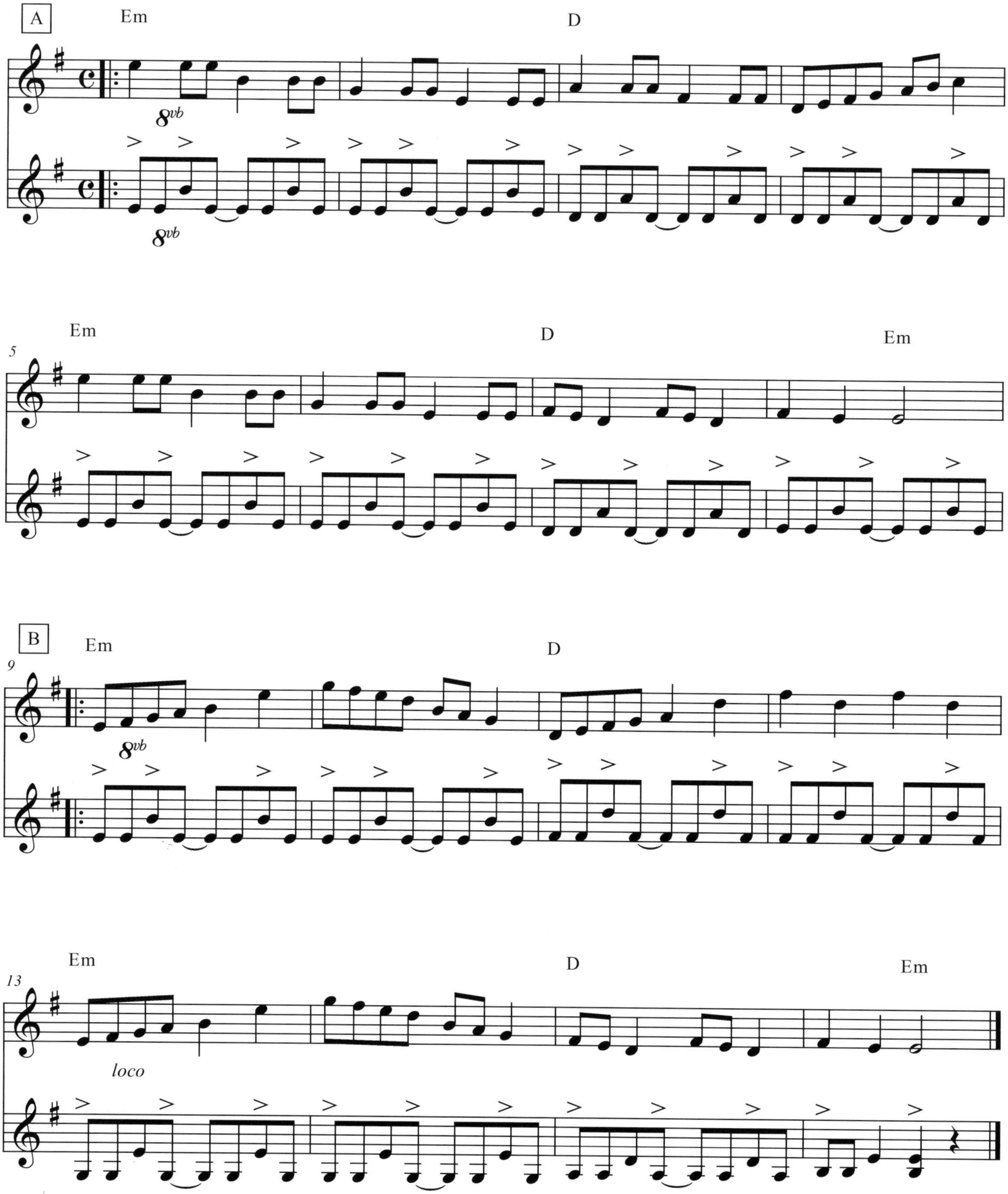

Missouri: melody, alternate accompaniment

Recorded on Mark Grobner and Ken Kolodner's "SunRise" (2011)

Mike Dappert: Arranged by © Ken Kolodner

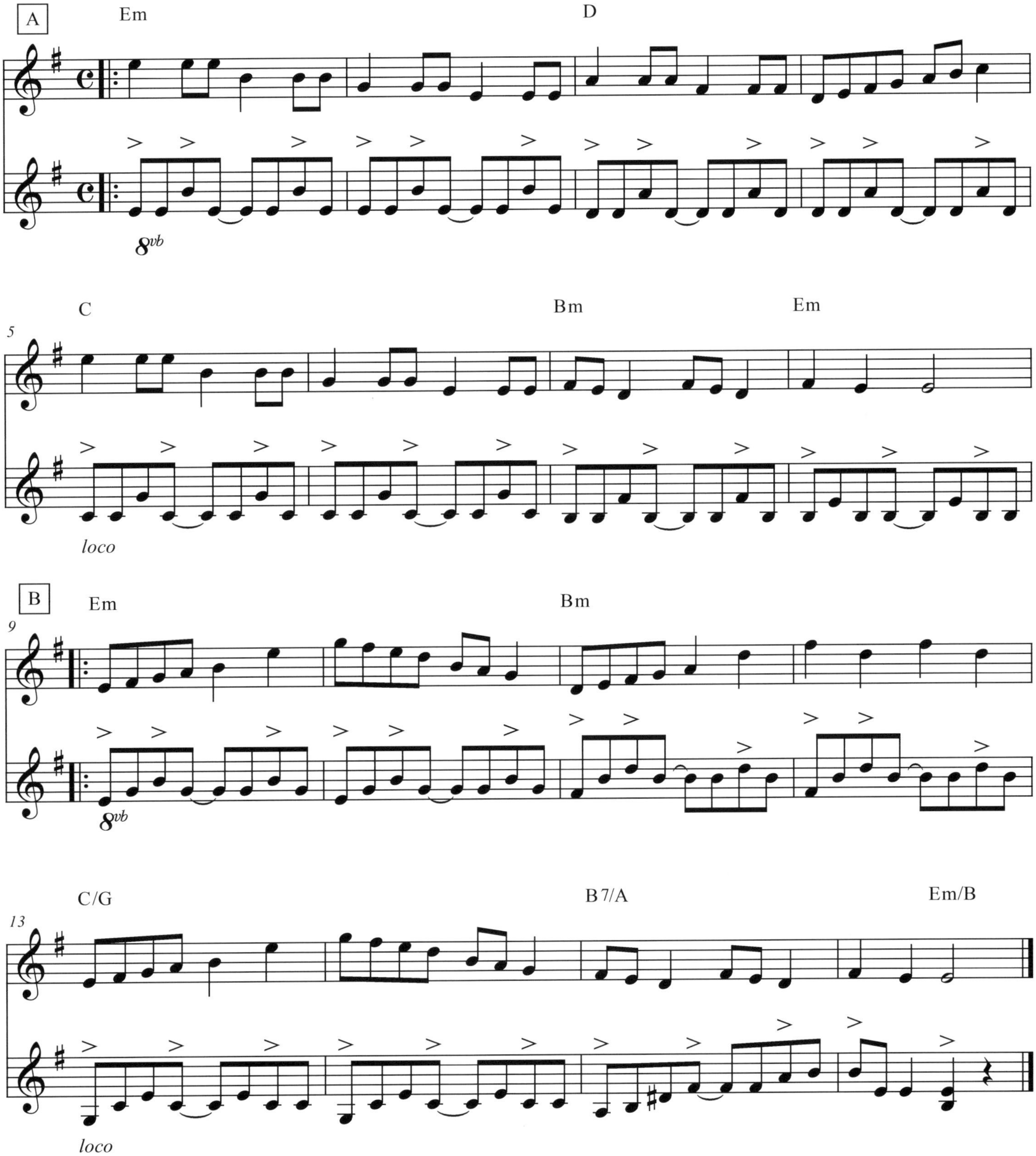

For the Em chord, I've substituted a C chord. For the D chord, I've substituted a Bm and a B7 chord. I start out with the standard chords (Em and D) but enjoy shaking things up with these more adventurous substitutions.

Missouri: variations

Recorded on Mark Grobner and Ken Kolodner's 2011 release "SunRise"

Mike Dappert: Arranged by © Ken Kolodner

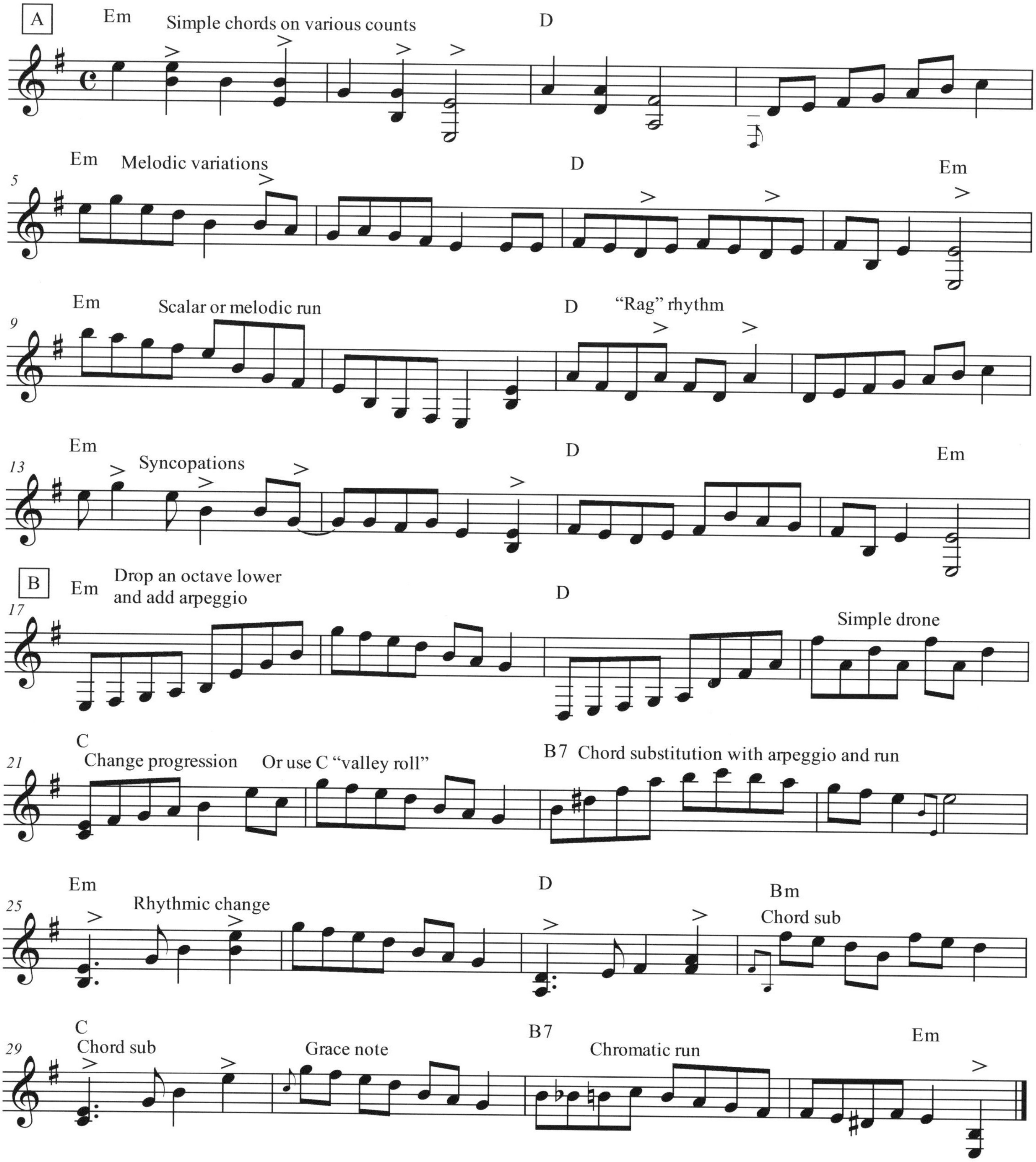

I've included all sorts of ideas here and would not play it EXACTLYthis way. This is largely an improvised version. Keep in mind that I would almost always start with a relatively simple statement of the basic tune with just a few additions. Please pick and choose!

North Carolina Breakdown

Recorded on Ken Kolodner's "Journey to the Heartland" (2005) and on "Hammered Dulcimer Arrangements: Fiddle Tunes Volume I" (2005)

Fiddlin' Arthur Smith: Arranged by © Ken Kolodner

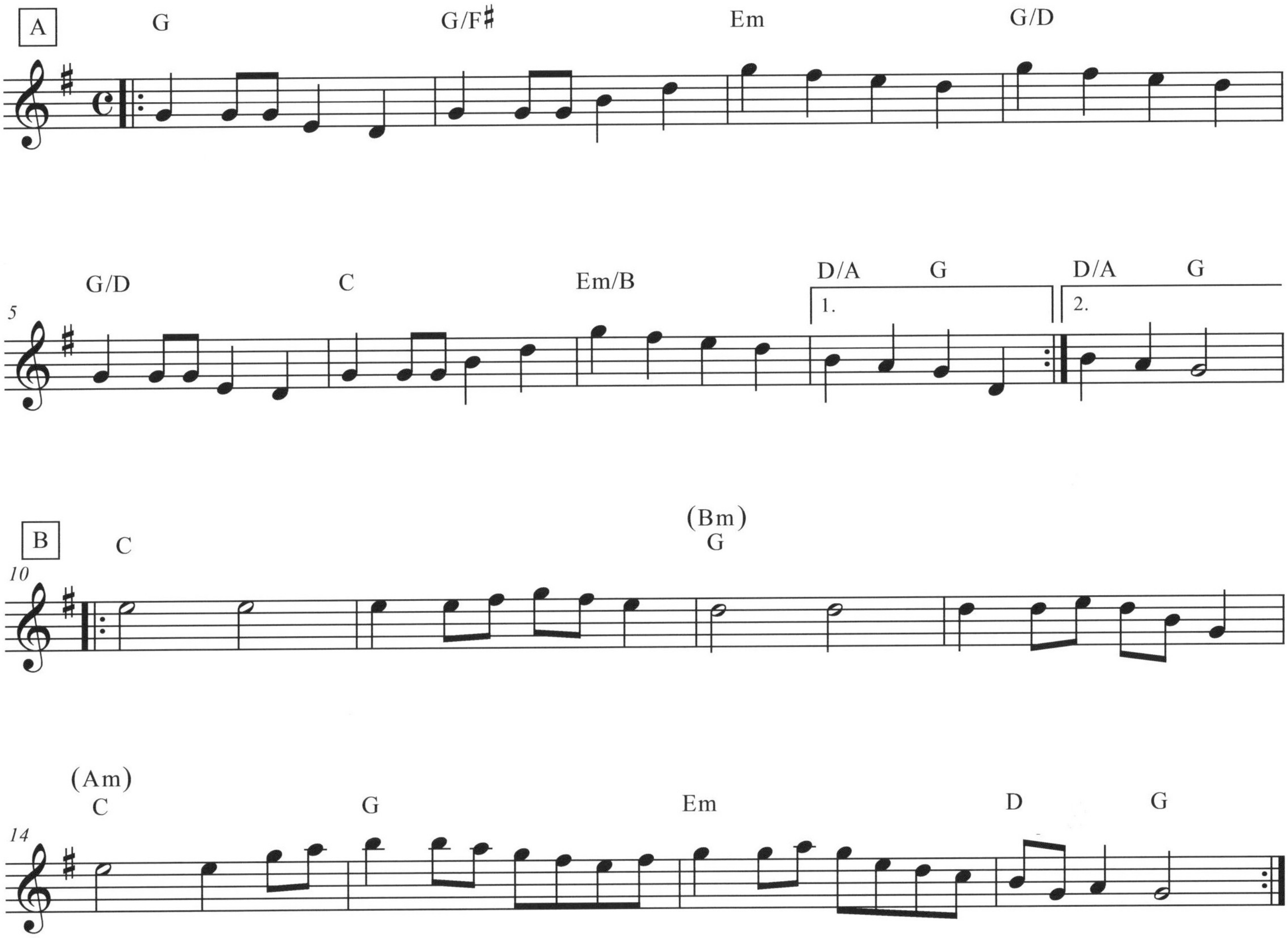

North Carolina Breakdown: variations

Recorded on Ken Kolodner's 2005 "Journey to the Heartland" and on "Hammered Dulcimer Arrangements: Fiddle Tunes Volume I" (2005)

Arthur Smith: Arranged by © Ken Kolodner

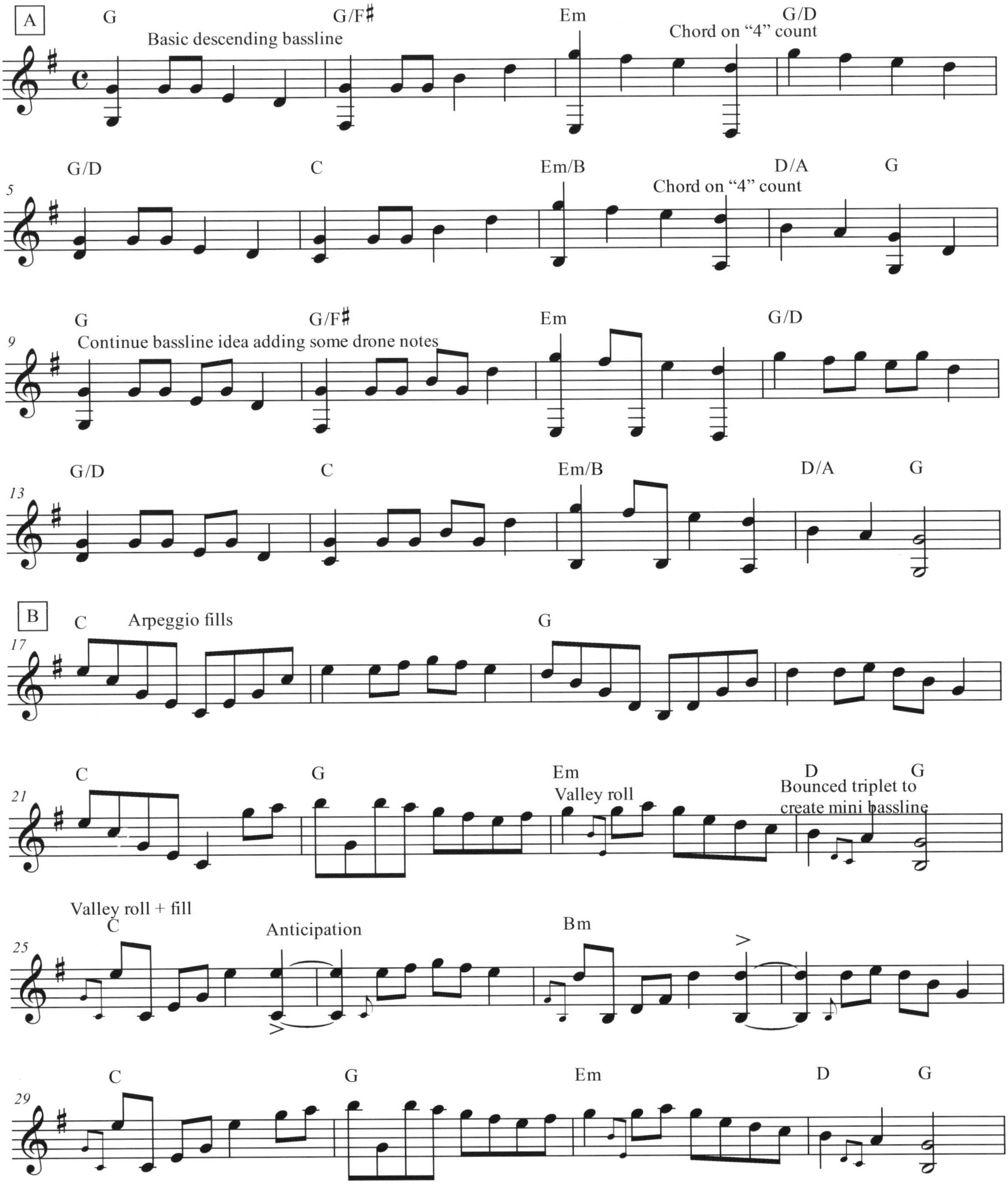

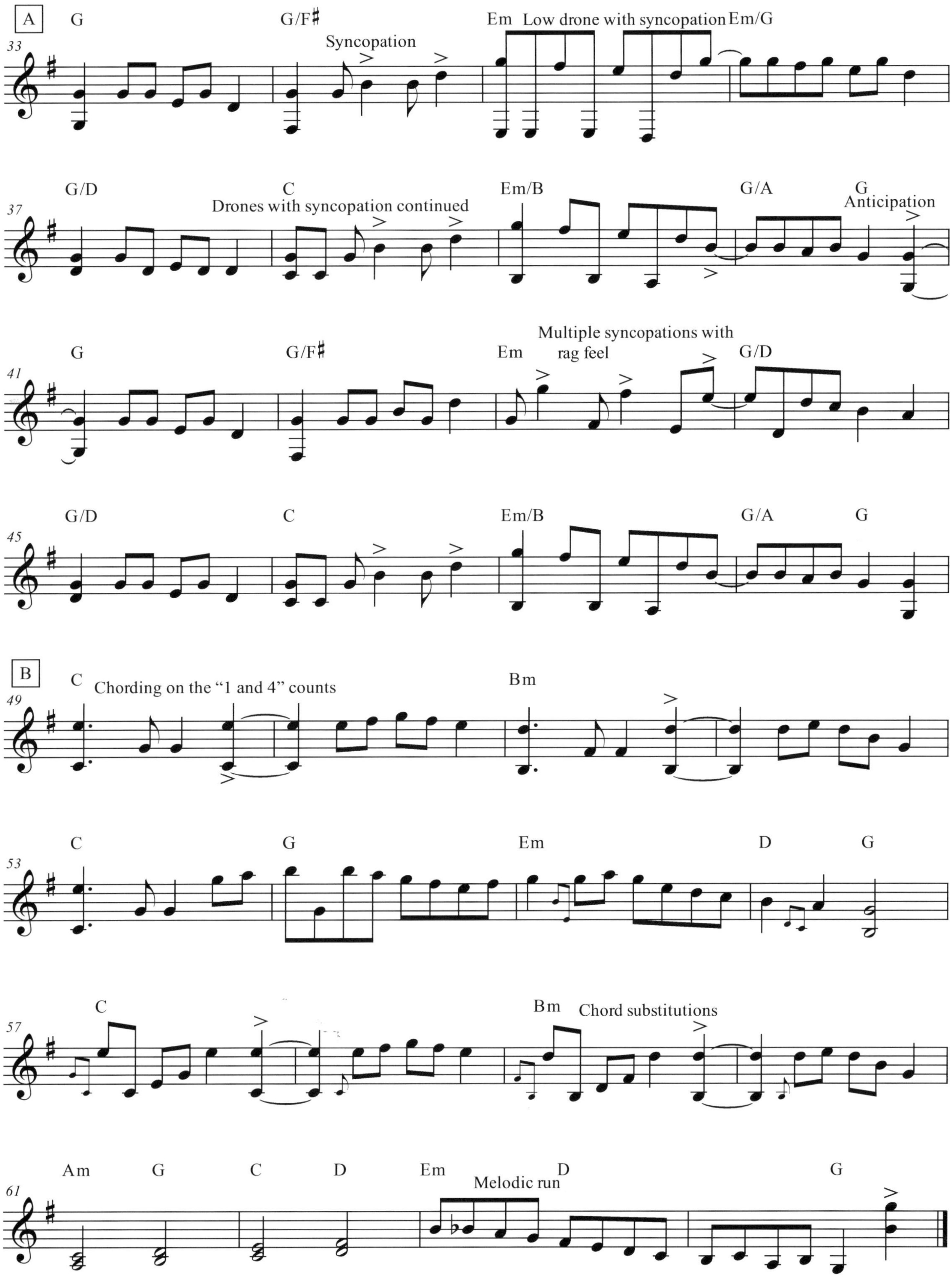
A
G
G/F♯
Syncopation
Em
Low drone with syncopation
Em/G
G/D
C
Drones with syncopation continued
Em/B
G/A
G
Anticipation
Multiple syncopations with
rag feel
B
Chording on the "1 and 4" counts
Bm
D
Chord substitutions
Am
Melodic run

O'Sullivan's Polka

Recorded on Ken Kolodner and Laura Risk's "A Roof for the Rain" (2001)

Ireland: Arranged by © Ken Kolodner

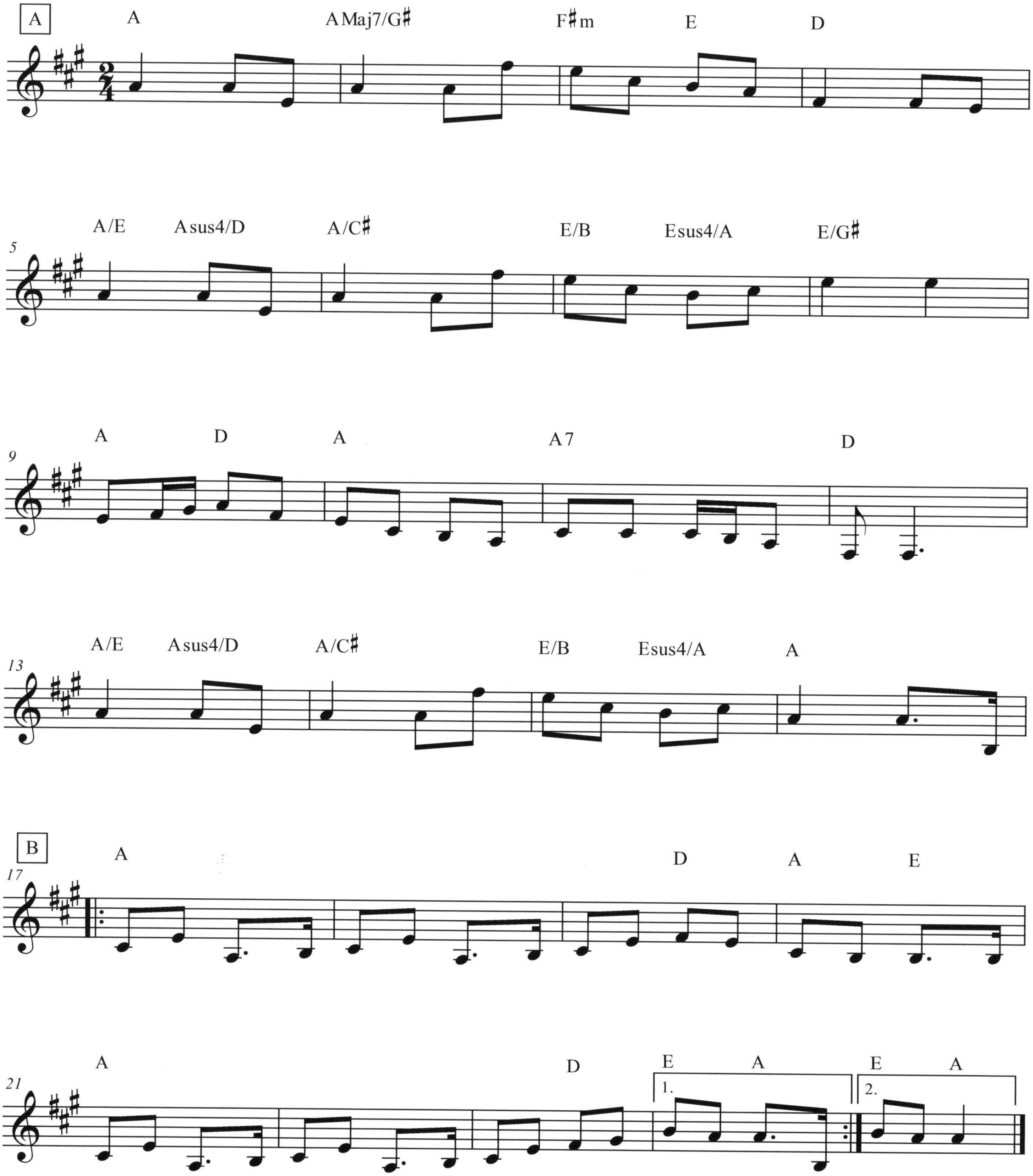

O'Sullivan's Polka: arrangement

Recorded on Ken Kolodner and Laura Risk's "Roof for the Rain" (2001)

Ireland: Arranged by © Ken Kolodner

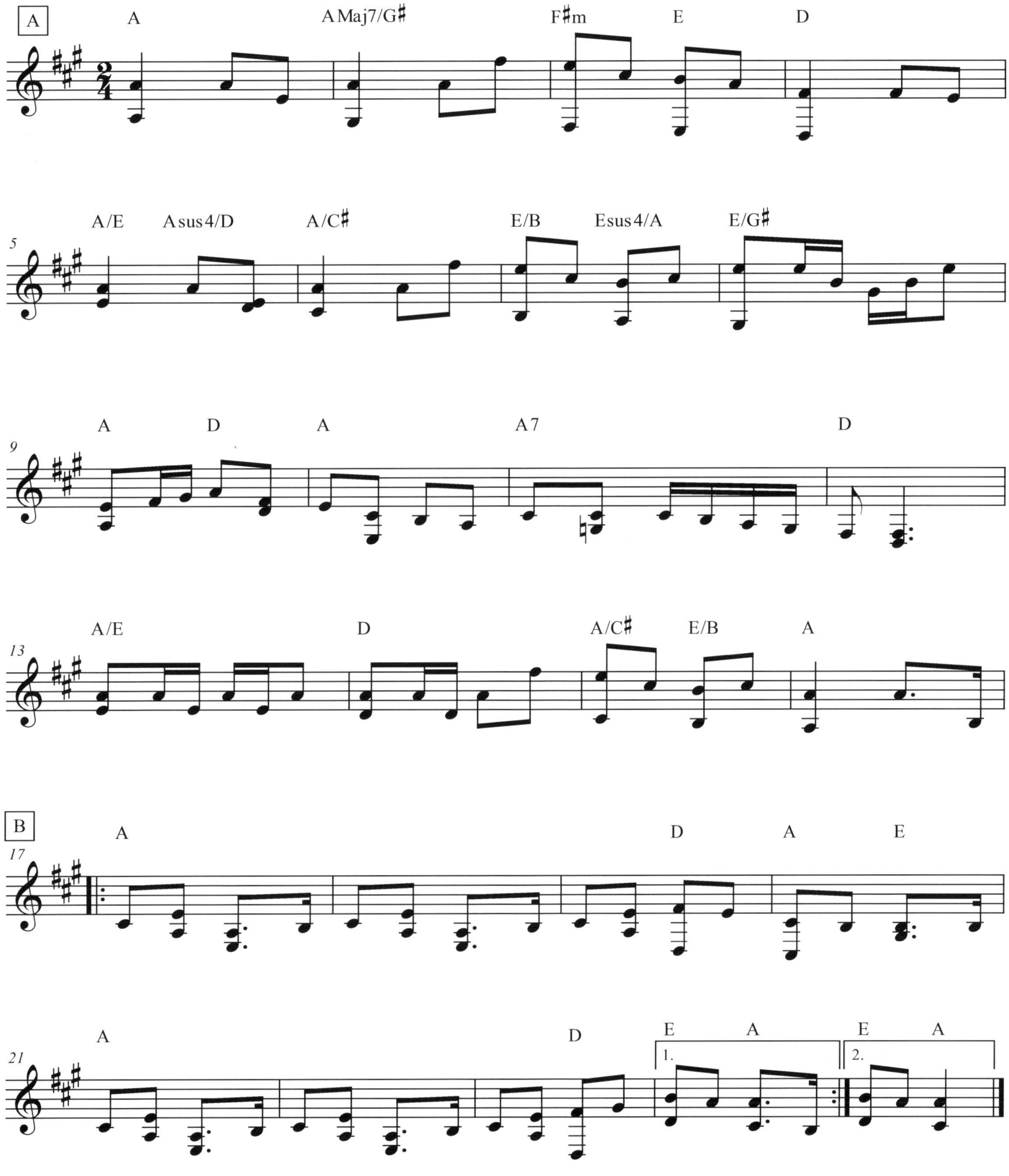

Oklahoma Rooster

Recorded on Helicon's "A Winter Solstice Celebration with Helicon" (1999)
and on "Hammered Dulcimer Arrangements: Fiddle Tunes Volume I" (2005)

U.S.: Arranged by © Ken Kolodner

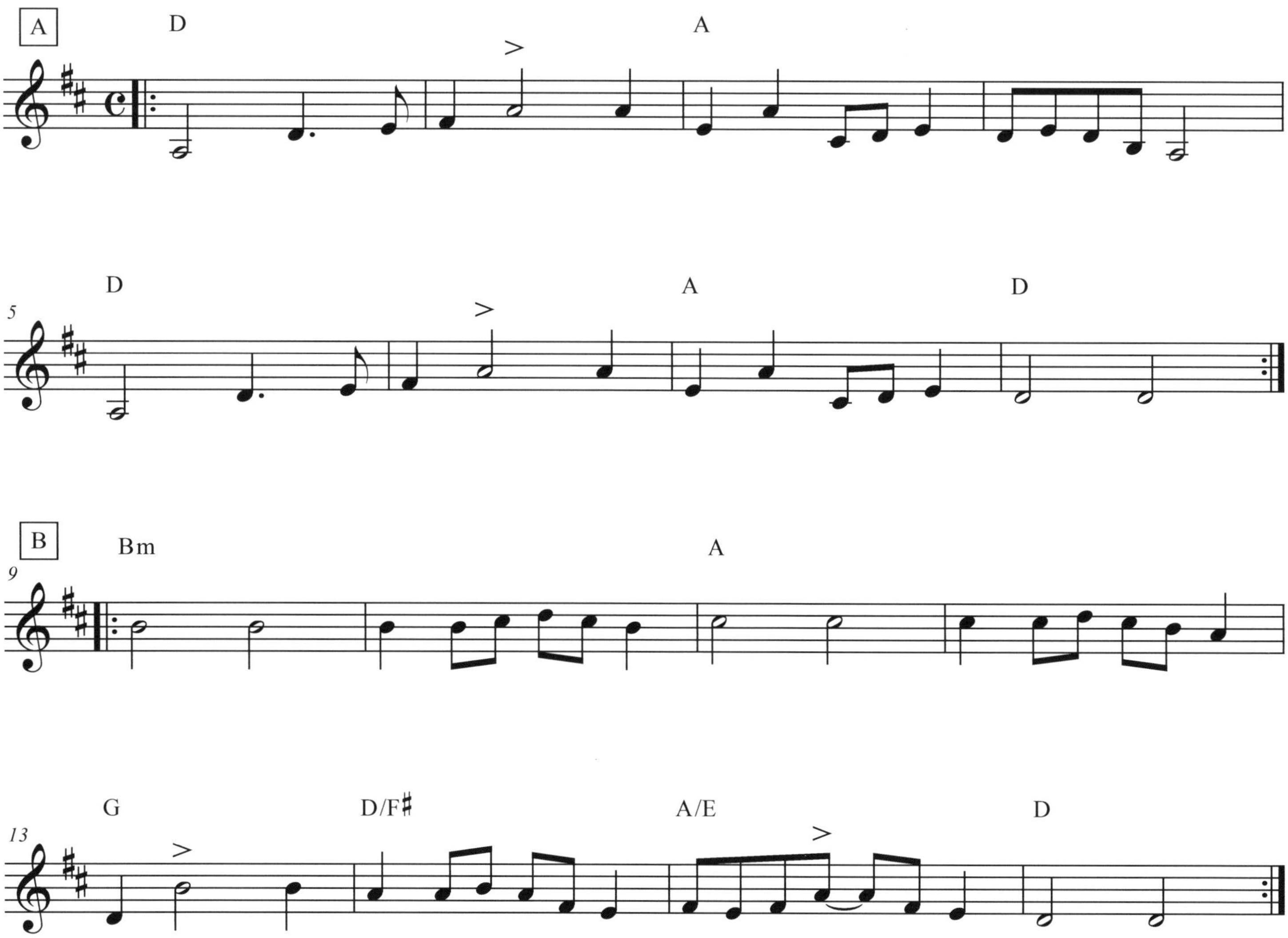

In old-time circles, many prefer a B major chord in place of the Bm in the B part. I sometimes insert an F♯7 between the two B parts or when moving to the B part.

Oklahoma Rooster: arranging ideas

Recorded on Helicon's "A Winter Solstice Celebration with Helicon" (1999)
and on "Hammered Dulcimer Arrangements: Fiddle Tunes Volume I" (2005)

U.S.: Arranged by © Ken Kolodner

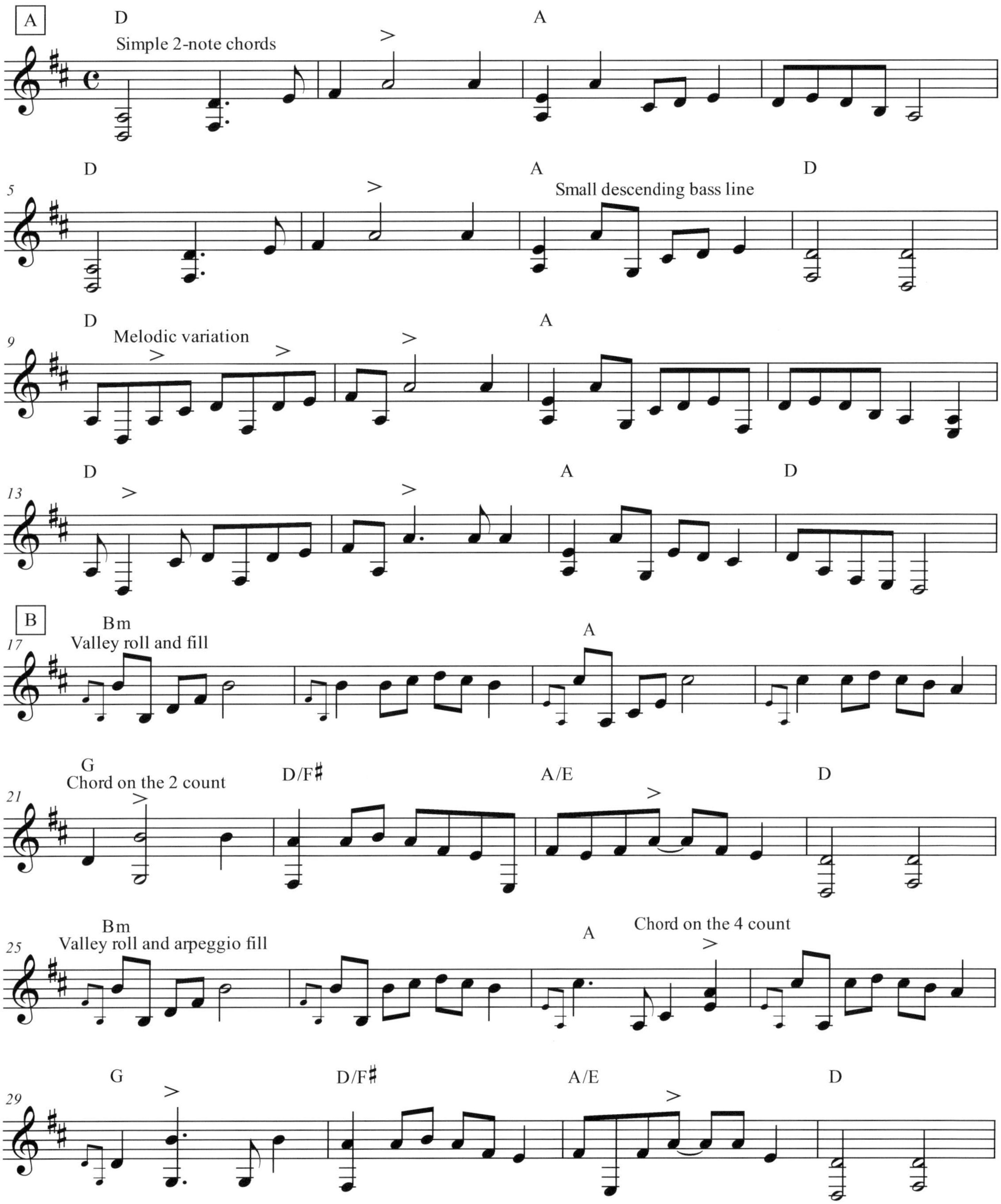

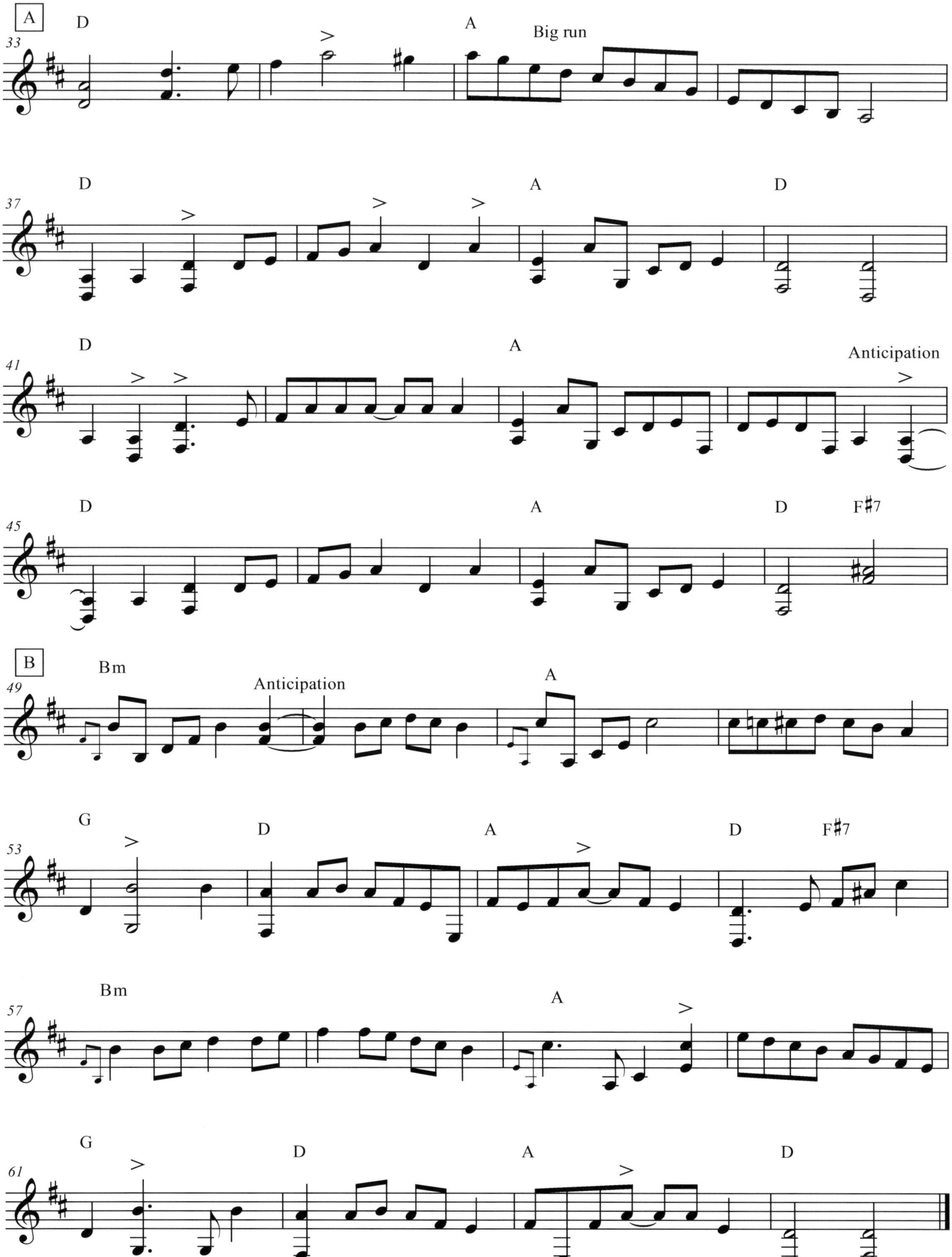
A
D
A
Big run
D
A
D
D
A
Anticipation
D
A
D
F♯7
B
Bm
Anticipation
A
G
D
A
D
F♯7
Bm
A
G
D
A
D

The Old Favorite

Recorded on Greenfire's "Greenfire" (1998) with
Ken Kolodner, Laura Risk, and Robin Bullock

Ireland: Arranged by © Ken Kolodner

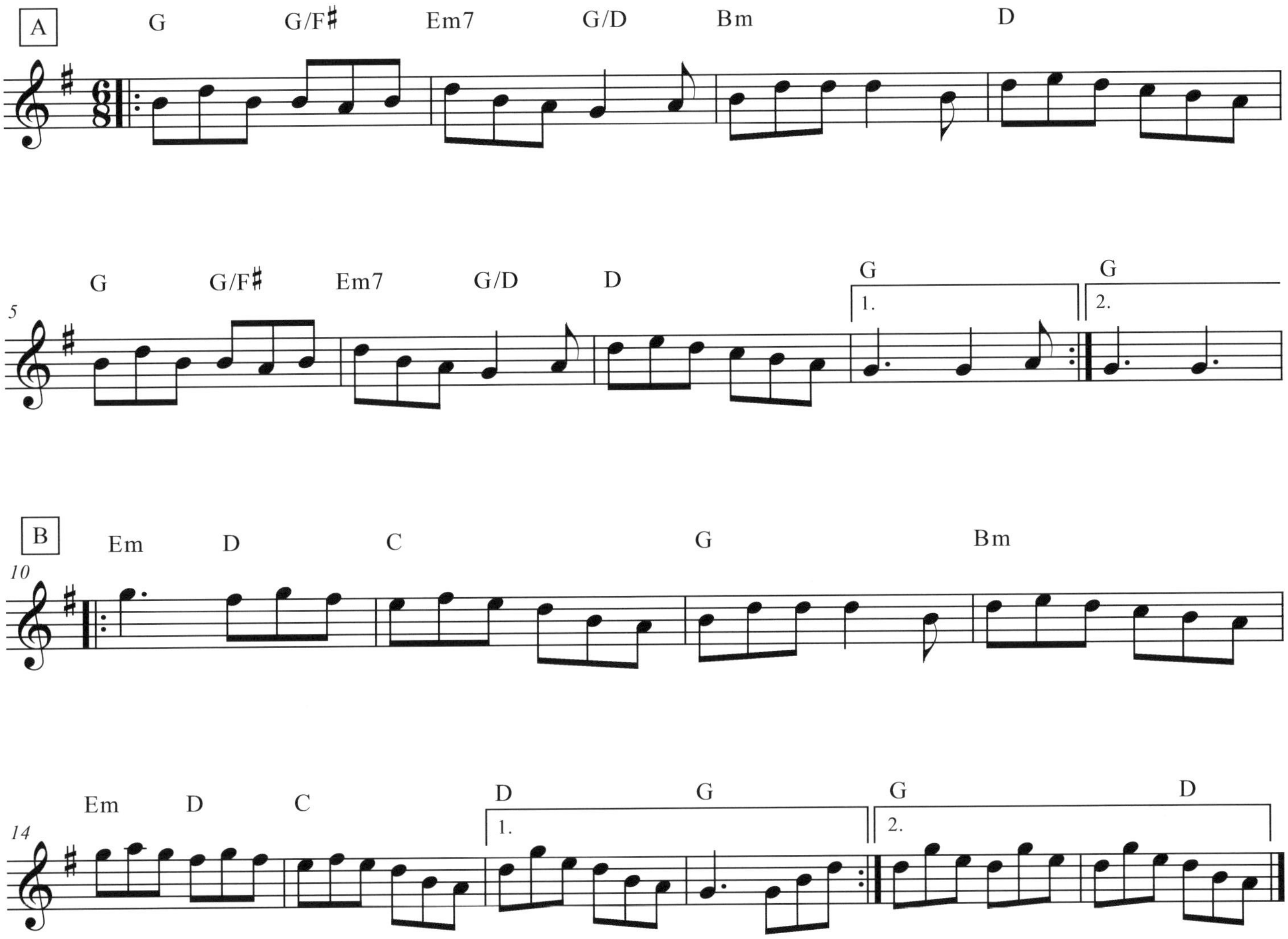

The Old Favorite: arranging ideas

Recorded on Greenfire's "Greenfire" (1998) with
Ken Kolodner, Laura Risk and Robin Bullock

Ireland: Arranged by © Ken Kolodner

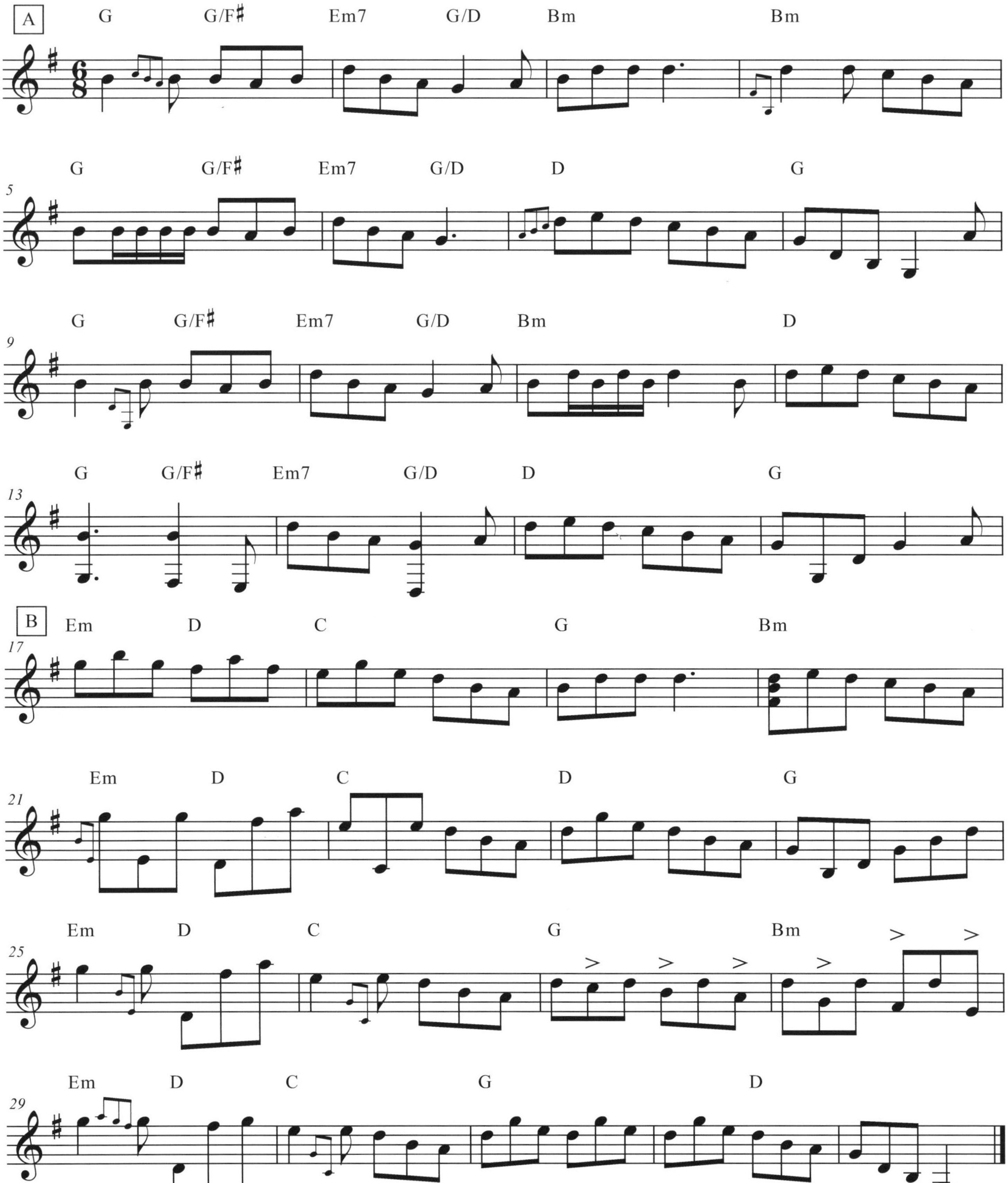

Over the Waterfall

U.S.: Arranged by © Ken Kolodner

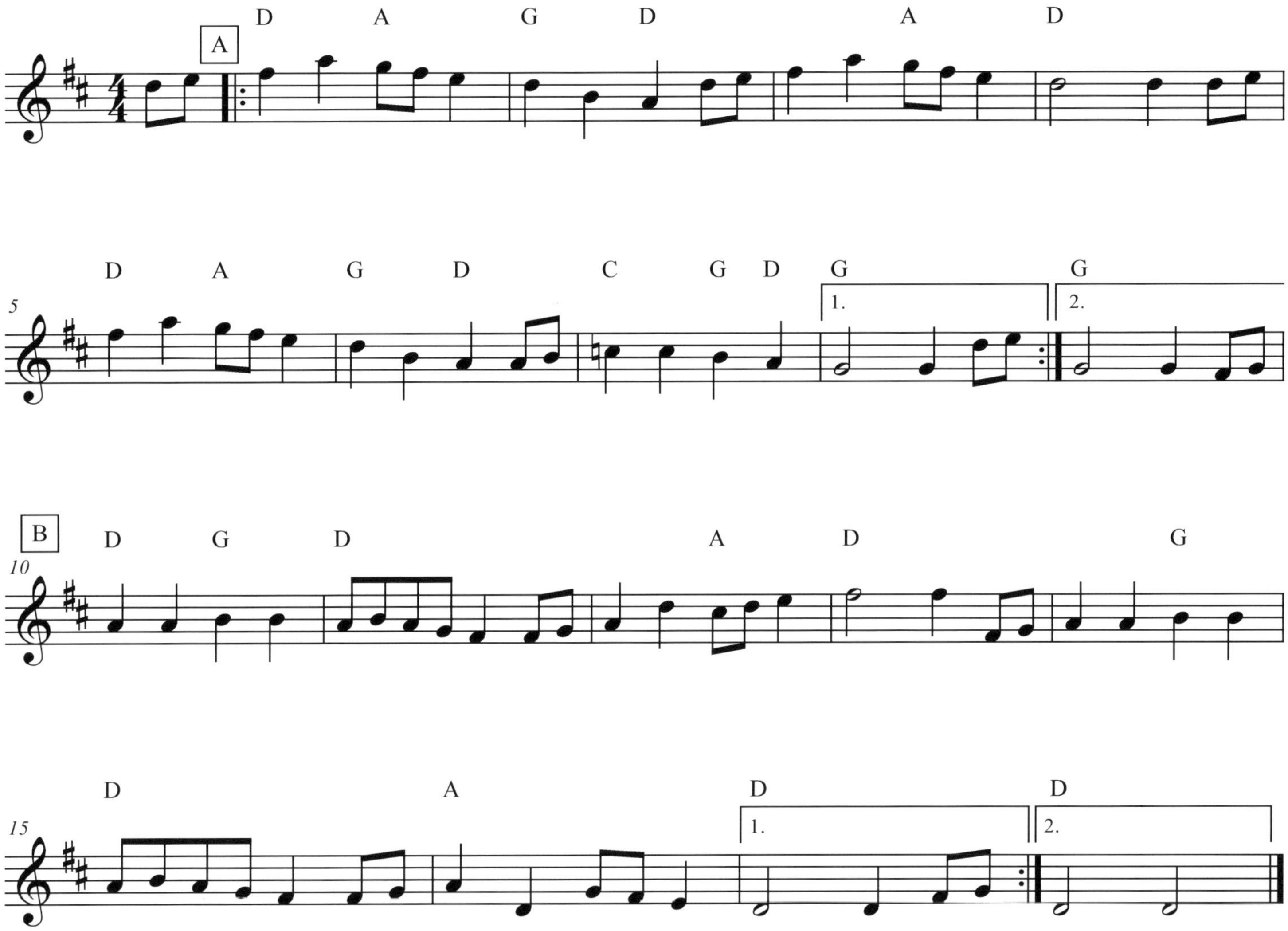

Over the Waterfall: arrangement #1

U.S.: Arranged by © Ken Kolodner

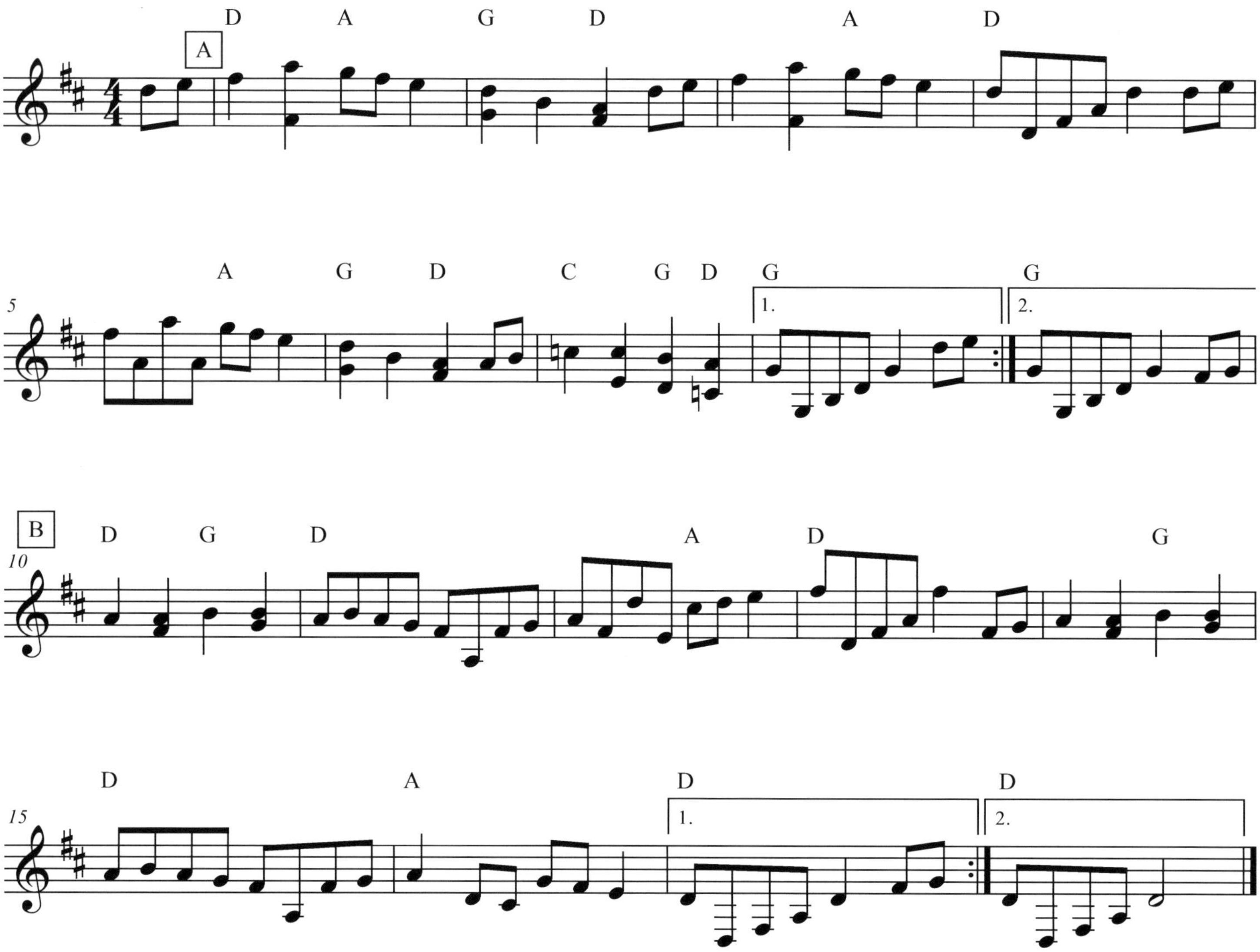

Over the Waterfall: variations

U.S.: Arranged by © Ken Kolodner

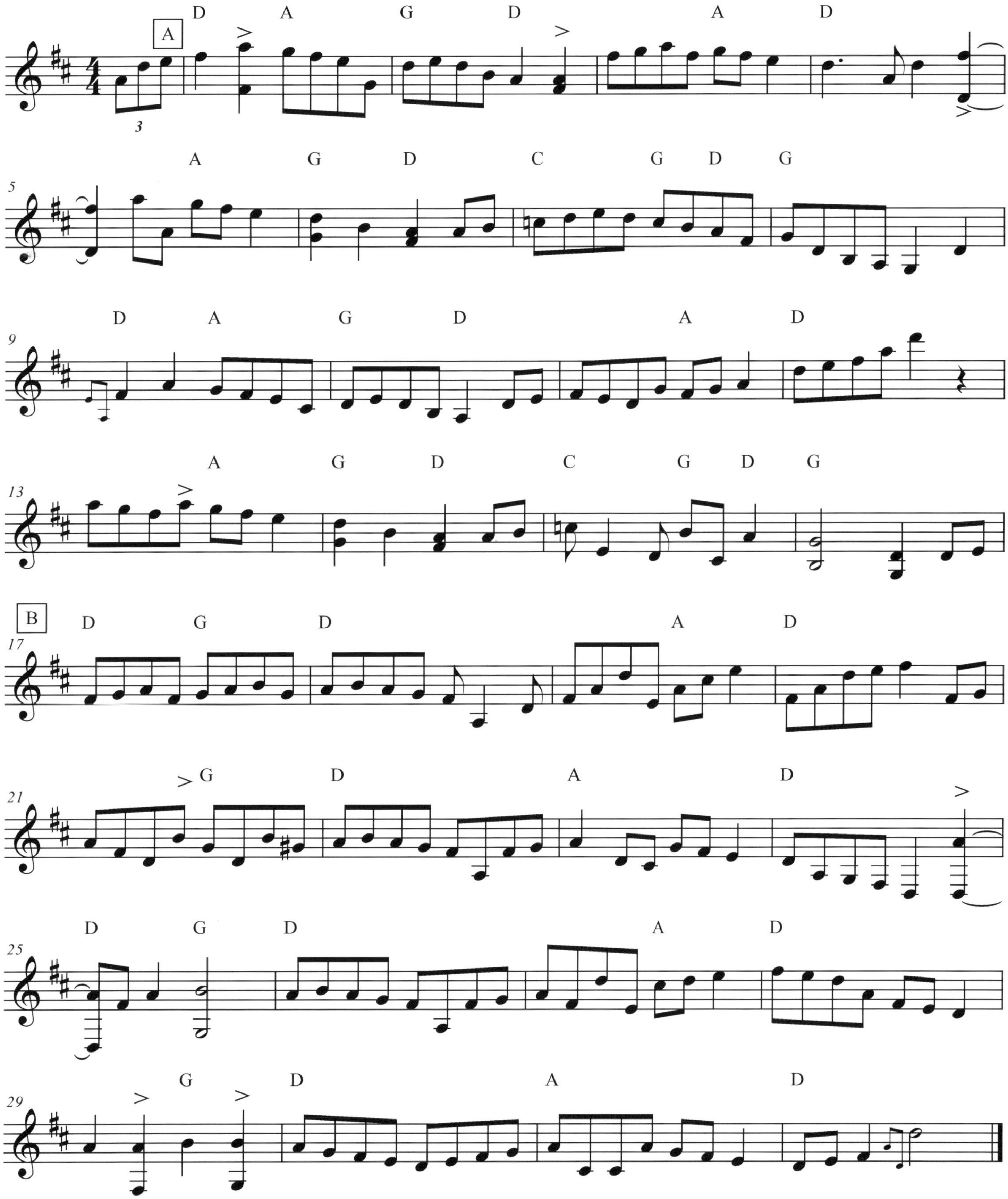

Reel du Nord

Quebec: Arranged by © Ken Kolodner

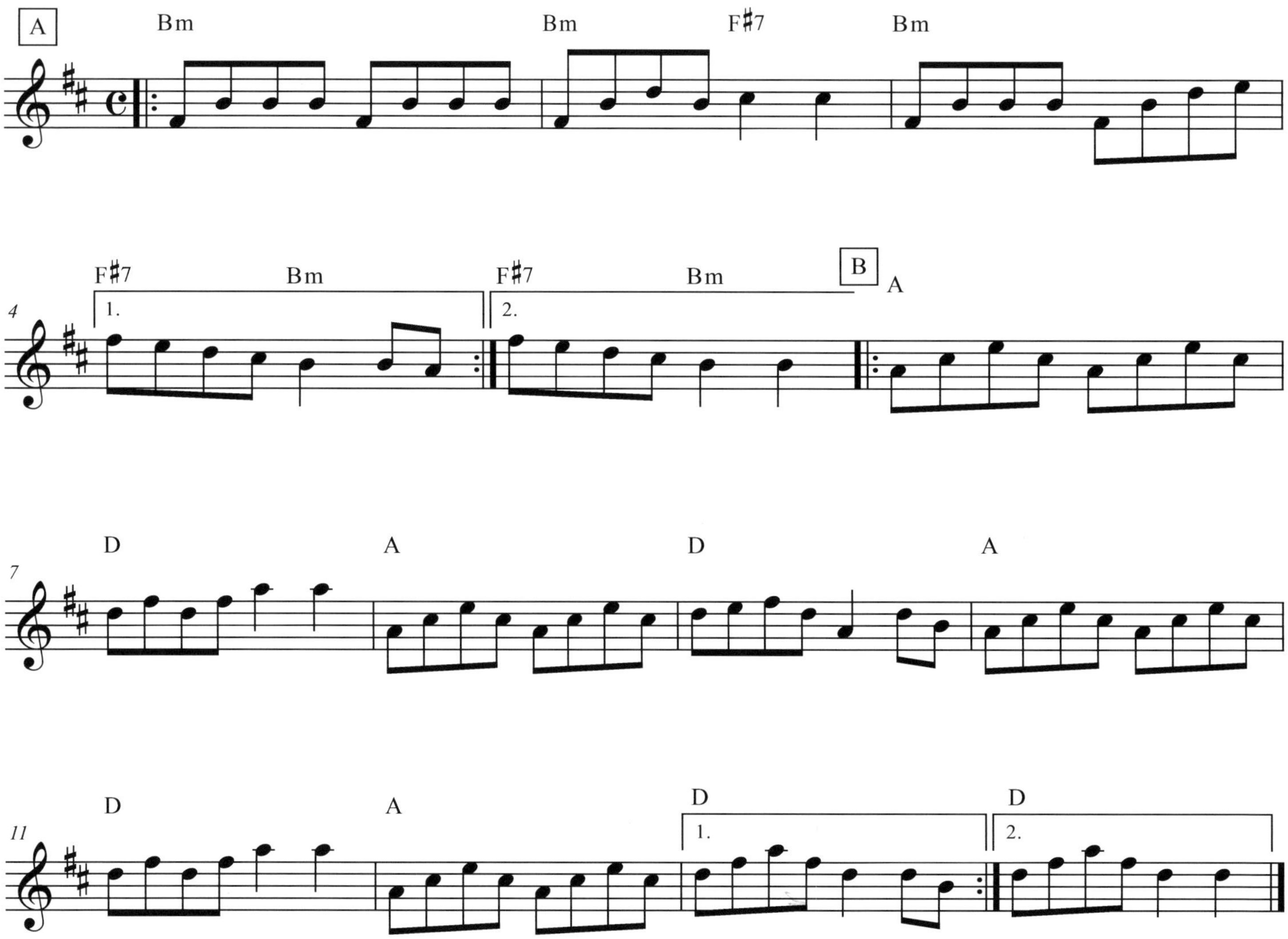

This simple tune uses just two chords in each part and is basically just arpeggios. The tune fits comfortably in two octaves and provides great opportunities for phrasing, accent shifts and creating variations.

Reel du Nord: arranging ideas

Quebec: Arranged by © Ken Kolodner

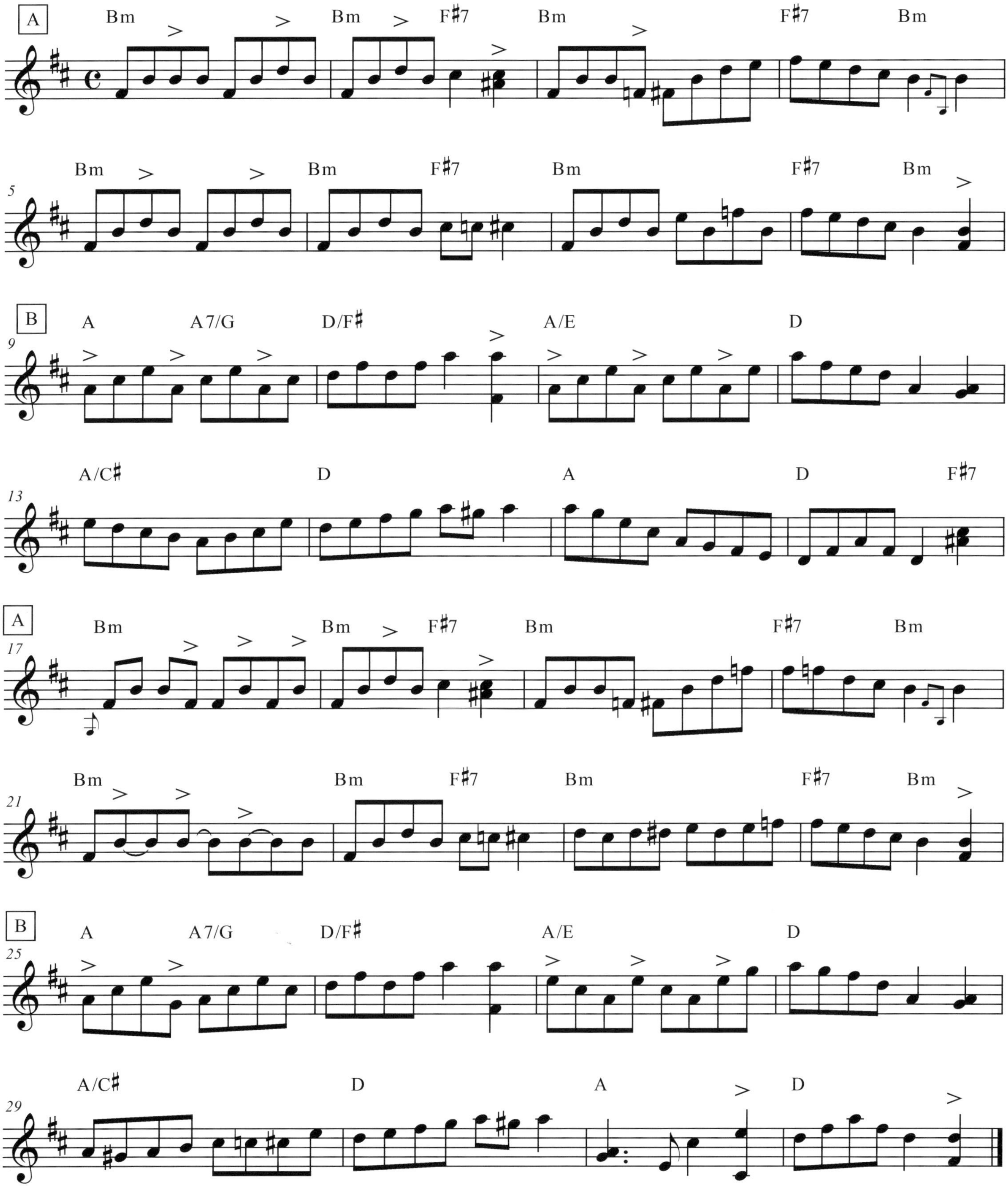

Reel St. Joseph: melody with accompaniment

On Ken Kolodner and Laura Risk's "Roof for the Rain" (2001) and on
"Hammered dulcimer arrangements: Reels and fiddle tunes Volume II" (2005)

Quebec: Arranged by © Ken Kolodner

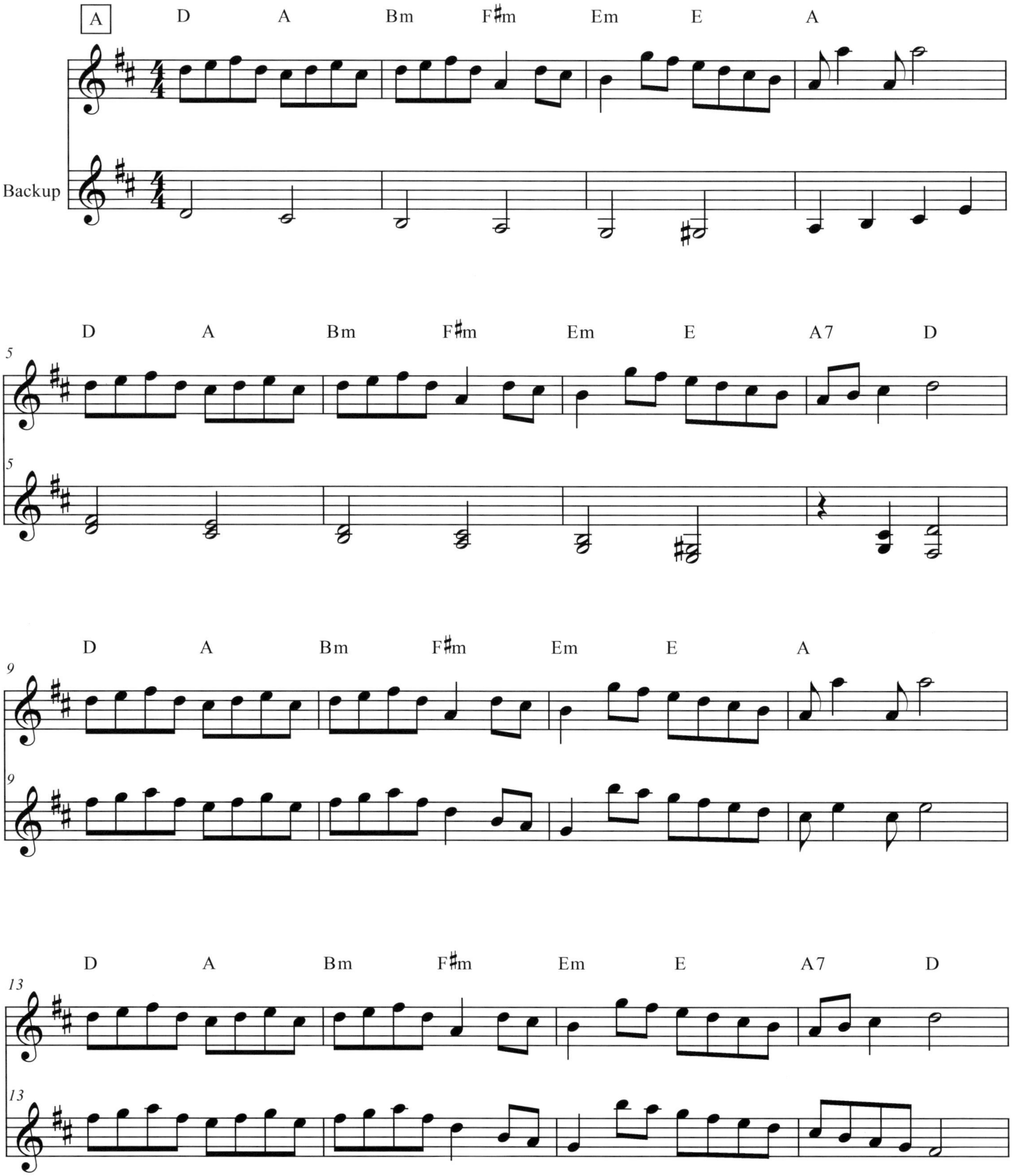

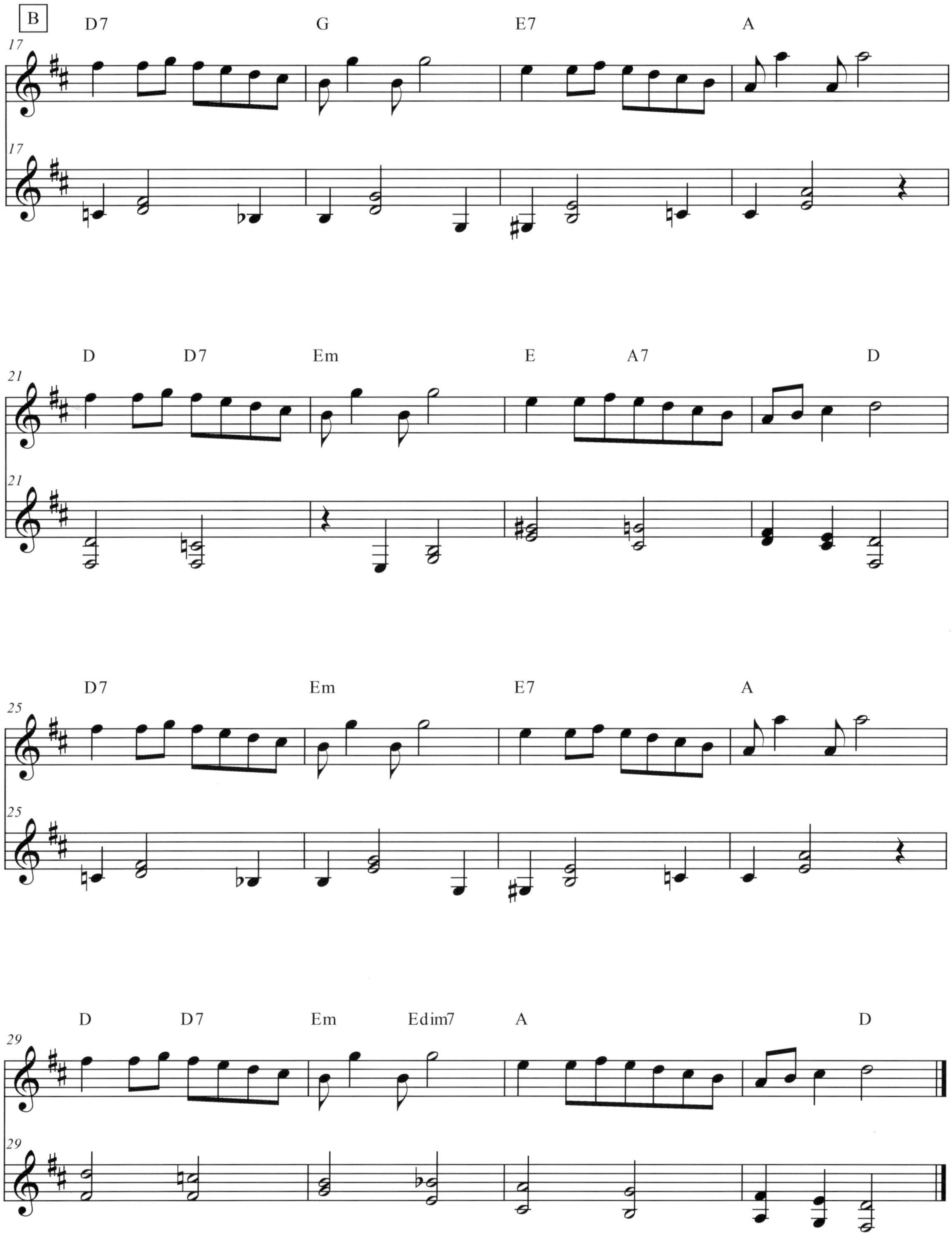

This is a simplified version of a classic ending! Much fun!!

Reel St. Joseph: arrangement #1

On Ken Kolodner and Laura Risk's "Roof for the Rain" (2001) and on
"Hammered dulcimer arrangements: Fiddle Tunes (Reels) Volume II (2005)"

Quebec: Arranged by © Ken Kolodner

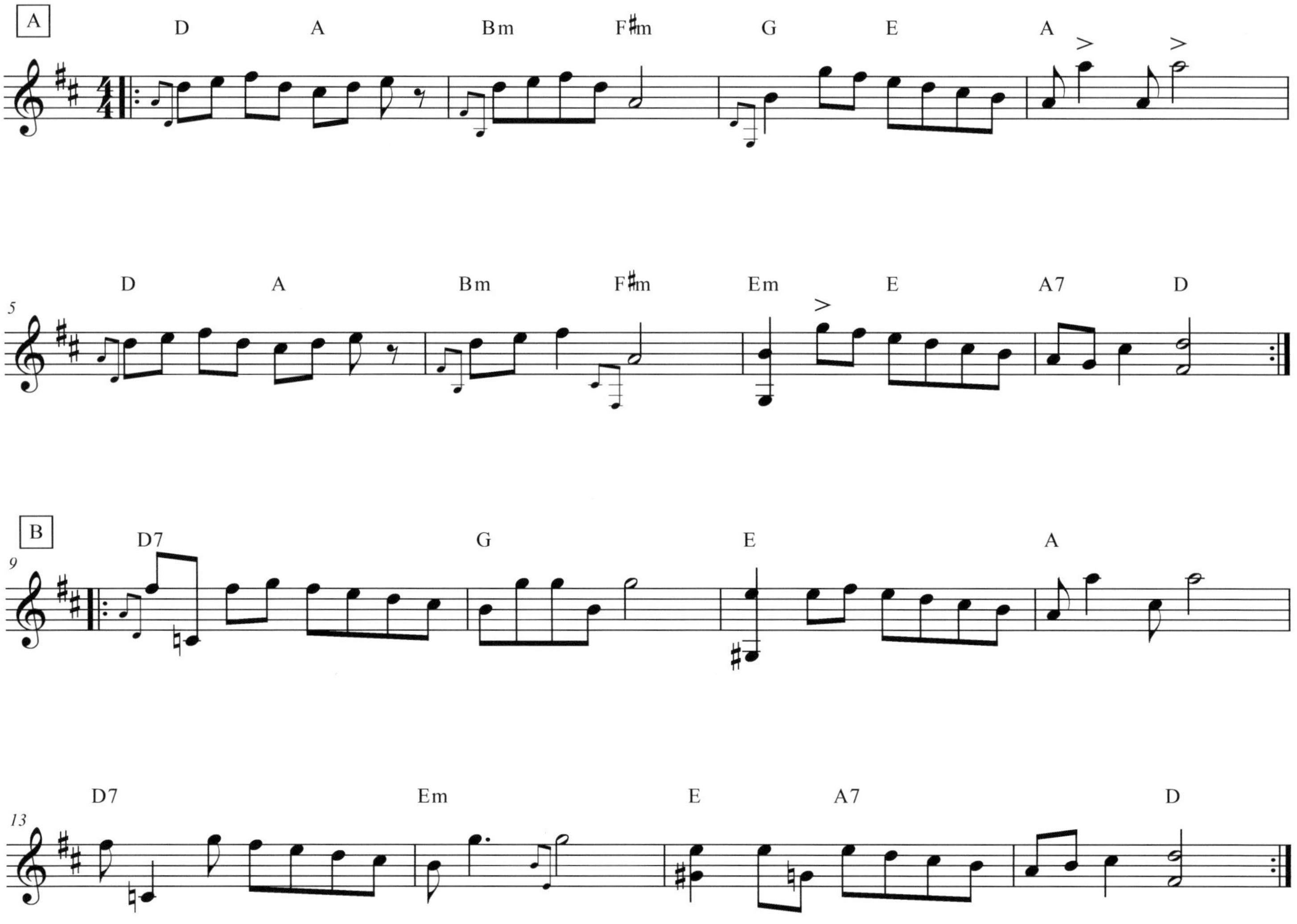

Reel St. Joseph: variations

On Ken Kolodner and Laura Risk's "Roof for the Rain" (2001) and on "Hammered dulcimer arrangements: Fiddle Tunes (Reels) Volume II (2005)"

Quebec: Arranged by © Ken Kolodner

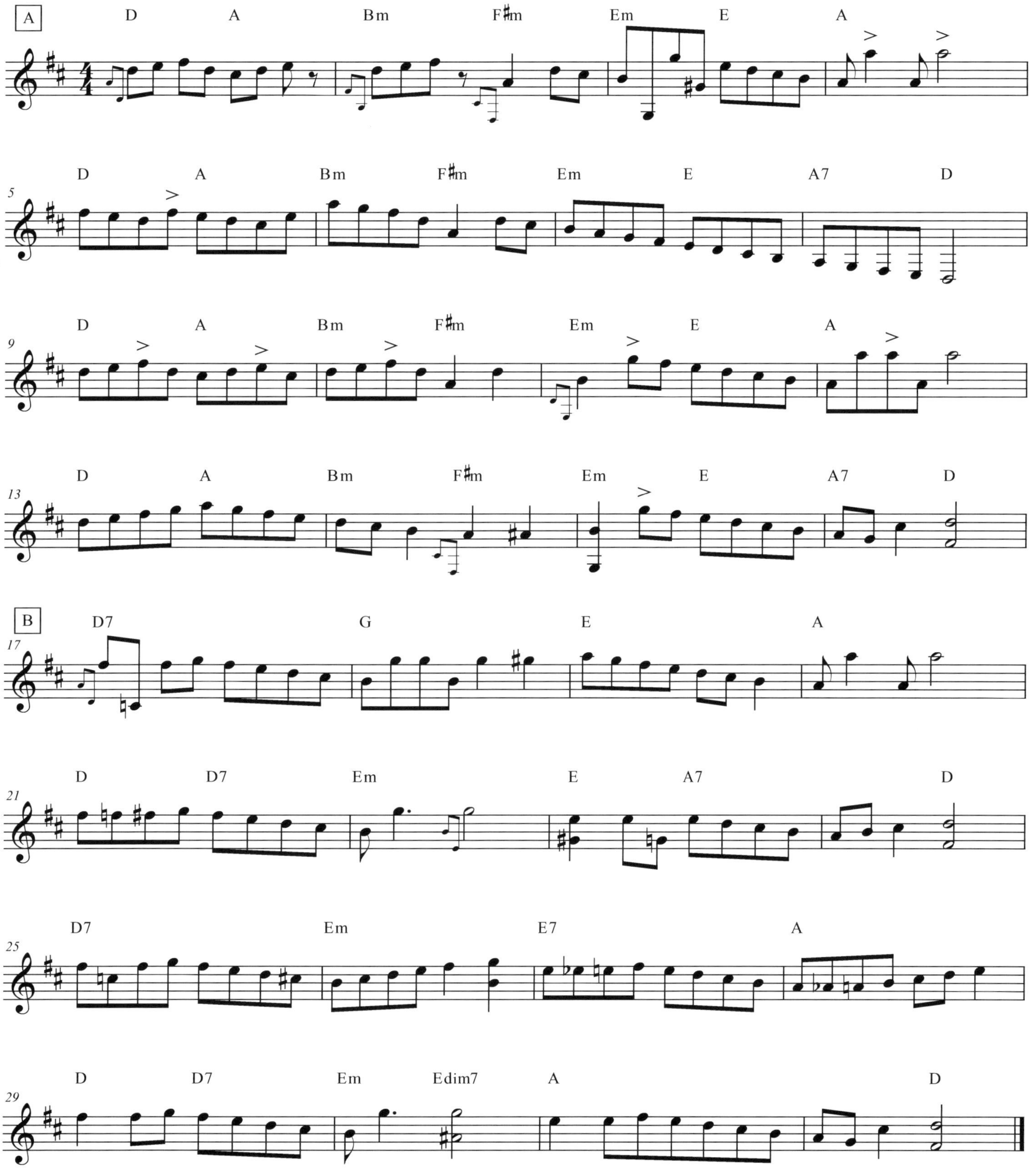

The Rights of Man

James Hill (Ireland): Arranged by © Ken Kolodner

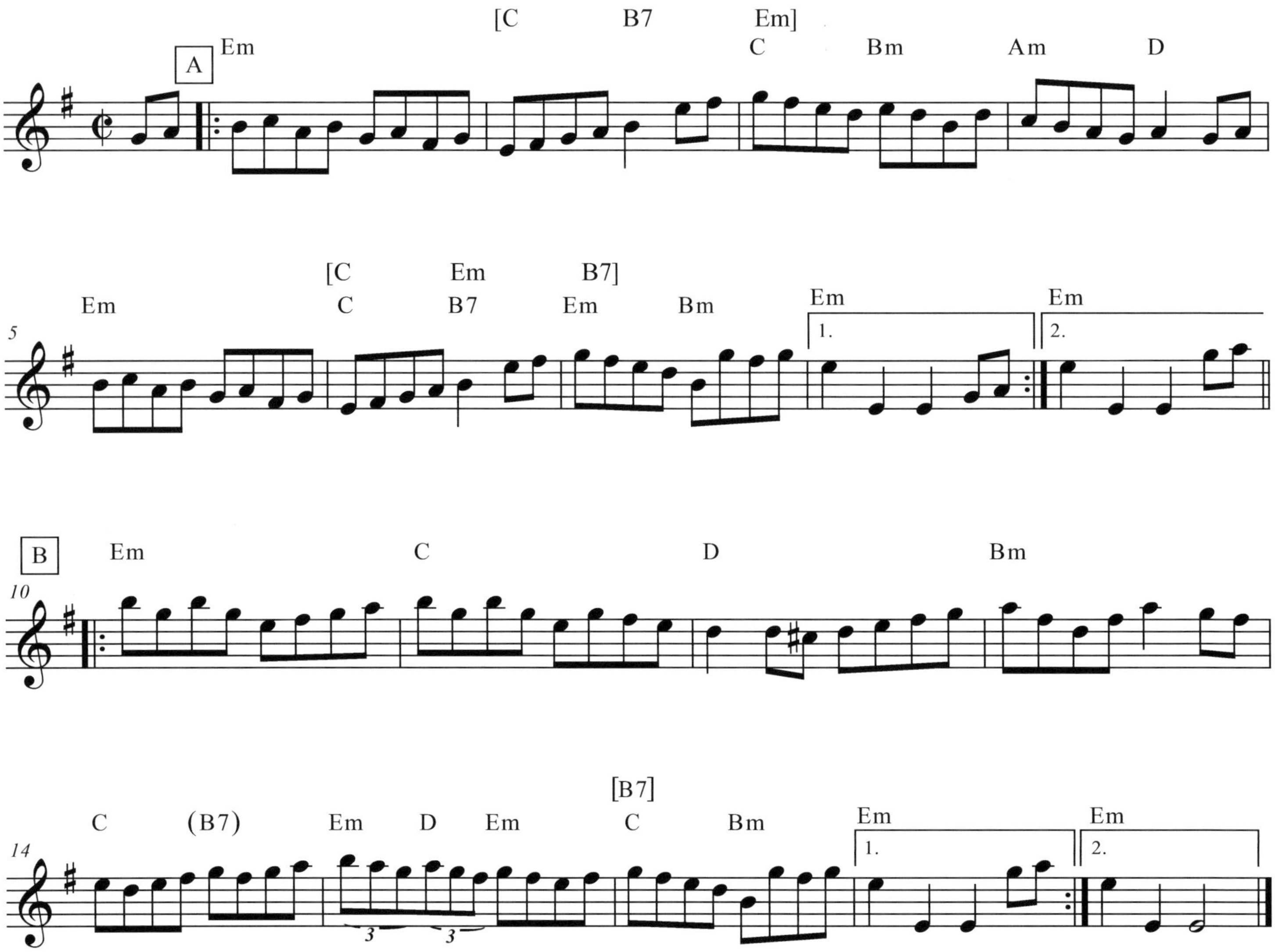

The Rights of Man: arranging ideas

James Hill (Ireland): Arranged by © Ken Kolodner

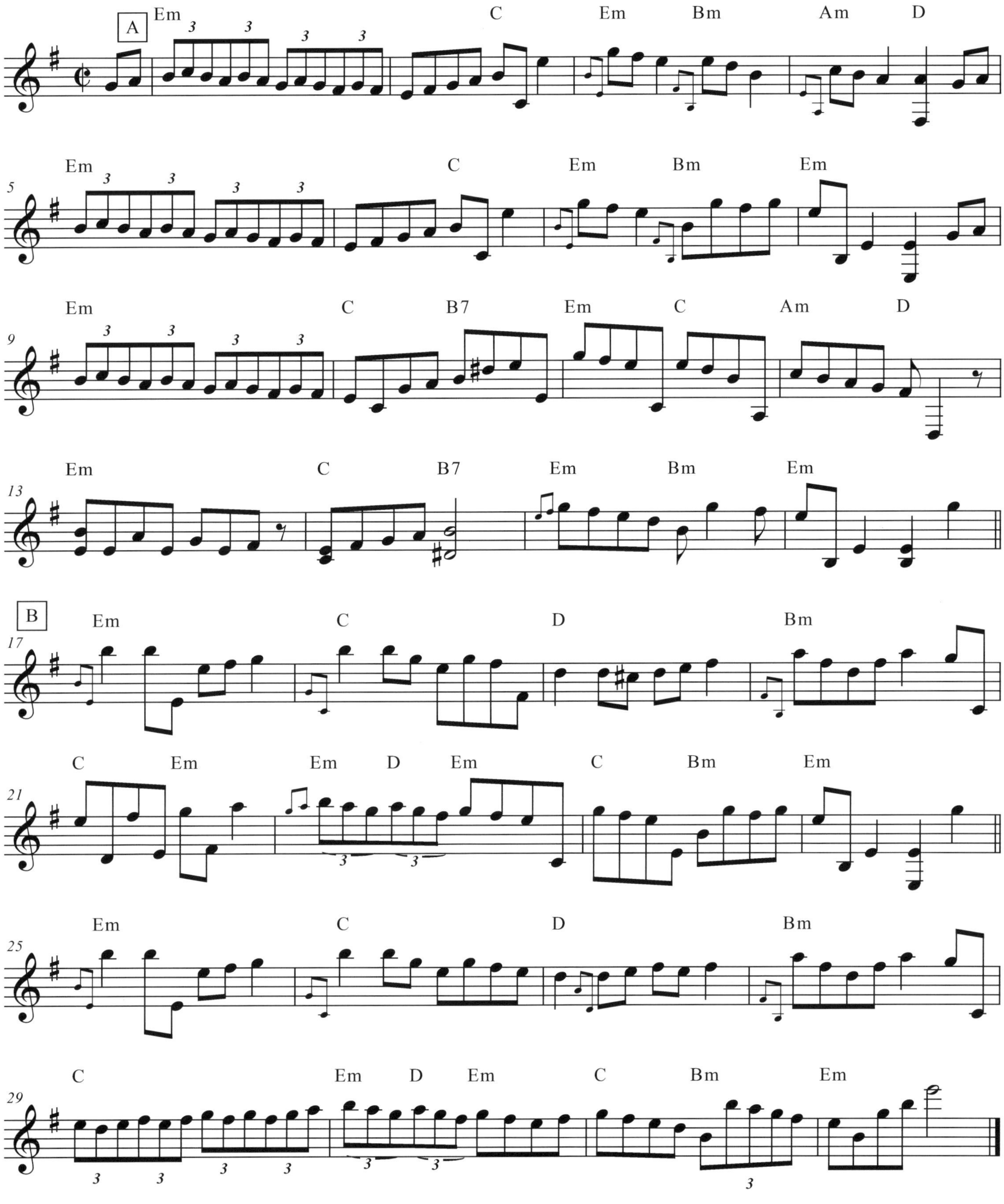

The Road to Banff

Recorded on Ken Kolodner and Elke Baker's "Out of the Wood" (2011)

Malcolm Reavell (Nineties Collection 31): Arranged by © Ken Kolodner

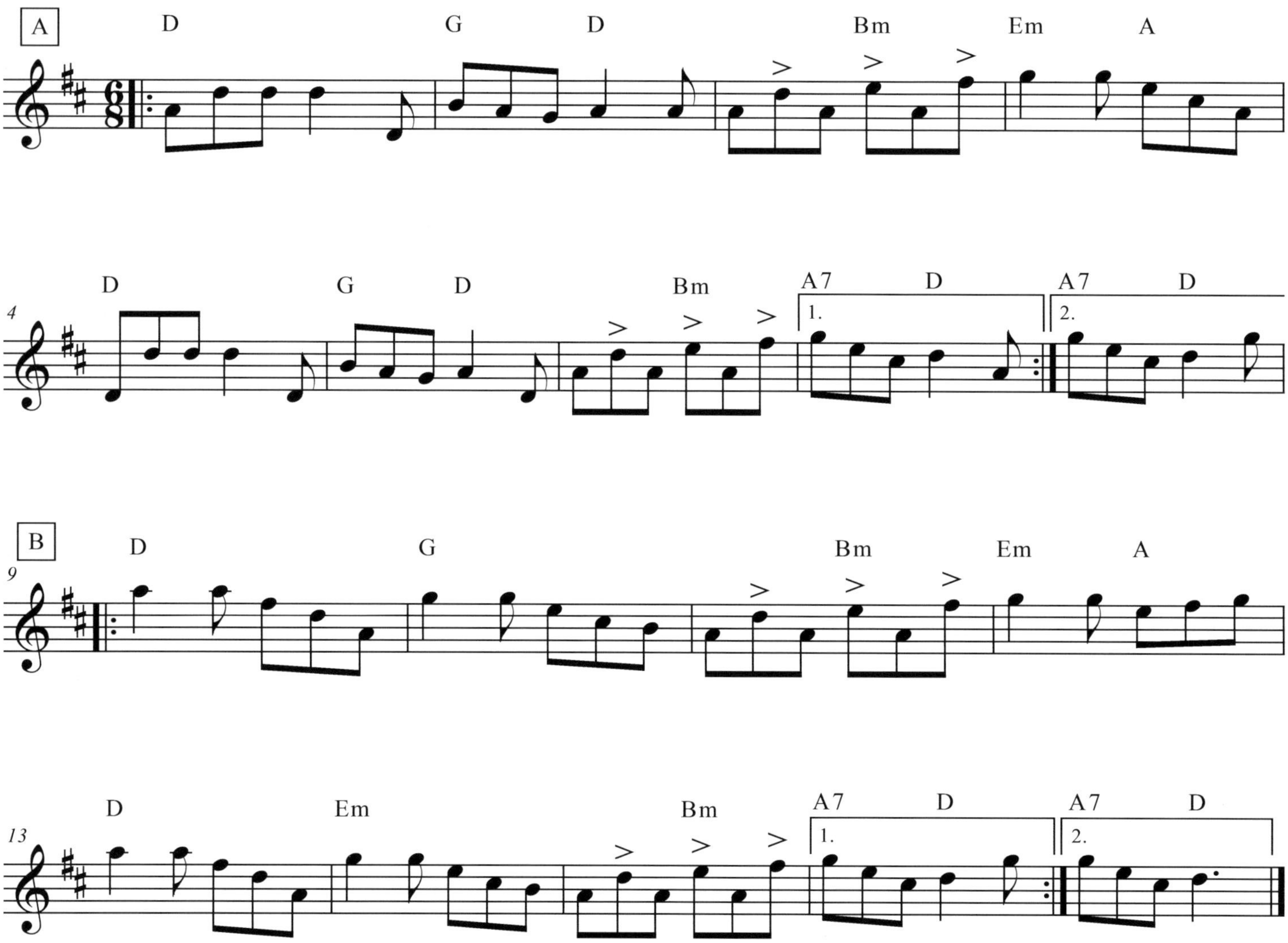

This tune can be played nicely in a lower octave as well.

The Road to Banff: arranging ideas

Recorded on Ken Kolodner and Elke Baker's "Out of the Wood" (2011)

Malcolm Reavell (Nineties Collection 31): Arranged by © Ken Kolodner

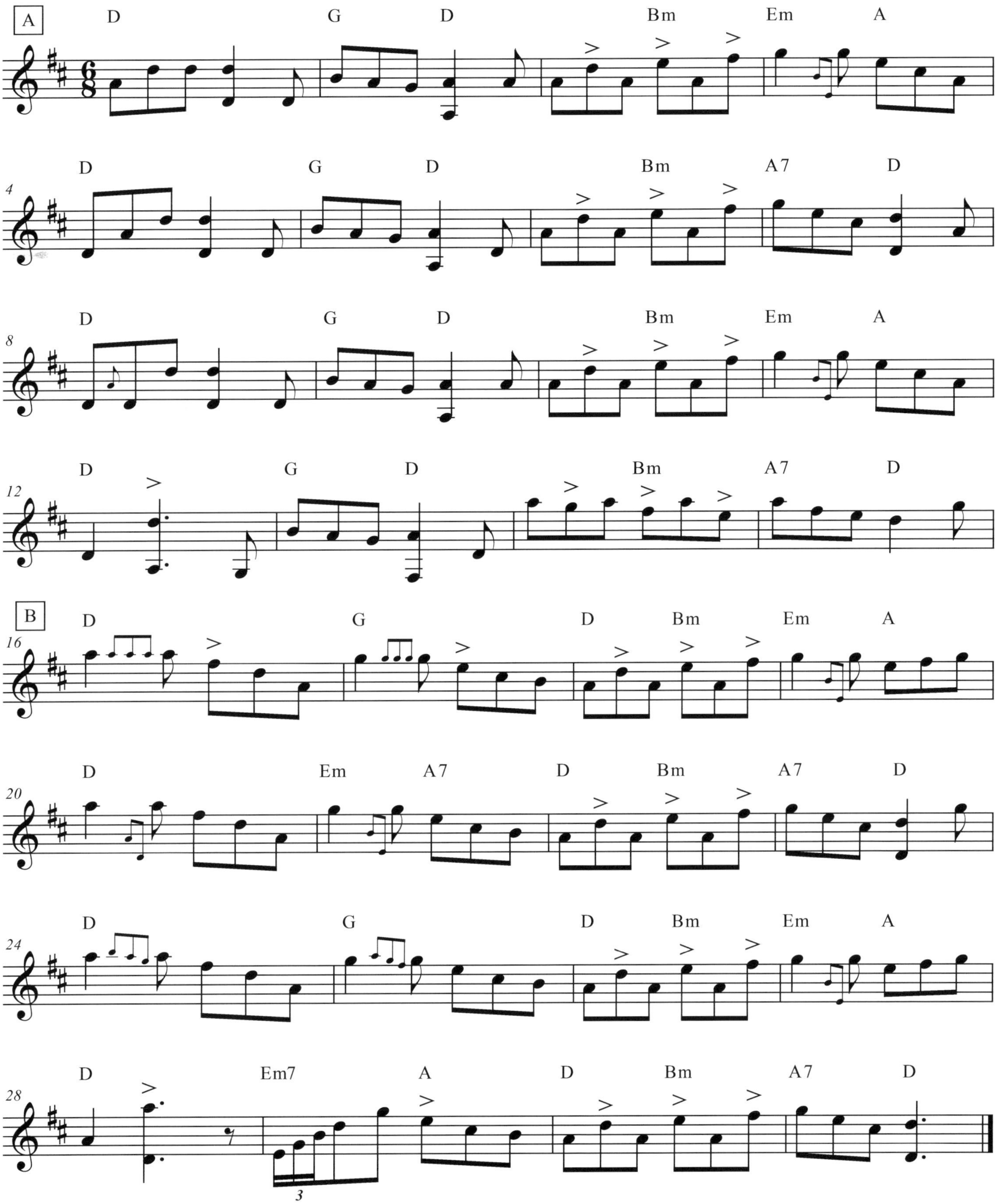

A Roof for the Rain: with chords and accompaniment

Recorded on Ken Kolodner and Laura Risk's "Roof for the Rain" (1999)
and on Brad and Ken Kolodner's "Otter Creek" (2011)

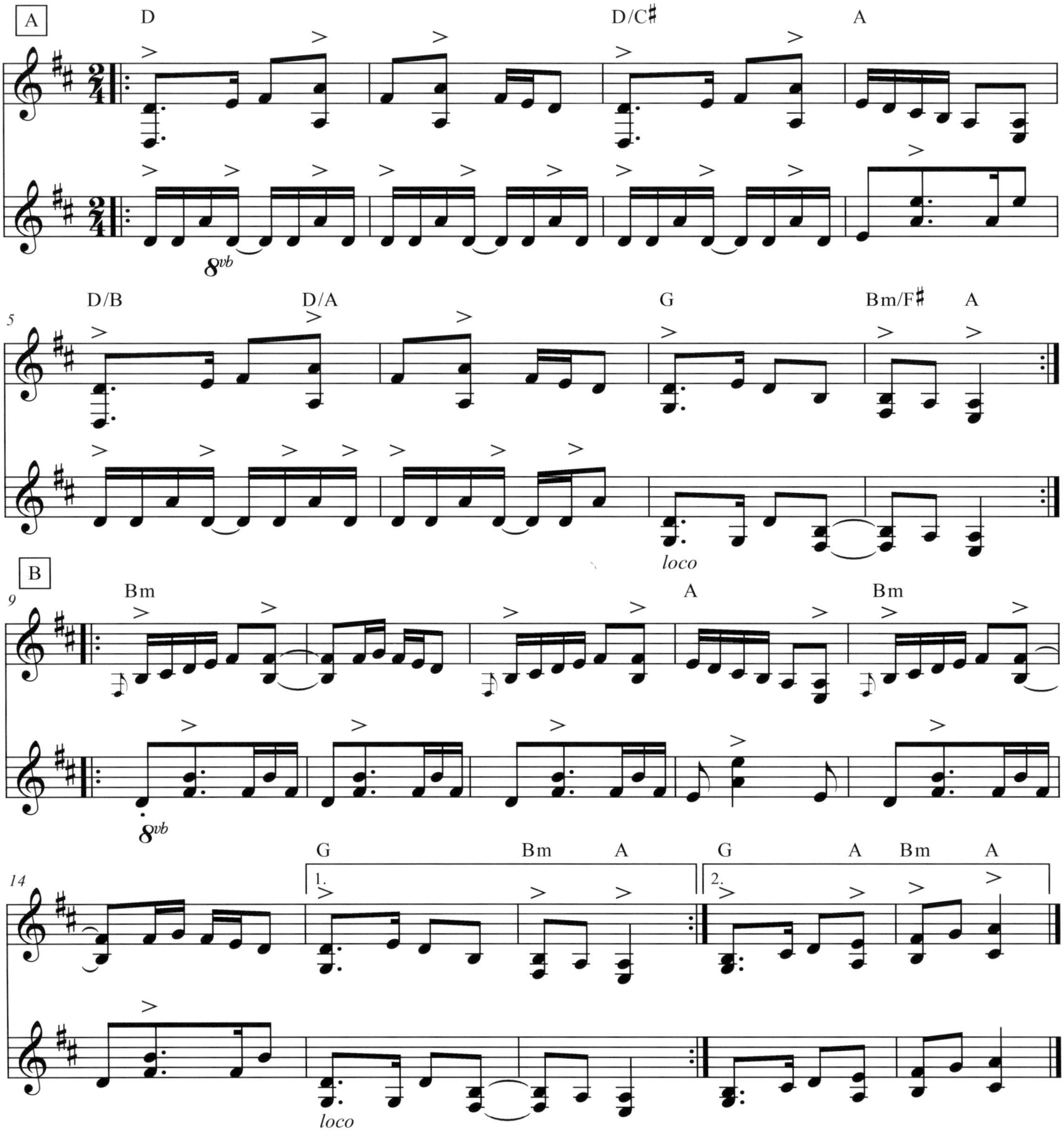

The key to making this tune drive is to really hit the accents. However, try playing the eighth notes very lightly but with almost no swing. To enhance readability, the backup was mostly written one octave higher than it should be played ("loco" indicates "return to original octave"). As a general rule of thumb, an accompaniment works best when it is played in a different range than the melody. Thinking in eighth notes, the backup in the A part uses an accent pattern on the counts of "1-4-7." The B part uses "1 3 6 7 8" with the primary accent on the "3."

Roscoe: melody, harmony, accompaniment

U.S.: Arranged by © Ken Kolodner

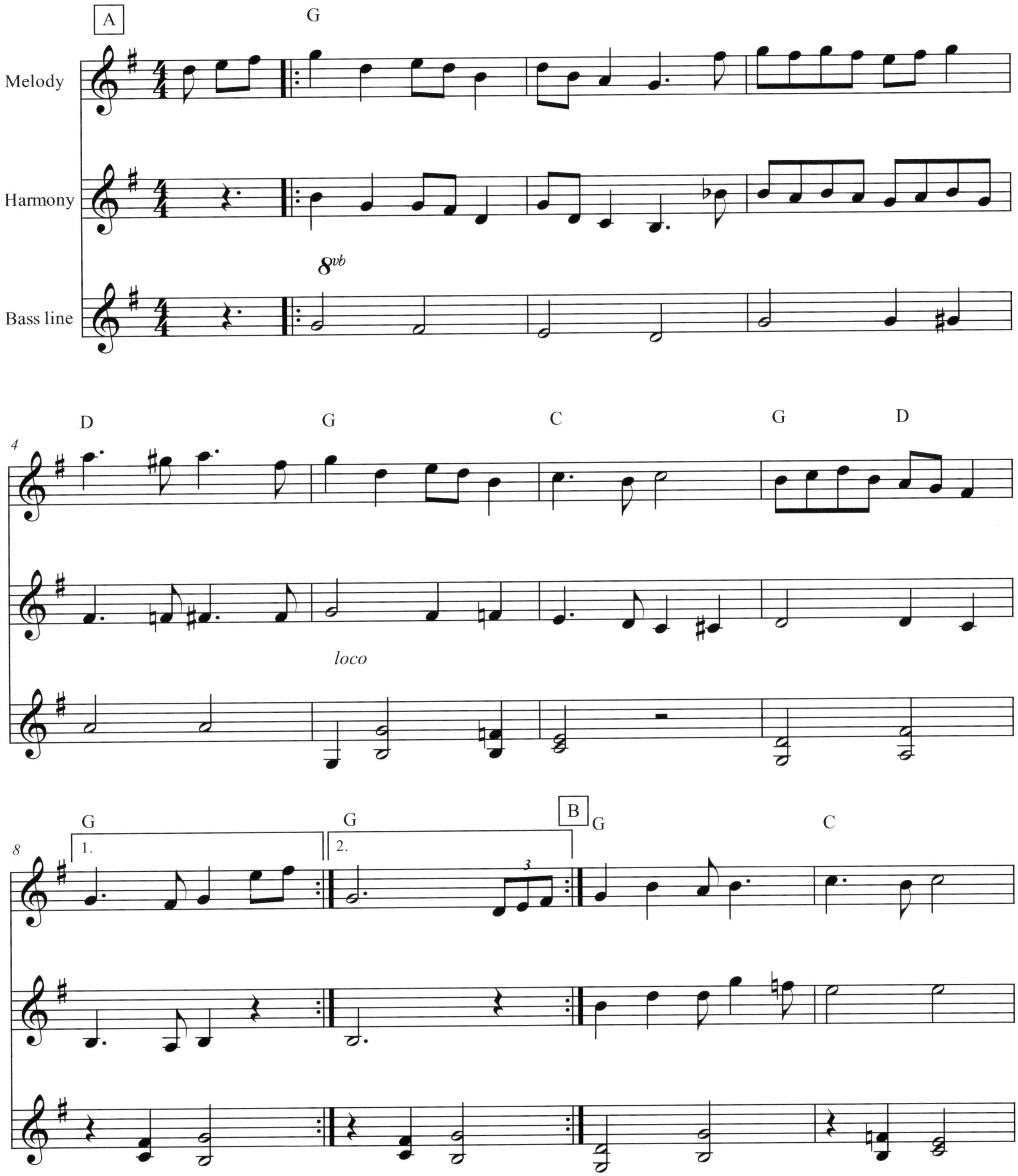

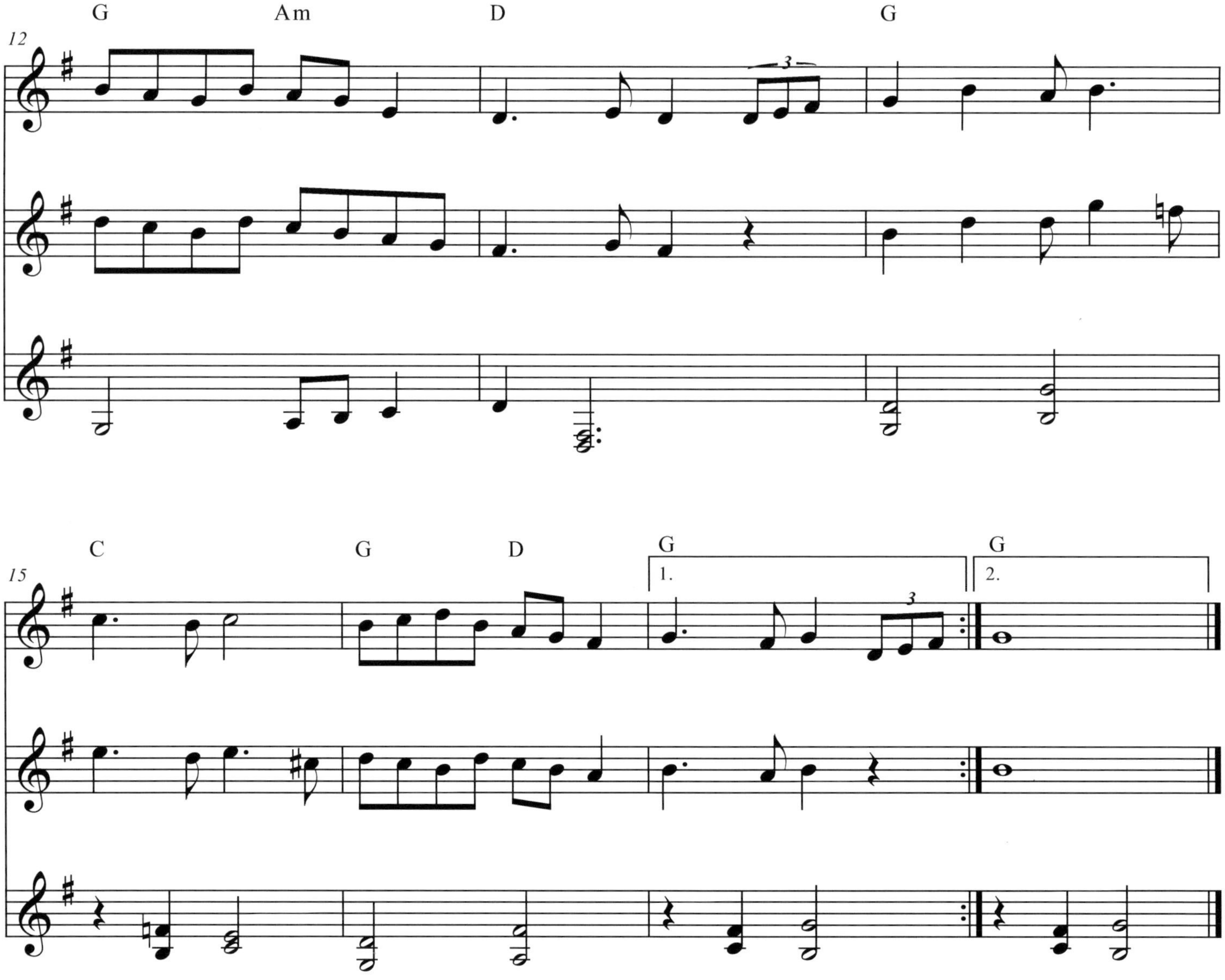
G
Am
D
G
12
3
C
G
D
G
1.
G
2.
15
3

Roscoe: variations

U.S.: Arranged by © Ken Kolodner

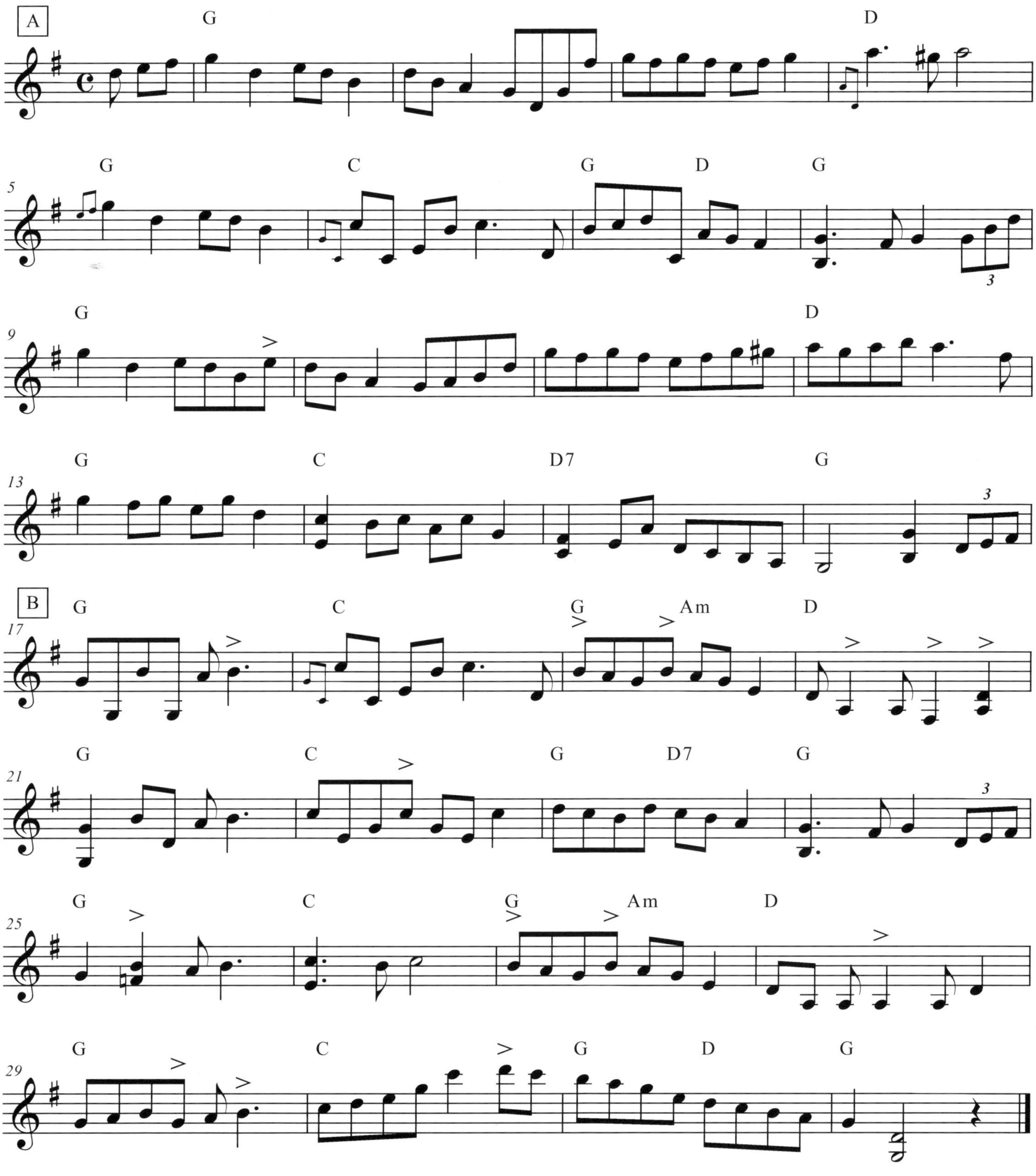

These variations are a sampling of ideas not intended to be played in one pass of the tune. The accent marks are offered as a general guide and as a reminder to shift accents. In the A part, try occasionally shifting to the "2 and 4" counts (away from the obvious "1 and 3").

Sail Away Ladies

Recorded on Ken and Brad Kolodner's "Otter Creek" (2011)

U.S.: Arranged by © Ken Kolodner

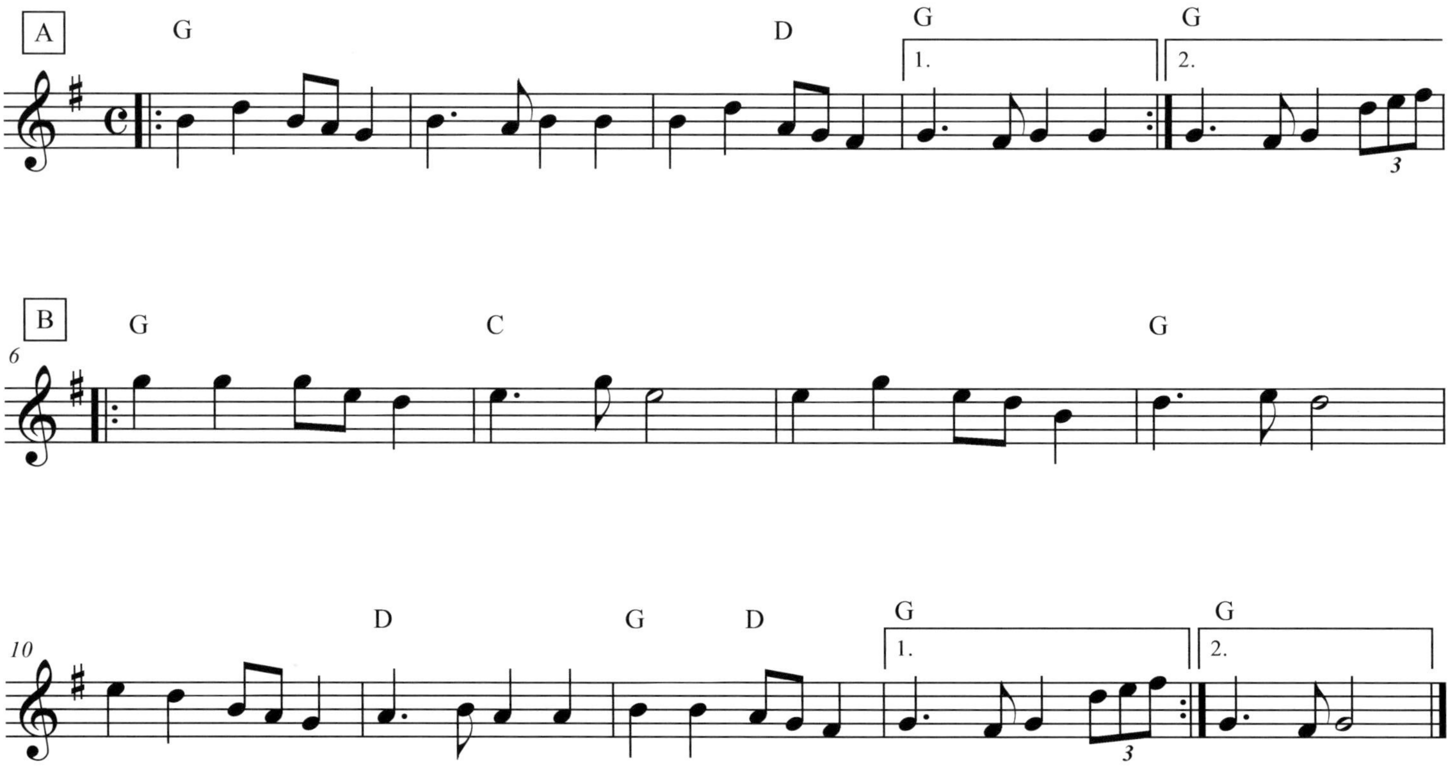

Sail Away Ladies: arranging ideas

Recorded on Ken and Brad Kolodner's "Otter Creek" (2011)

U.S.: Arranged by © Ken Kolodner

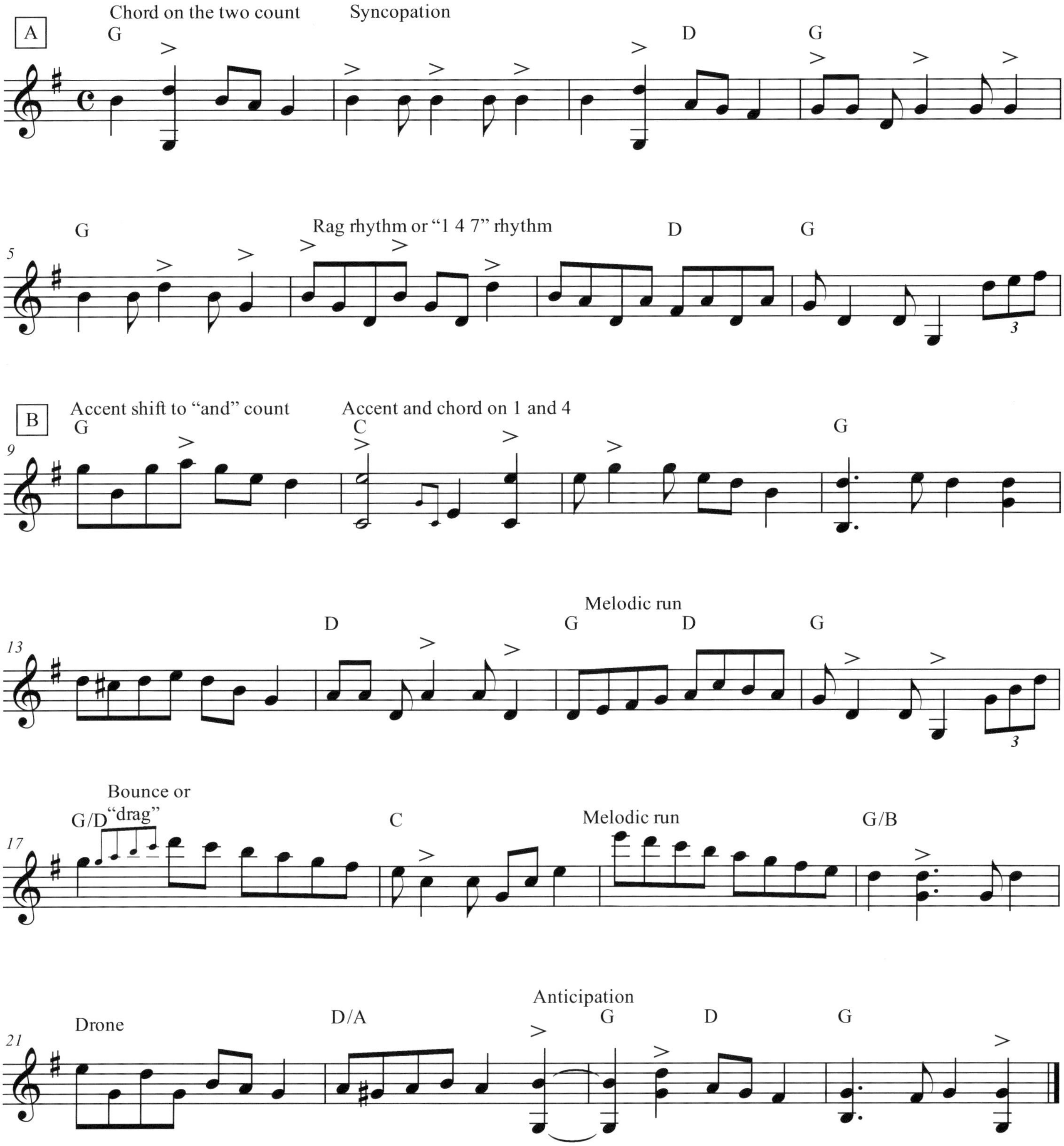

I like to use this simple tune to explore many rhythm ideas such as accent shifts, chords on counts other than "one" and "three," various syncopations, "rag" rhythms, and anticipation. Swing the eighth notes.

St. Anne's Reel: melody, accompaniment

Quebec/U.S./Ireland: Arranged by © Ken Kolodner

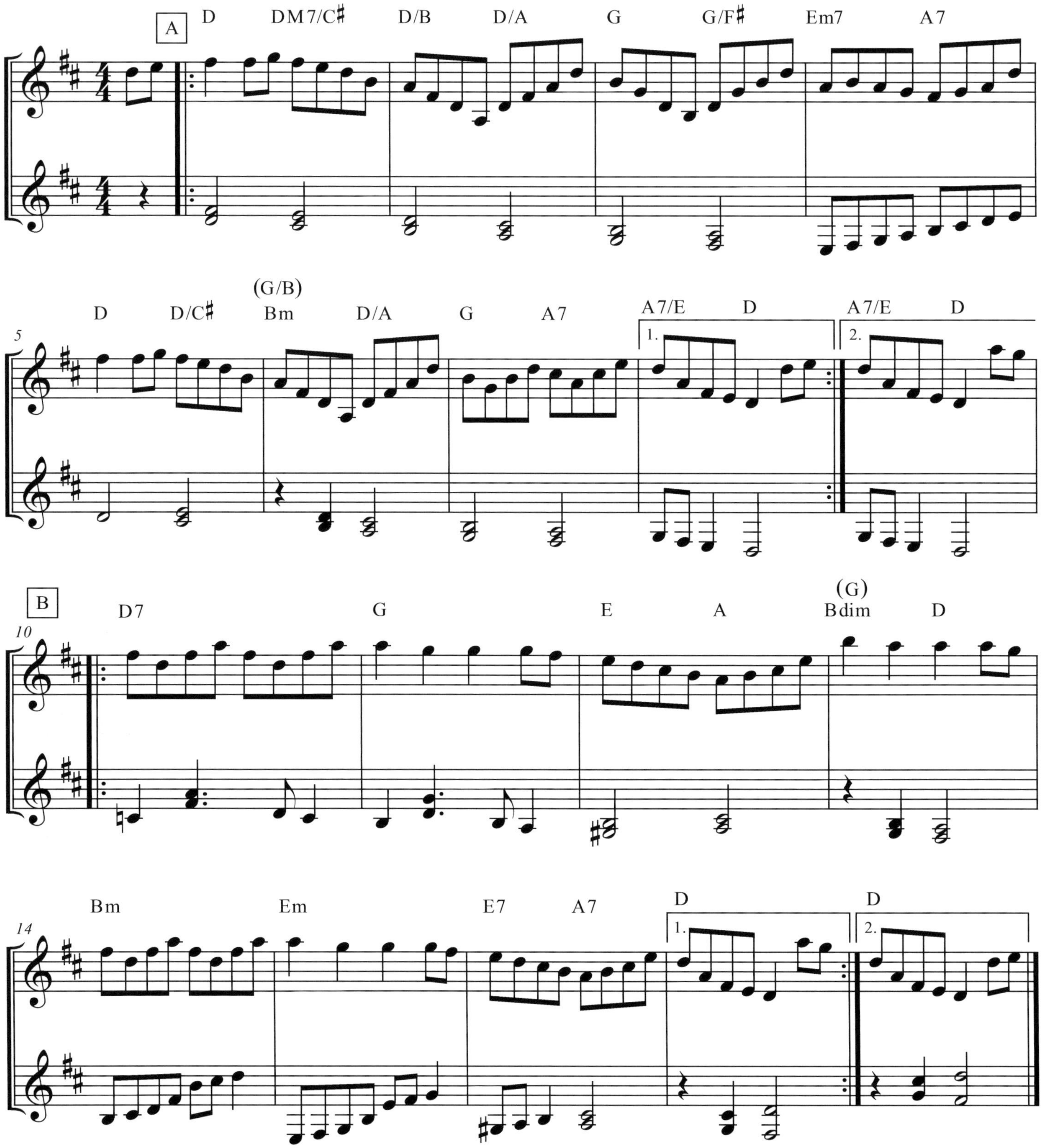

This is definitely not a standard harmonization of St. Anne's Reel. D, G and A chords work just fine but I think these chords work as well. I especially can't imagine playing the tune without the Bm moving to Em in the B part!

St. Anne's Reel: variations and arranging ideas

Quebec/Ireland/U.S.: Arranged by © Ken Kolodner

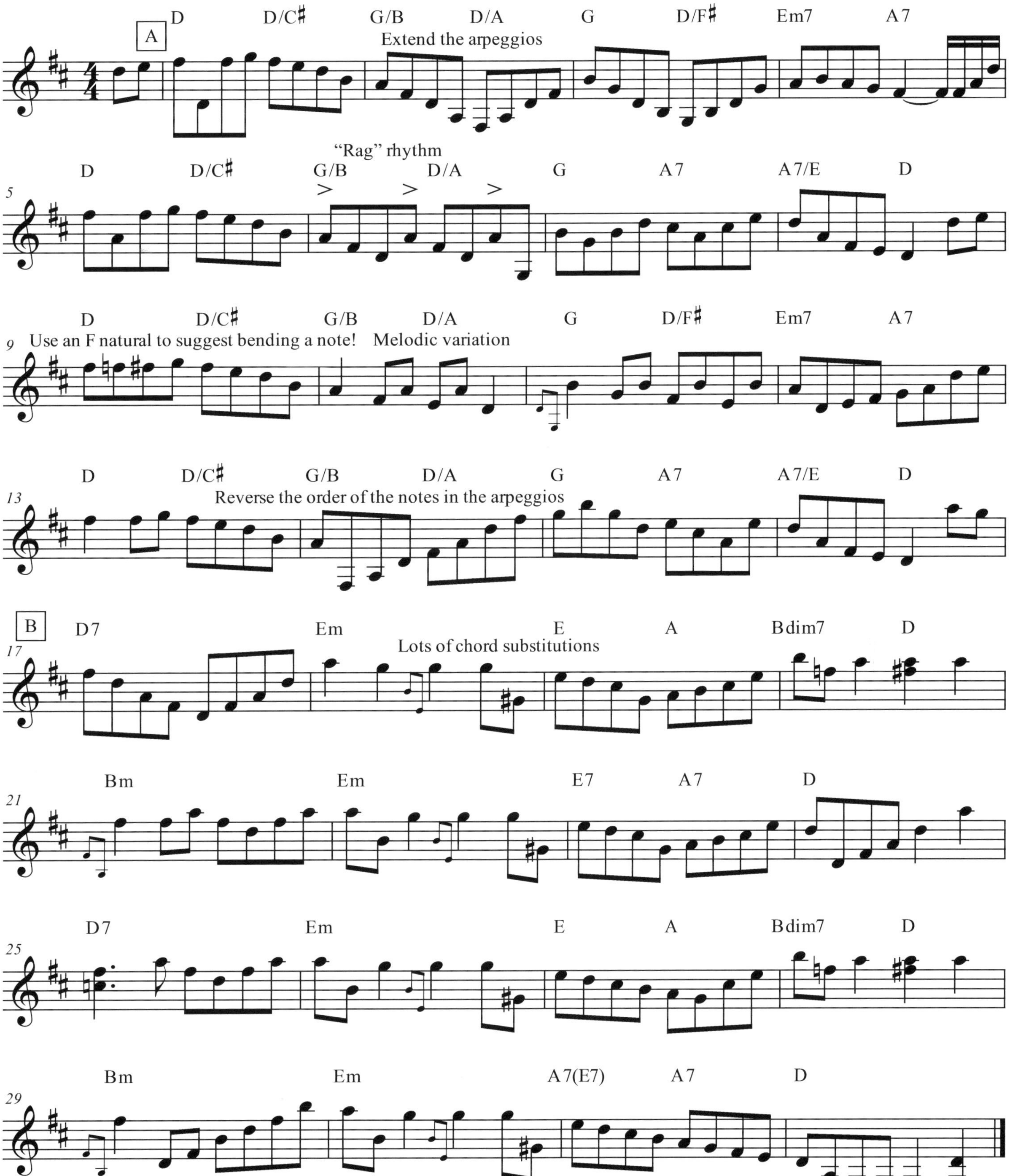

Salmon Tails up the Water

Recorded on “Greenfire” (1998) with Ken Kolodner, Laura Risk and Robin Bullock

Ireland: Arranged by © Ken Kolodner

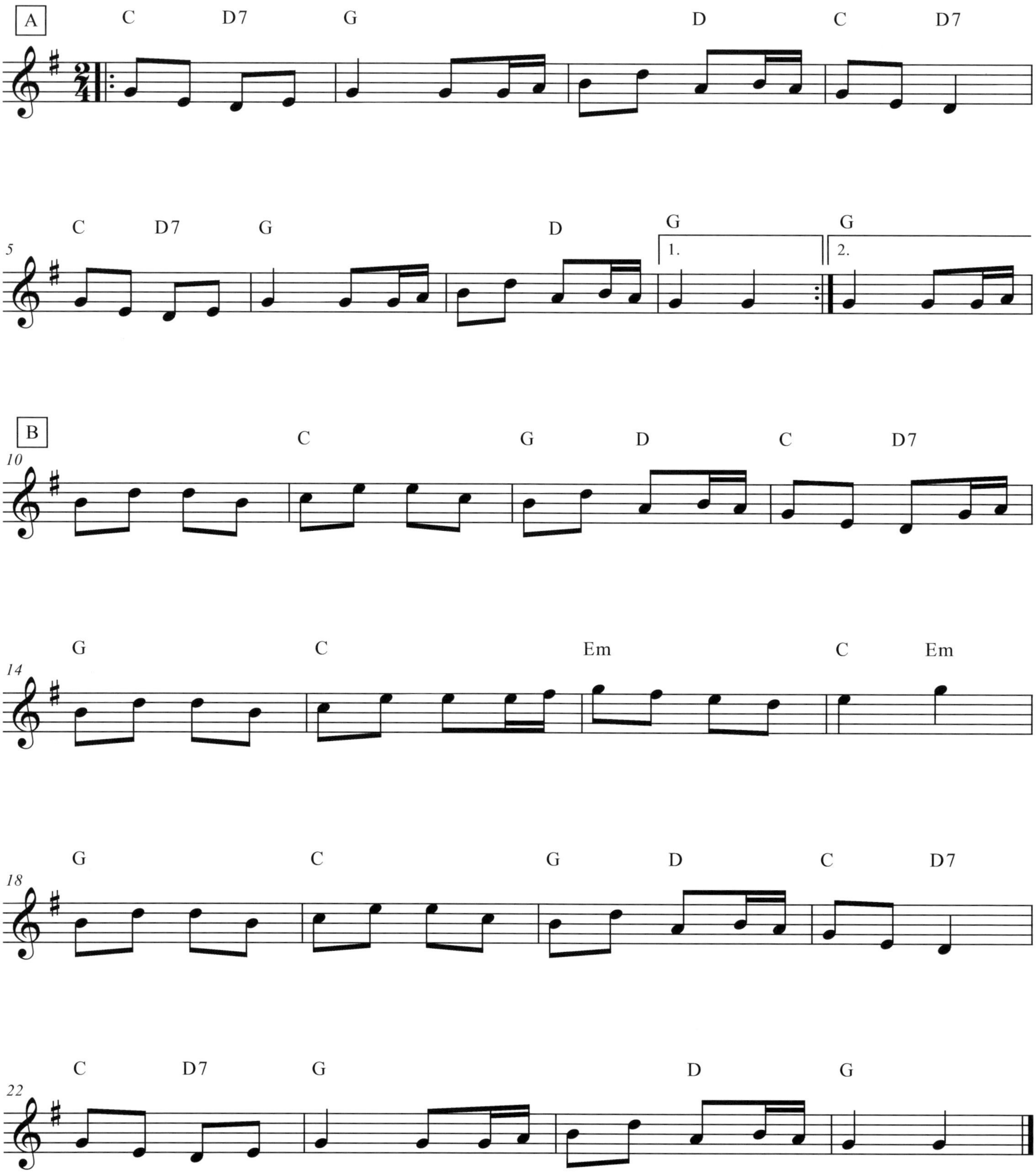

Salmon Tails up the Water: arranging ideas

Recorded on "Greenfire" (1998) with Ken Kolodner, Laura Risk and Robin Bullock

Ireland: Arranged by © Ken Kolodner

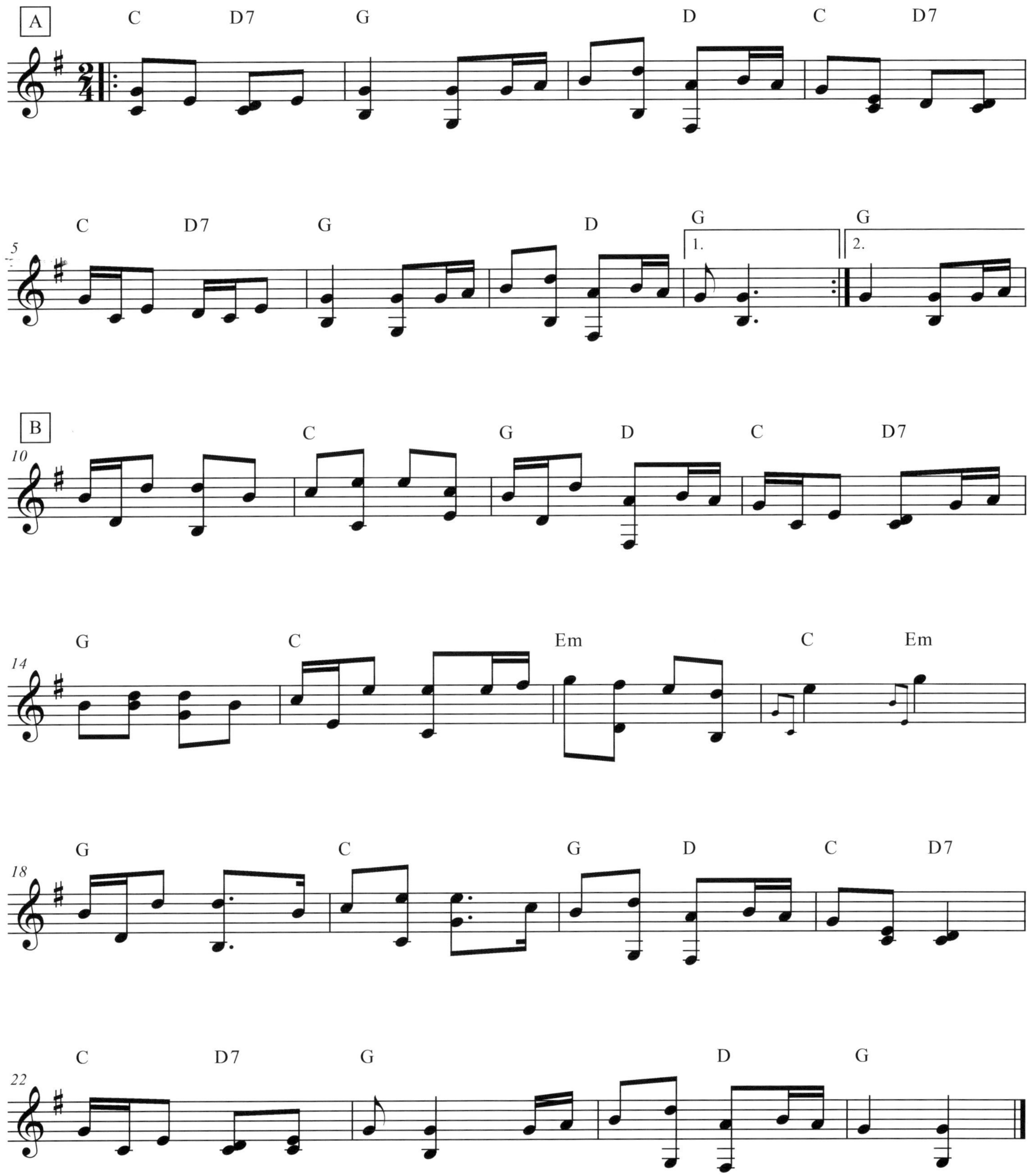

Shenandoah Falls: melody, harmony, accompaniment

Recorded on Ken Kolodner's "Journey to the Heartland" (2005) and on "Hammered Dulcimer Arrangements: Fiddle Tunes Volume II" (2005)

U.S.: Arranged by © Ken Kolodner

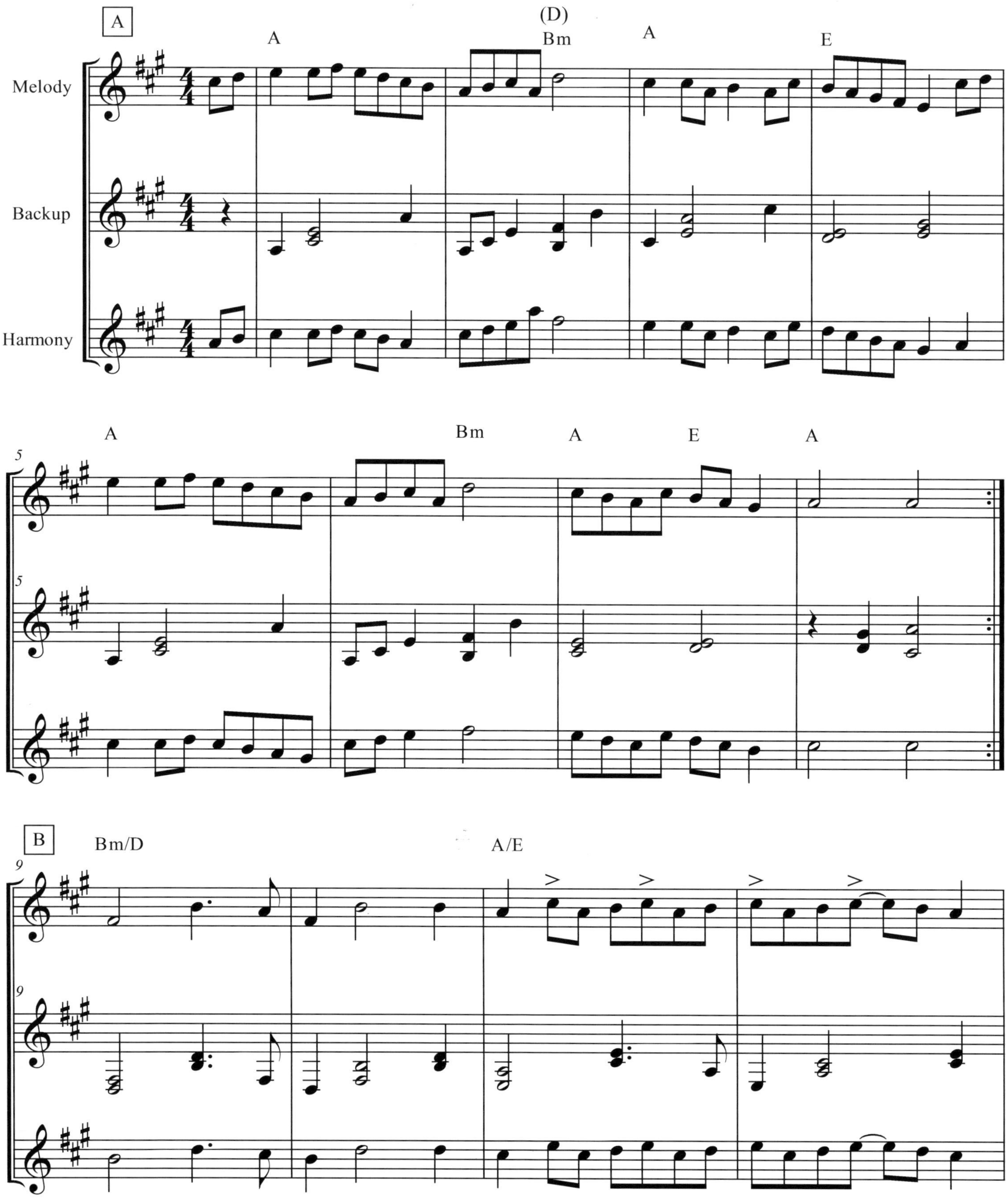

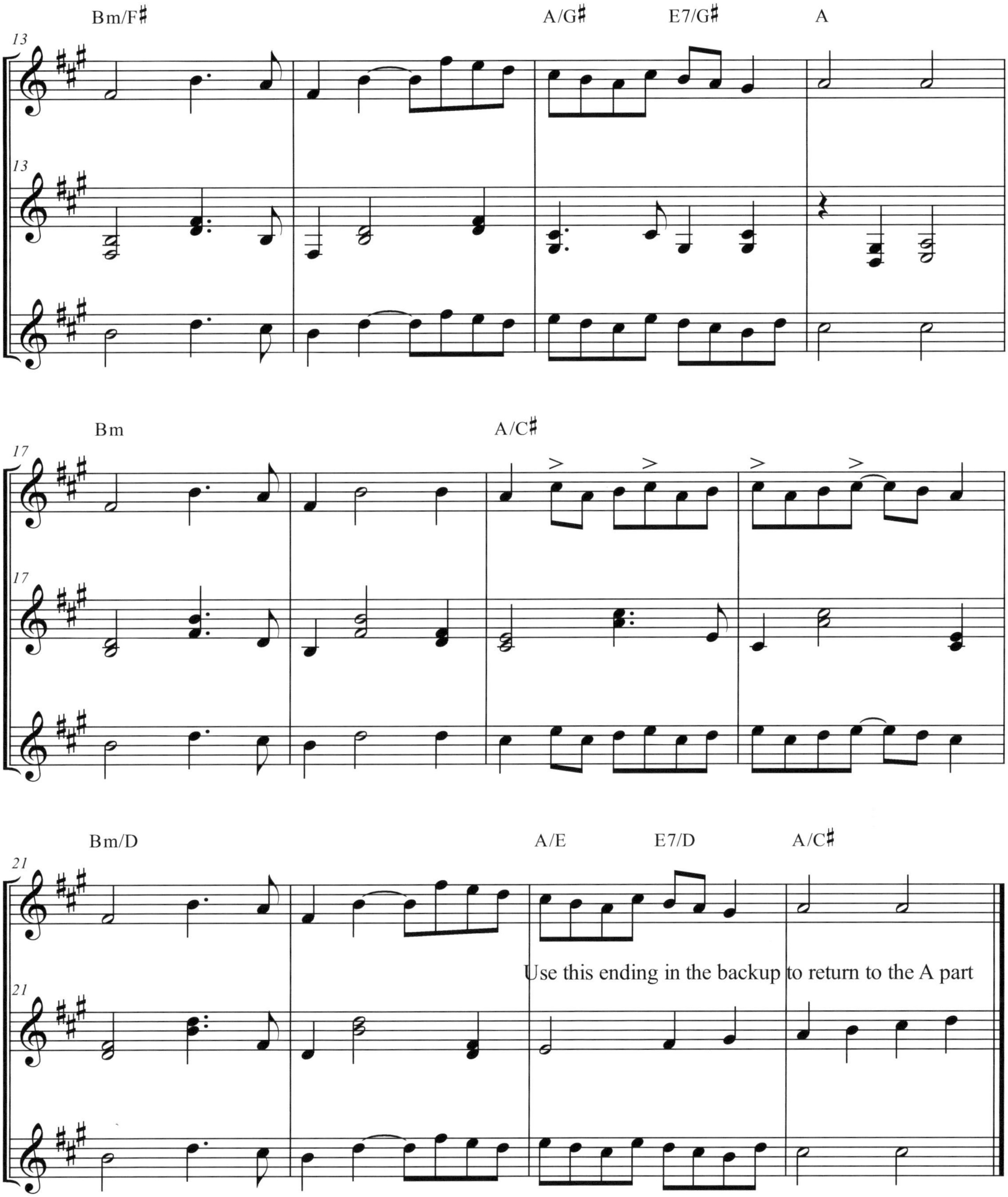

The backup in the first A part begins with chording only on the "one" for measures 1 and 2 and then moves to a simple pattern of chording on the "one" and "three" counts followed by the "two" and "three" of the following measure. The second A part uses a "one-four-one" pattern but the accent is on the "two". The B parts exploit a rising bass line that begins on your low D on the bass bridge and runs through two octaves, concluding with a scale that can be used to return to the melody. The "vamp" rhythm of the B part mimics the rhythm of the first two measures of the B part. The harmony is fairly straightforward and primarily uses thirds above and below the melody.

Shenandoah Falls: variations

Recorded on Ken Kolodner's "Journey to the Heartland" (2005) and on
"Hammered Dulcimer Arrangements: Fiddle Tunes Volume II" (2005)

U.S.: Arranged by © Ken Kolodner

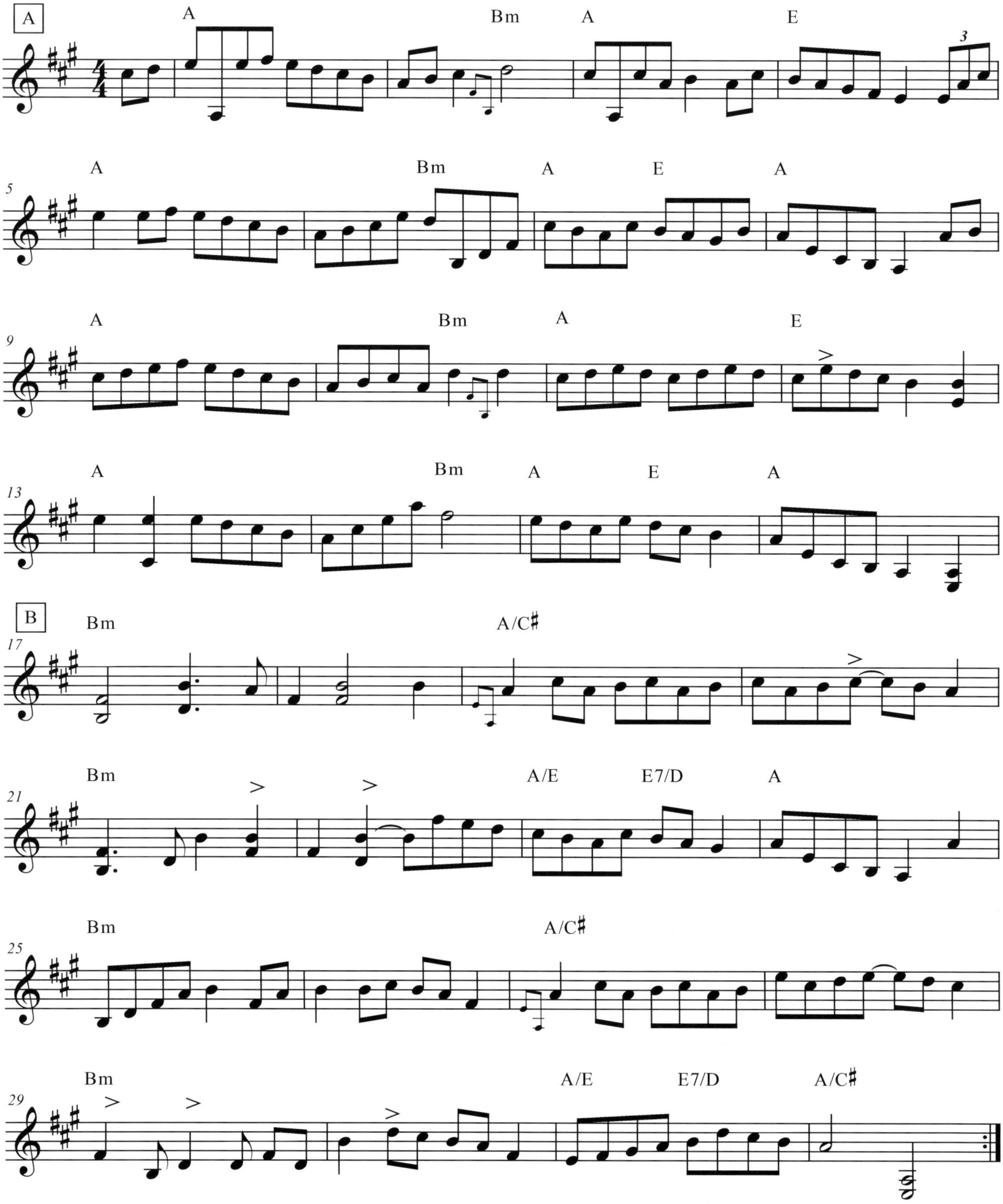

Silver and Gold Two-Step

Recorded on Ken Kolodner and Elke Baker's "Out of the Wood" (2011)

Canada: Arranged by © Ken Kolodner

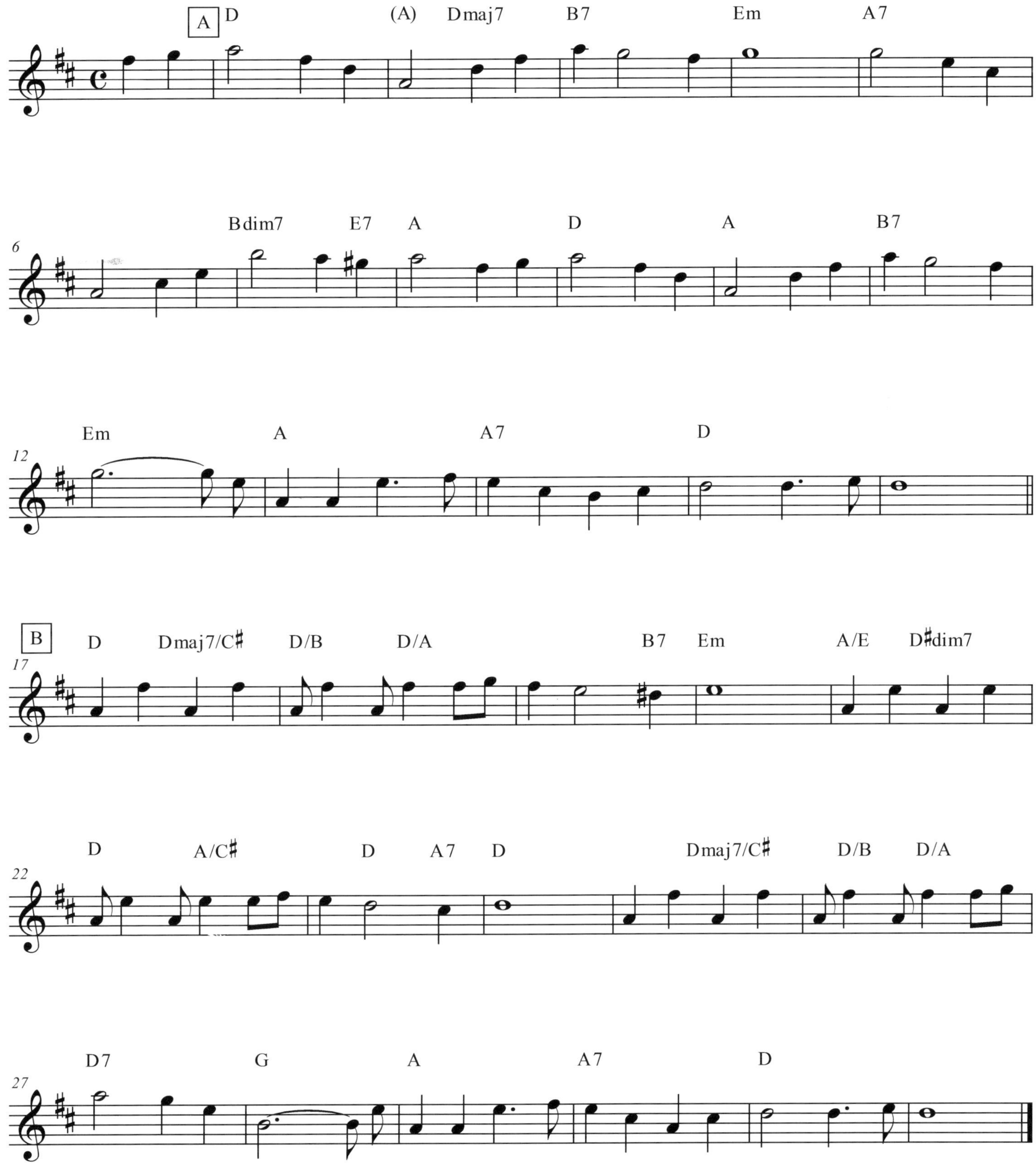

Silver and Gold Two-Step: arranging ideas

Recorded on Ken Kolodner and Elke Baker's "Out of the Wood" (2011)

Canada: Arranged by © Ken Kolodner

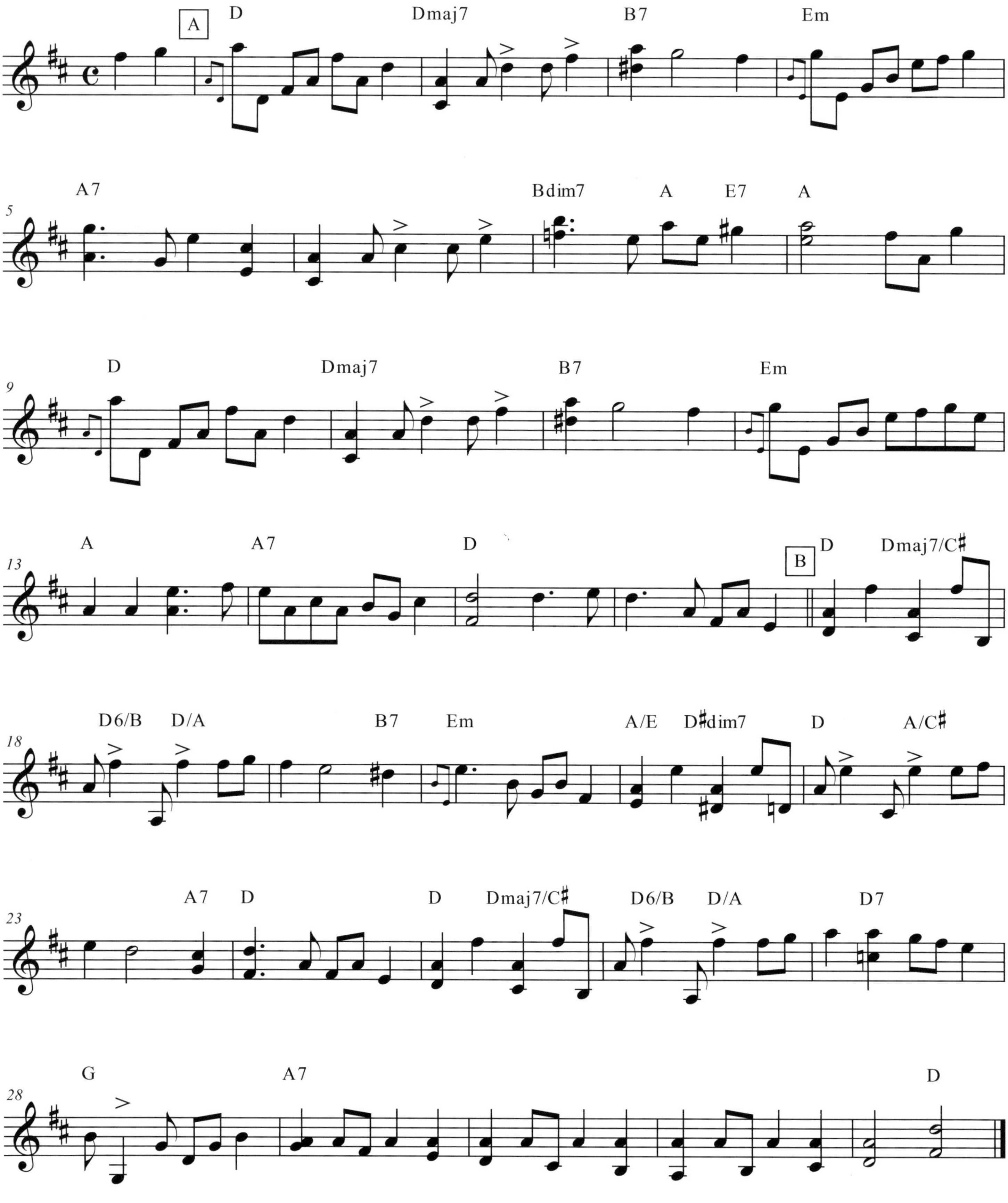

Snow Drop

Recorded on Brad and Ken Kolodner's "Otter Creek" (2011)

U.S.: Arranged by © Ken Kolodner

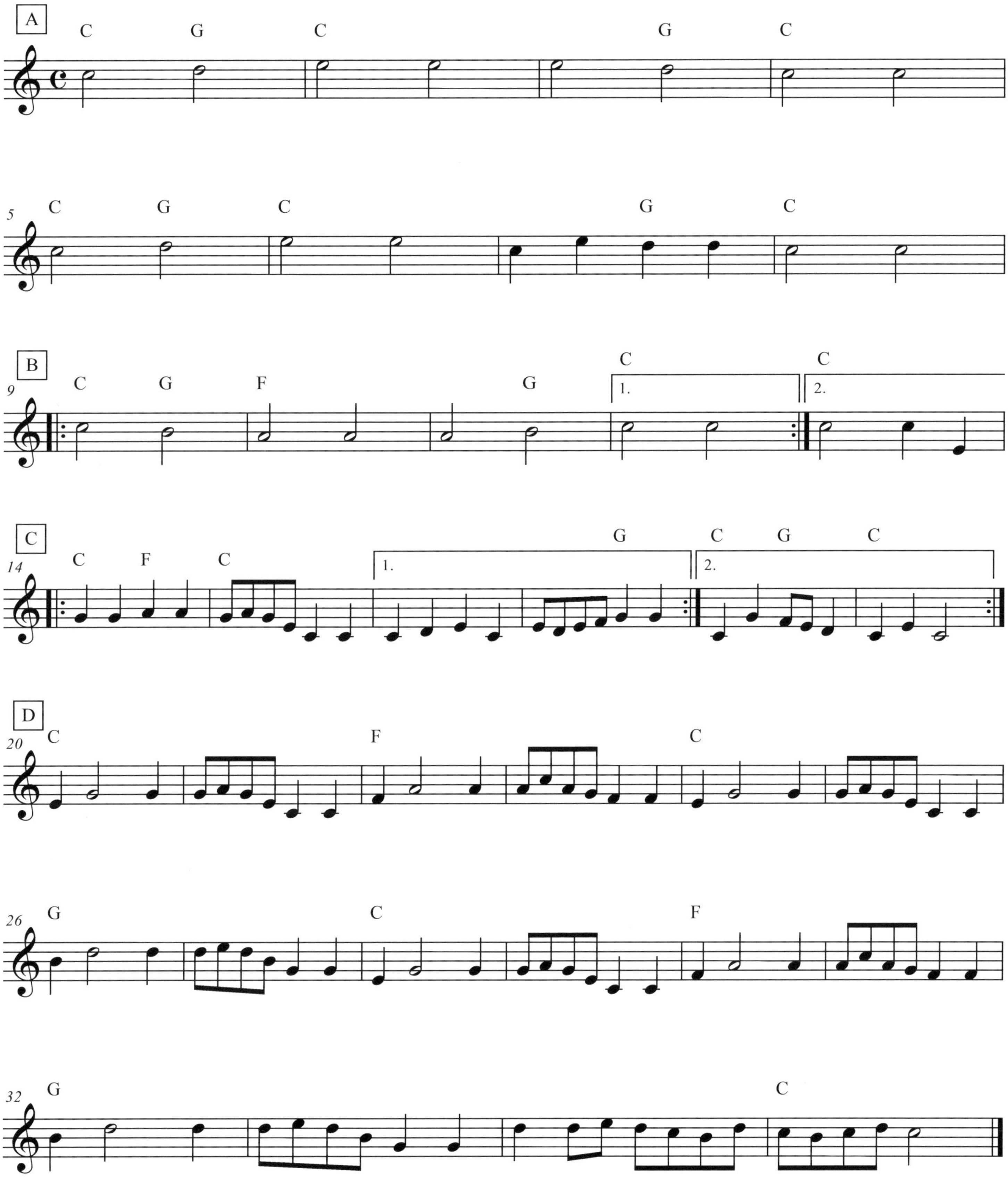

Snow Drop: arranging ideas

Recorded on Brad and Ken Kolodner's "Otter Creek" (2011)

U.S.: Arranged by © Ken Kolodner

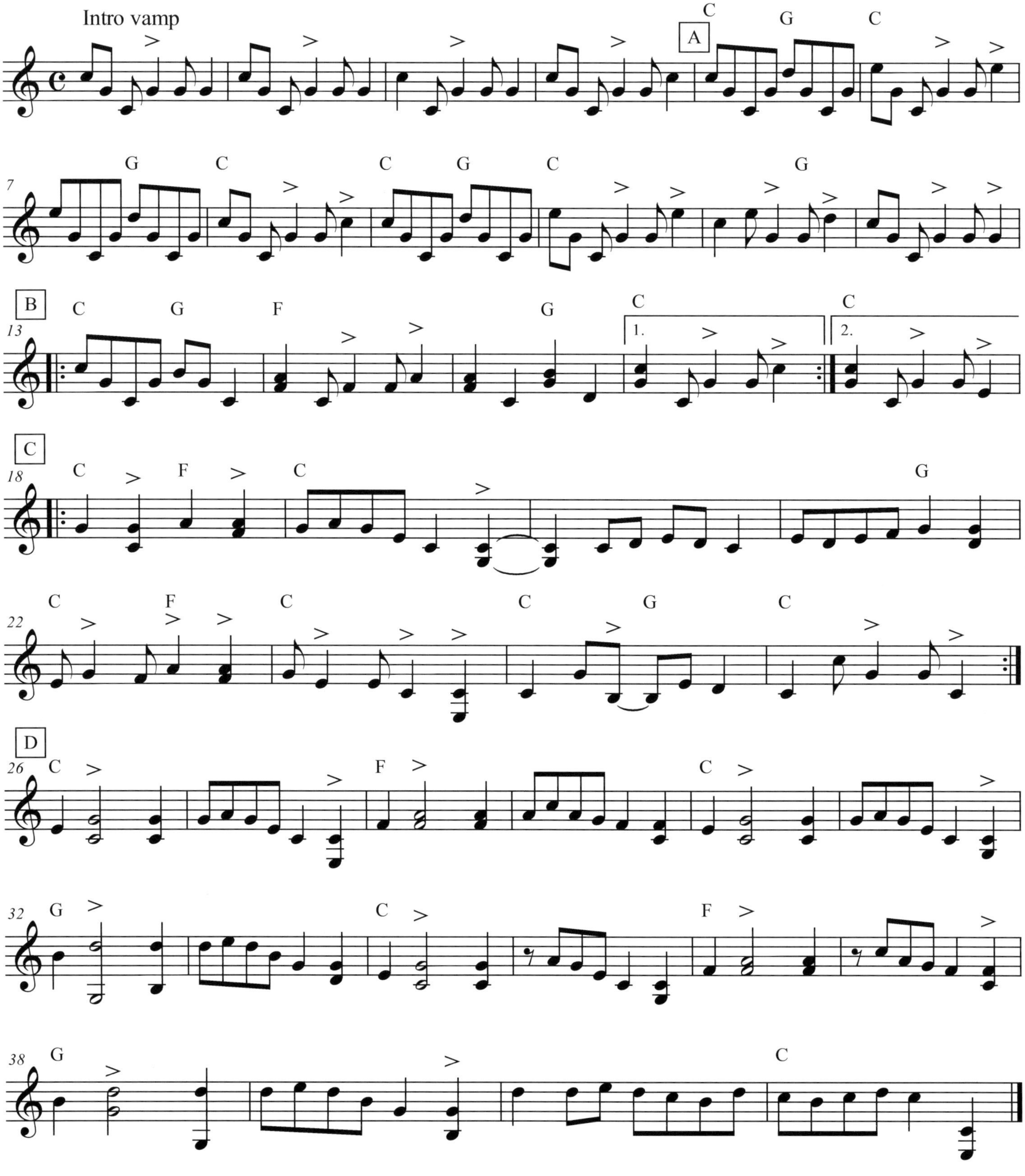

This wonderful tune provides a great exploration of rhythm: e.g. I used a vamp in the A part, lots of chording on the counts OTHER than 1 and 3, various syncopations, etc...Have fun!

Swift House

Recorded on Brad and Ken Kolodner's "Otter Creek" (2011)

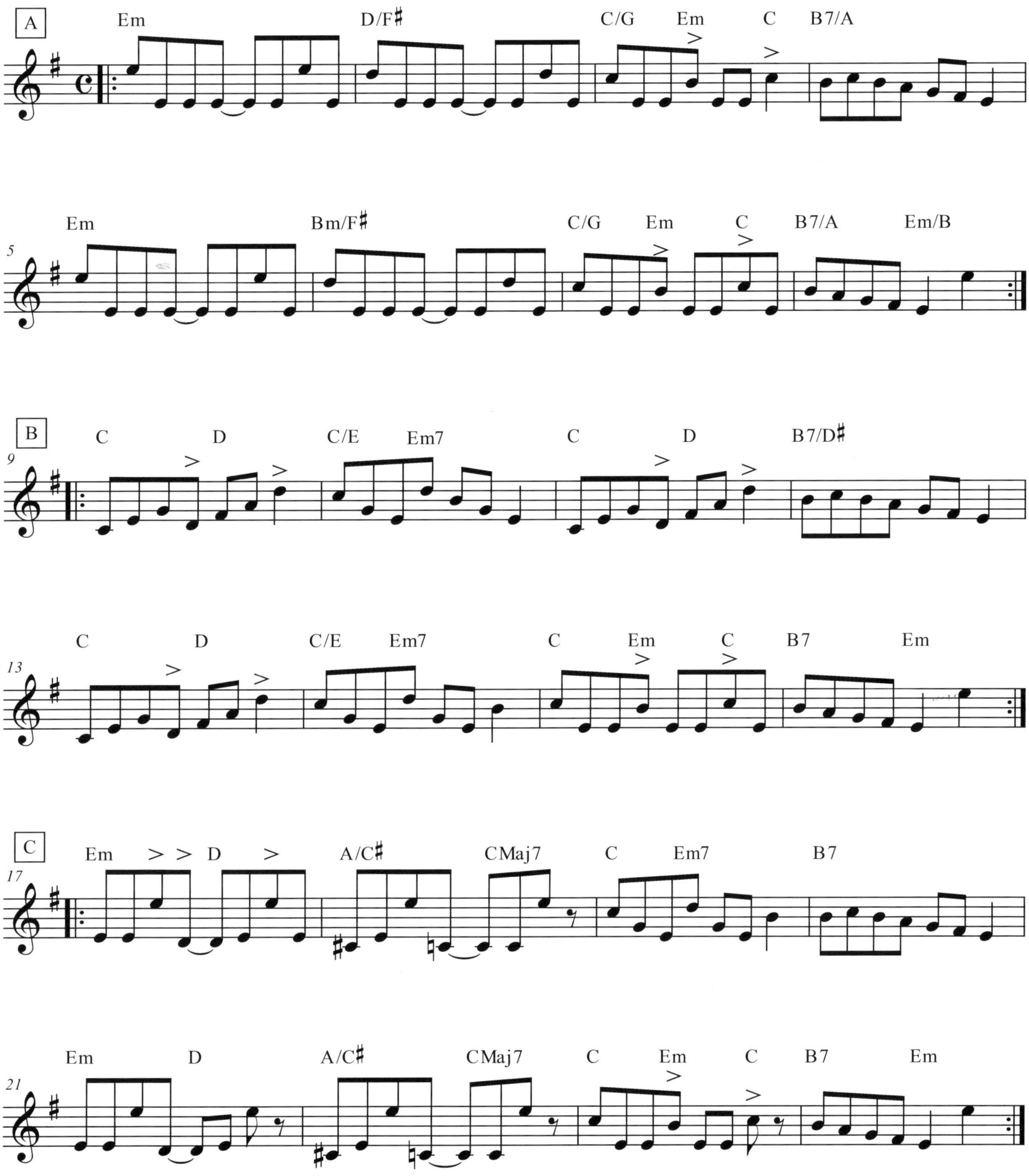

This is one tune that I just play exactly as written! The rhythms should keep you busy.

Tom Morrison's

Recorded on Ken Kolodner's "Walking Stones" (1997, re-released 2006)
with Laura Risk and Robin Bullock

Ireland: Arranged by © Ken Kolodner

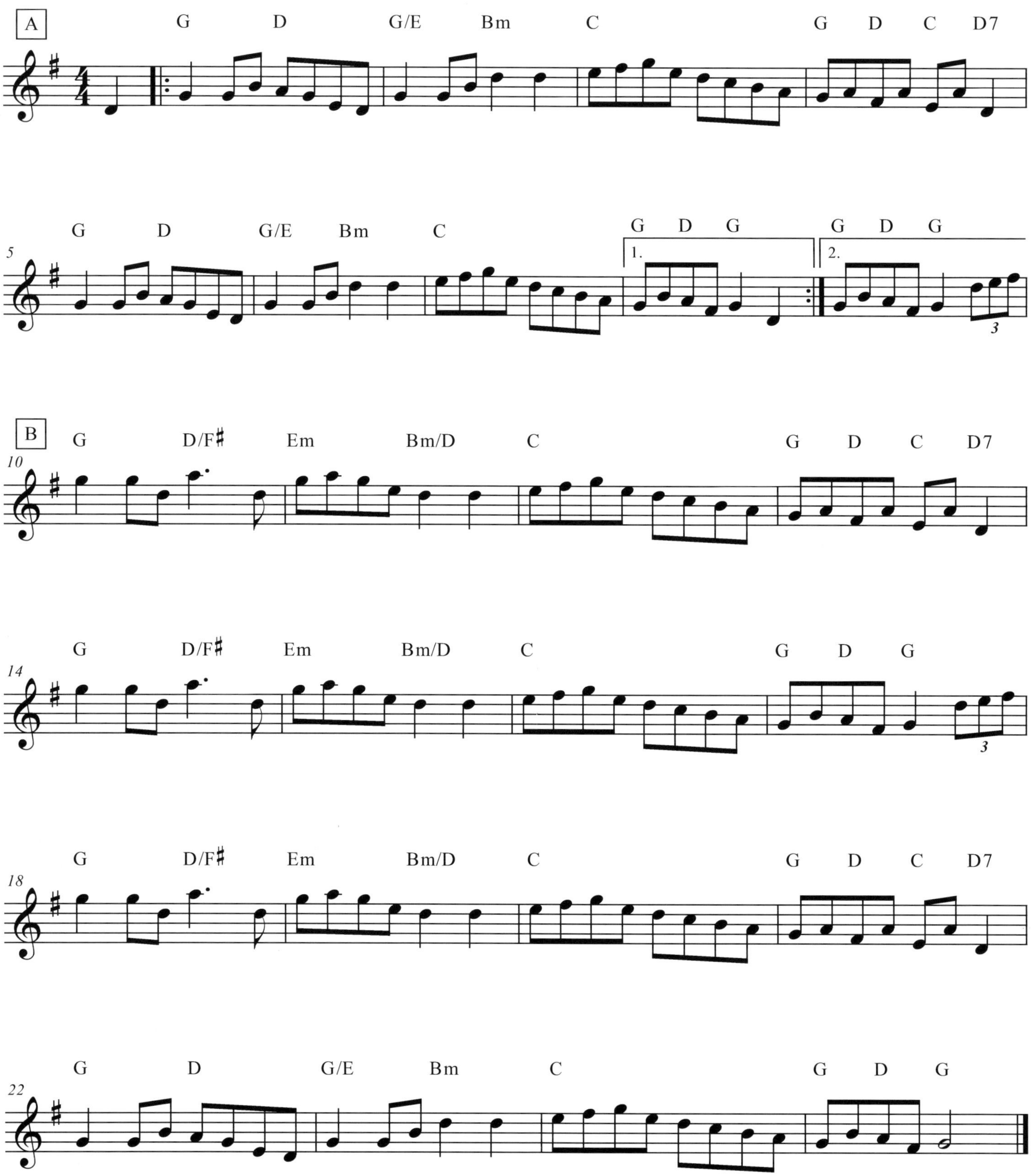

Tom Morrison's: arranging ideas

Recorded on Ken Kolodner's "Walking Stones" (1997, re-released 2006) with Laura Risk and Robin Bullock

Ireland: Arranged by © Ken Kolodner

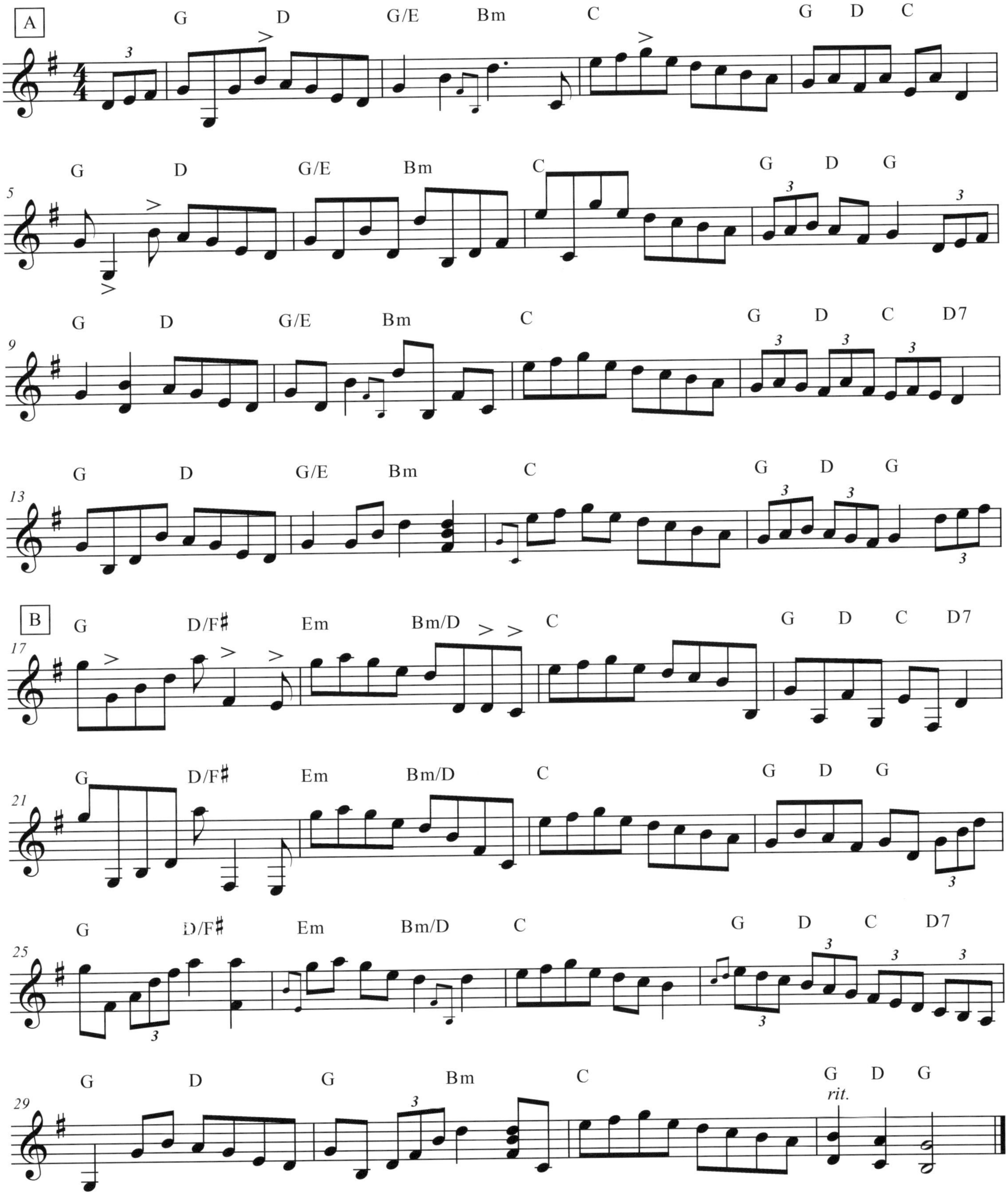

Washington's Hornpipe: melody with harmony

Also known as "The Stony Steps" (Ireland) and "Good for the Tongue"

England: Arranged by © Ken Kolodner

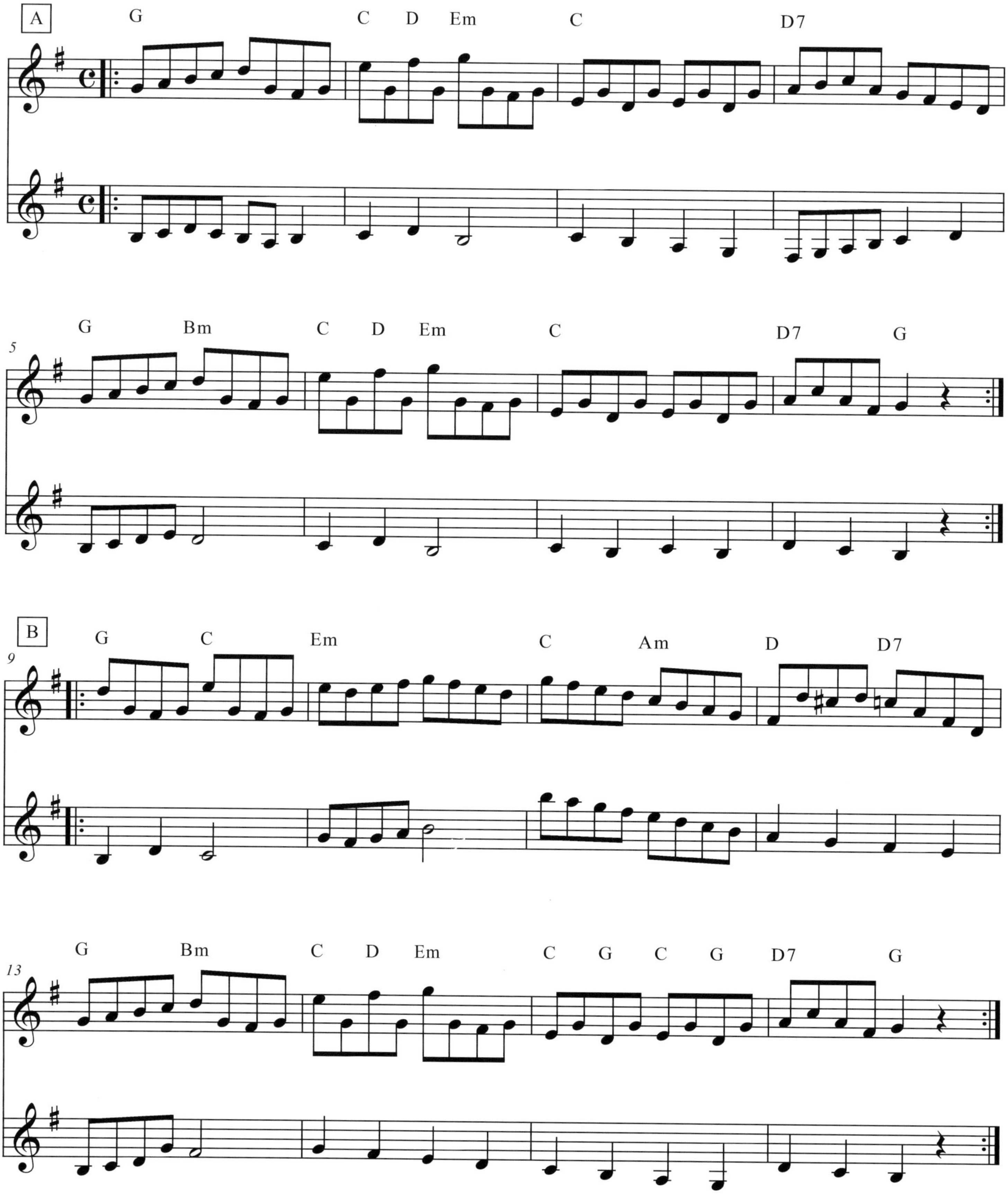

Washington's Hornpipe: arranging ideas #1

Also known as "The Stony Steps" (Ireland) and "Good for the Tongue"

England: Arranged by © Ken Kolodner

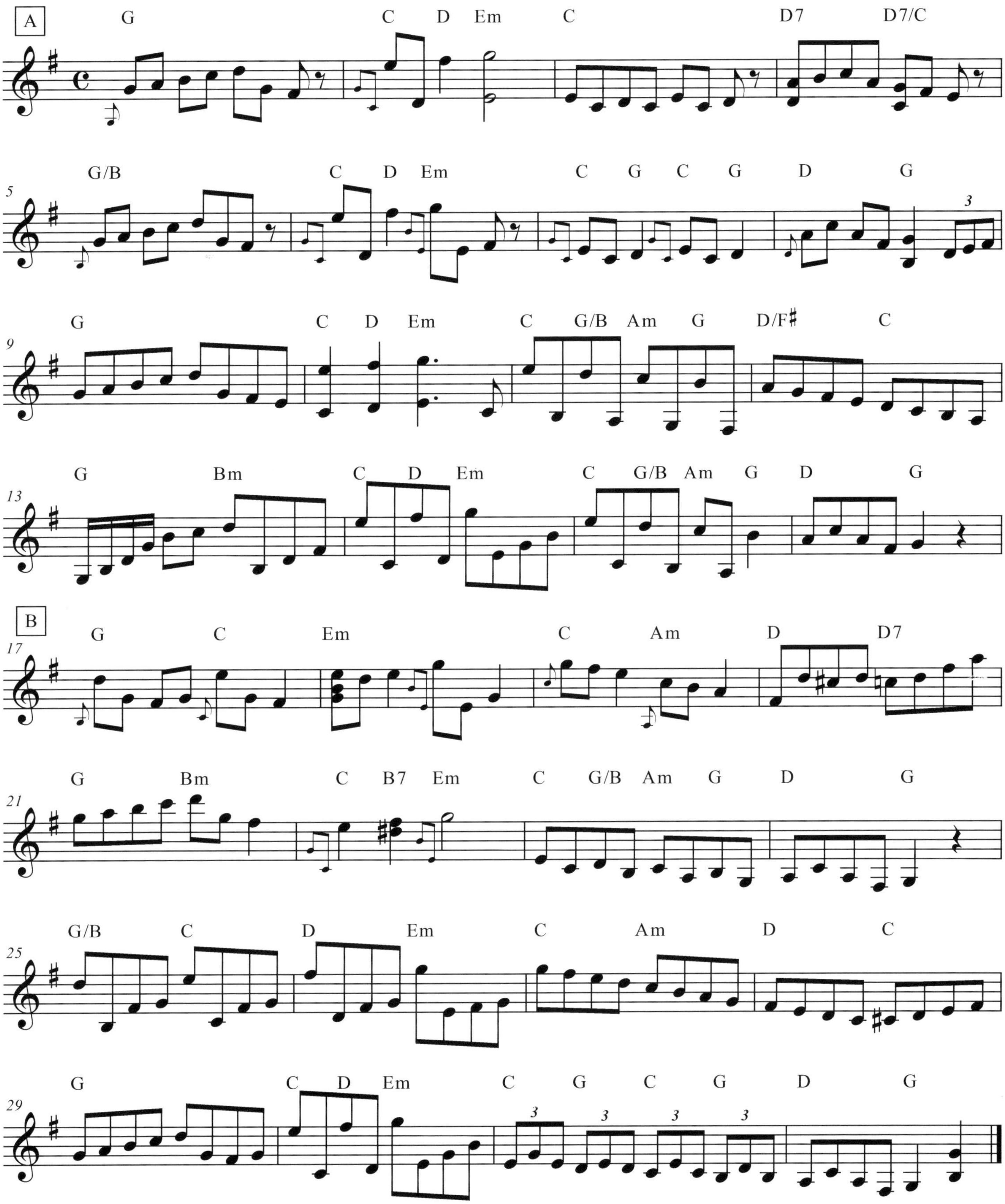

Washington's Hornpipe: additional arranging ideas

Also known as "The Stony Steps" (Ireland) and "Good for the Tongue"

England: Arranged by © Ken Kolodner

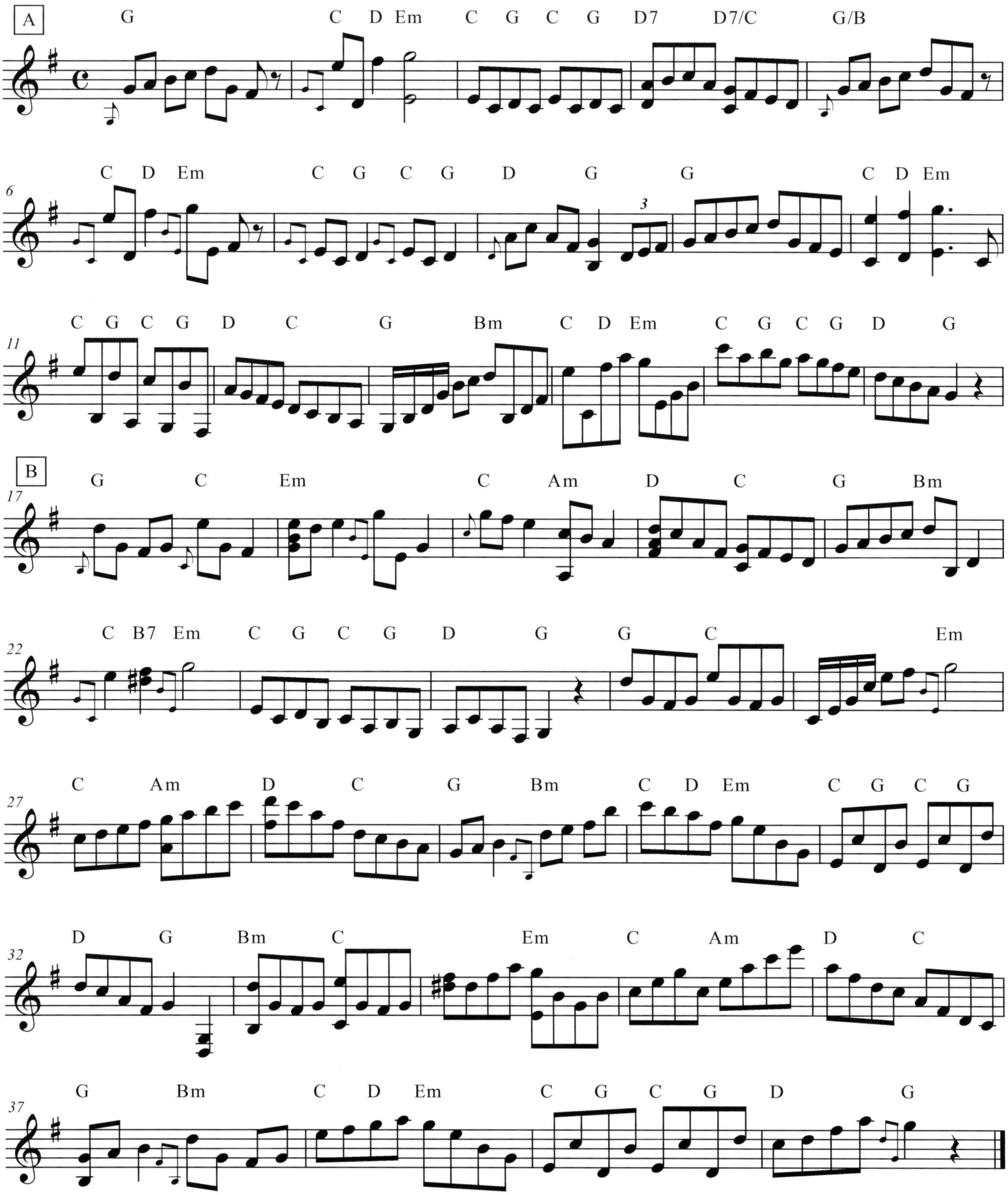

Willafjord: melody, harmony, arranging ideas

Recorded on Mark Grobner and Ken Kolodner's "SunRise" (2011)

Shetland Islands/Greenland: Arranged by © Ken Kolodner

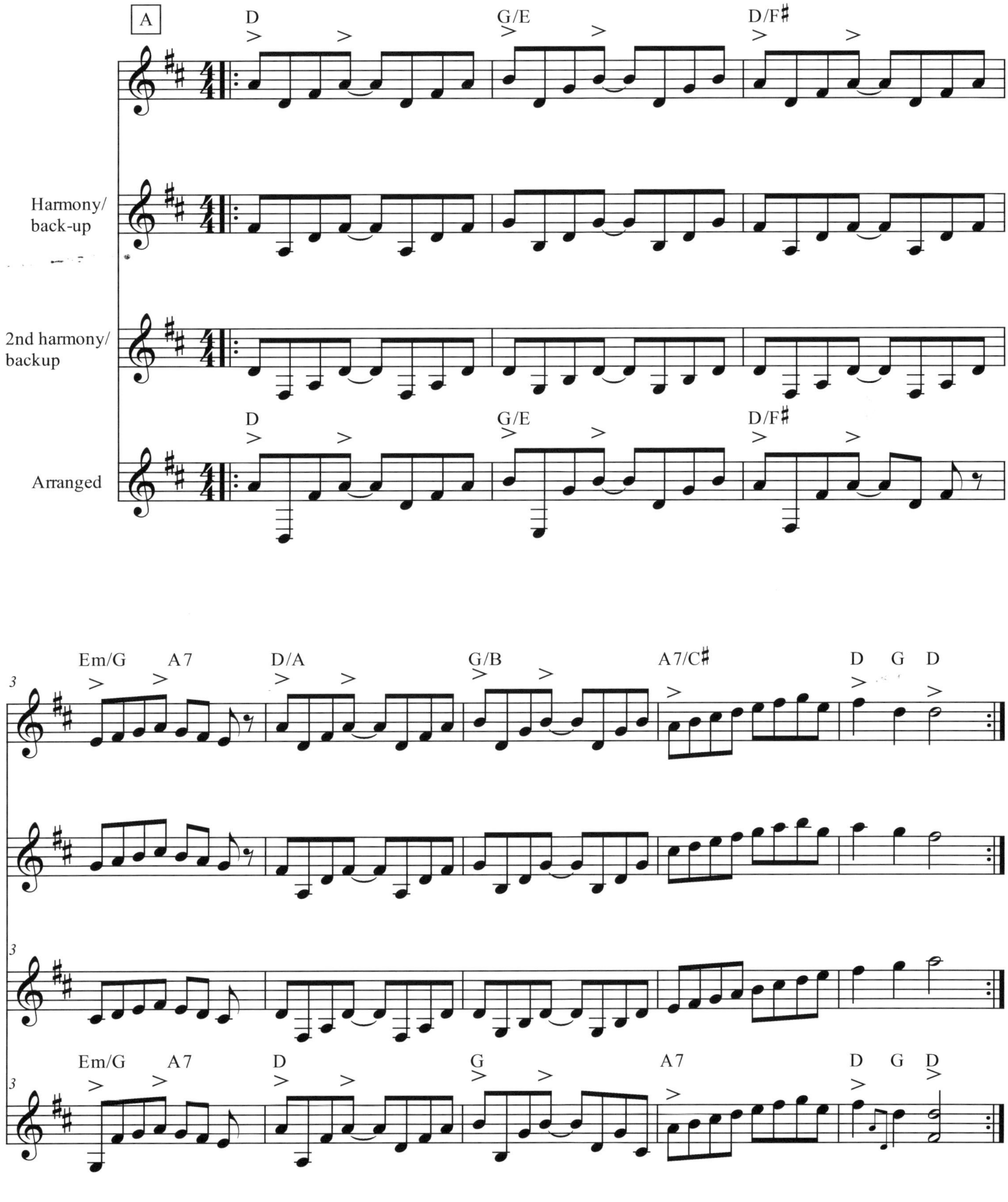

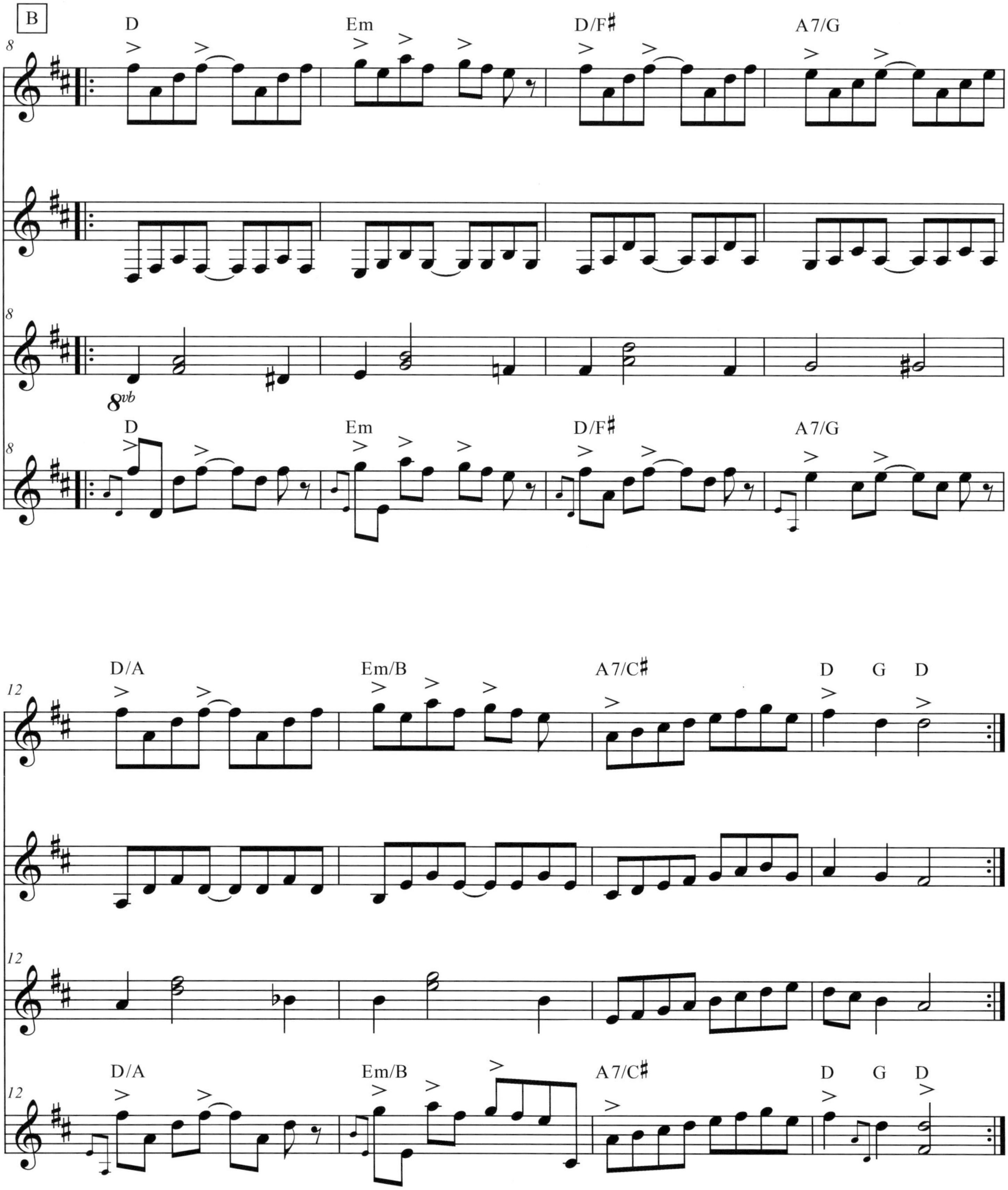
B
D
Em
D/F♯
A7/G
8vb
D
Em
D/F♯
A7/G
D/A
Em/B
A7/C♯
D G D
D/A
Em/B
A7/C♯
D G D

The Wren's Polka

Ireland: Arranged by © Ken Kolodner

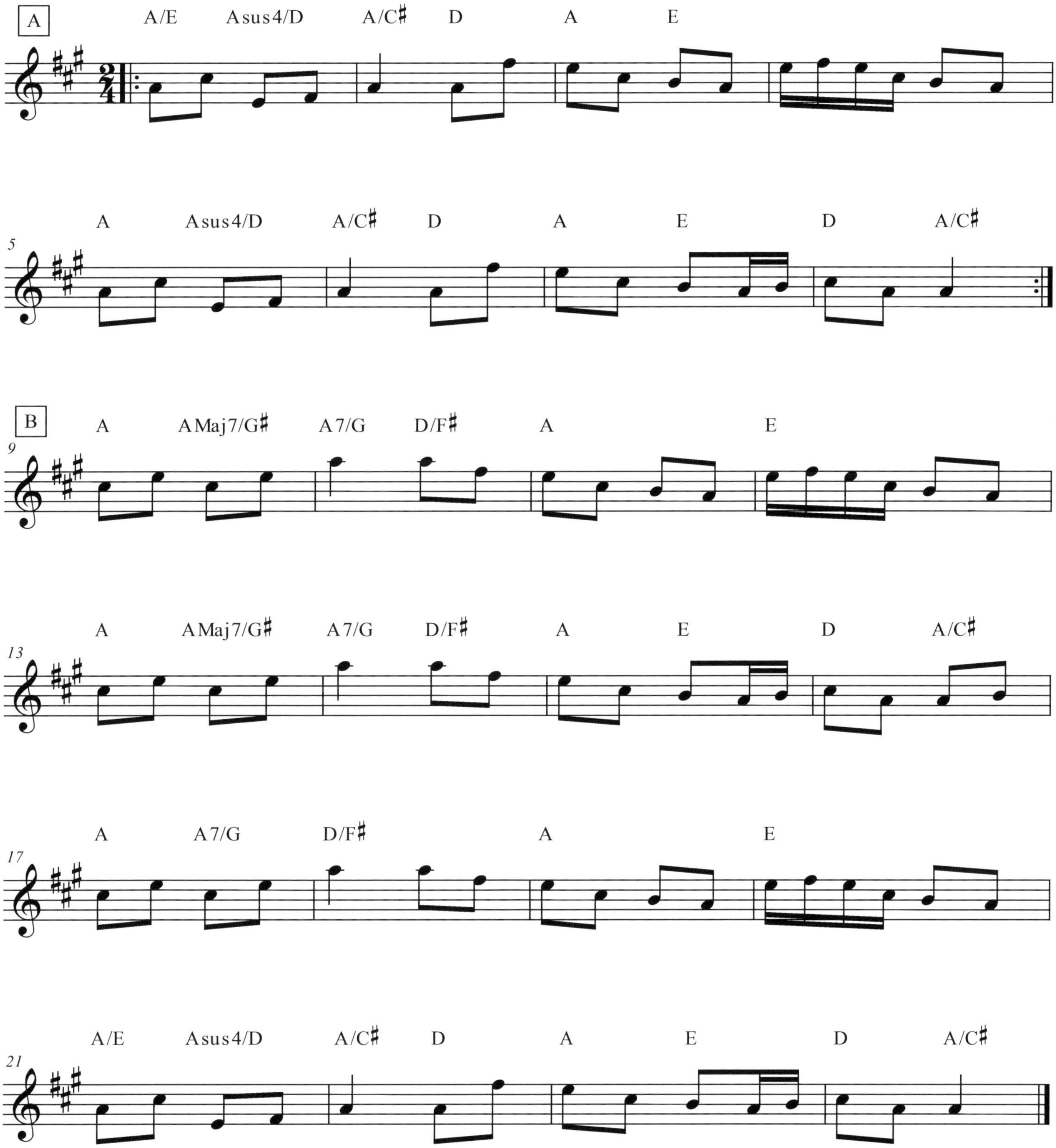

The A7 chord might be a bit of a stretch to use every time. A more conservative alternative is to stay with an A chord throughout the B part instead of the AMaj7 and A7.

The Wren's Polka: arrangement

Ireland: Arranged by © Ken Kolodner

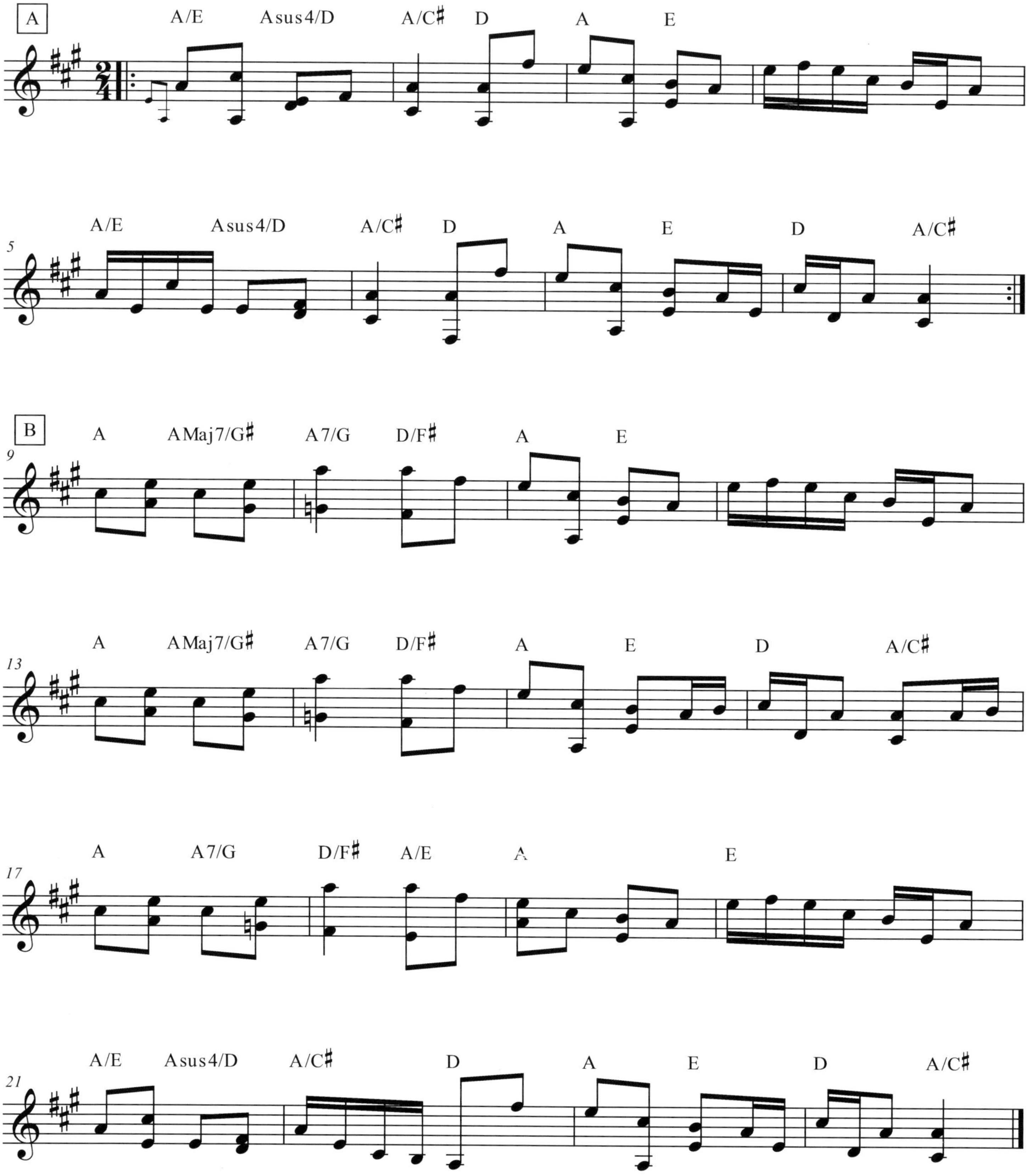

Y.Z. Hamilton's Breakdown

Recorded on Ken Kolodner's "Journey to the Heartland" (2005) and on
"Hammered Dulcimer Arrangements for Fiddle Tunes (Reels): Volume II"

U.S.: Arranged by © Ken Kolodner

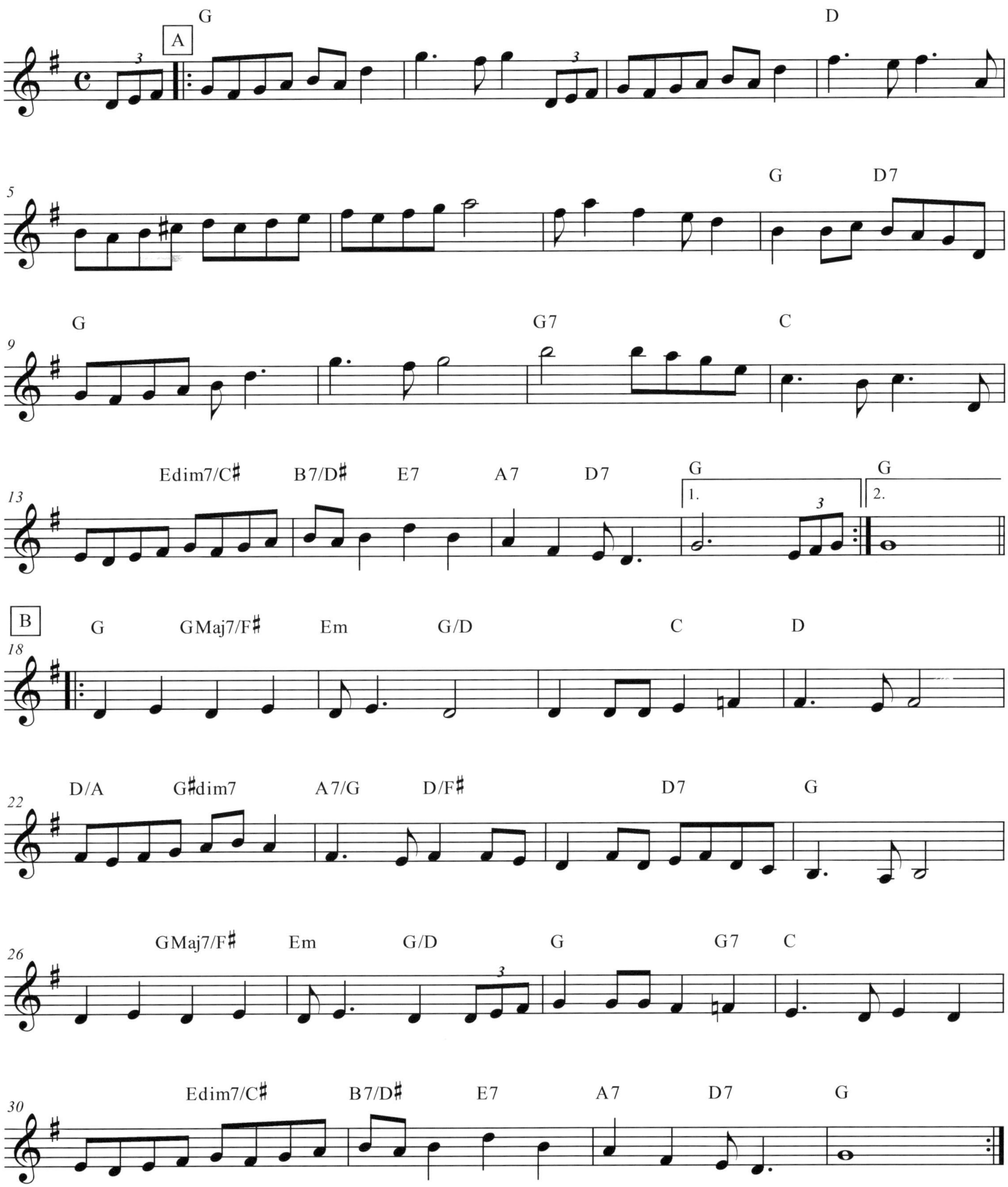

Y.Z. Hamilton's Breakdown: arranging ideas

Recorded on Ken Kolodner's "Journey to the Heartland" (2005) and
"Hammered Dulcimer Arrangements: Fiddle Tunes: Volume II" (2005)

U.S.: Arranged by © Ken Kolodner

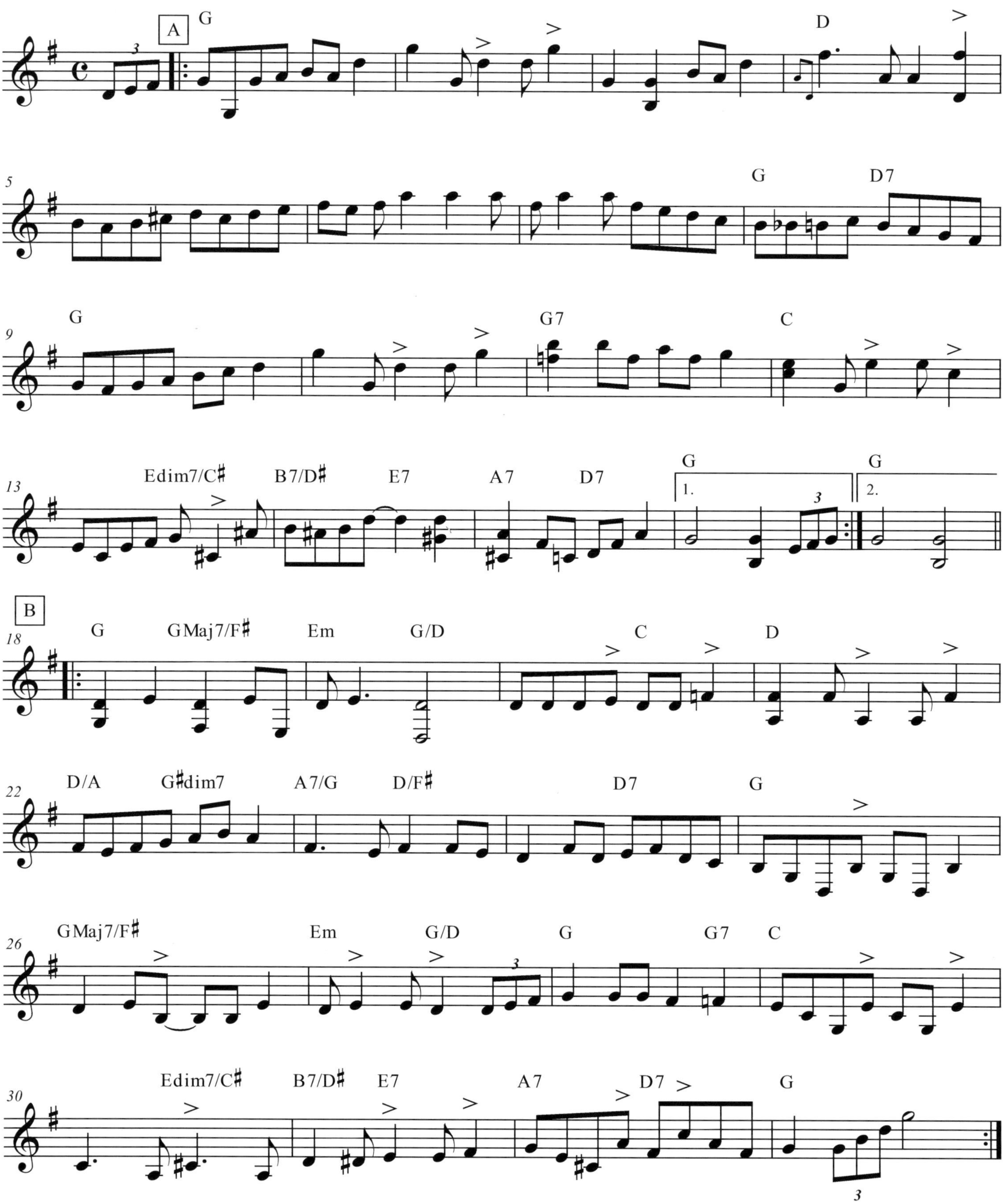

APPENDICES

I. INDEX OF TUNES BY TYPE OF TUNE

Reels

Jigs

Hornpipes

Polkas

Rags

II. INDEX OF TUNES RECORDED BY KEN KOLODNER

Many of the tunes in this volume may be found on YouTube and/or on one of Ken's recordings. Here is a listing of CDs on which the following tunes can be heard.

On Daybreak:
Kitchen Girl

On Helicon:
Bill Cheatham

On Helicon's Winter Solstice:
Oklahoma Rooster

On Walking Stones:
Cuckoo's Nest
Lad O'Bierne's
Tom Morrison's

On Greenfire:
Old Favorite, The
Salmon Tails Up the Water

On A Roof for the Rain:
The Galway
O'Sullivan's
A Roof for the Rain
Reel St. Joseph's

On Journey to the Heartland:
North Carolina Breakdown
Shenandoah Falls
Y.Z. Hamilton's Breakdown

On Otter Creek:
Big Scioty
Lonesome John
Sail Away Ladies
Snow Drop
Swift House

On Out of the Wood:
Carnaval
Road to Banff, The
Silver and Gold Two Step, The

On SunRise:
Frenchie's Reel
Johnny Cope
Missouri
Willafjord

On Skipping Rocks:
Billy in the Lowground
Grub Spring's
John Brown's March

III. SELECTED DISCOGRAPHY:

- DAYBREAK, Chris Norman and Ken Kolodner, JEB 001, 1985, re-released 2010, JEB Records, 3806 Fenchurch Rd., Baltimore, MD 21218; 410-243-7254.
- HELICON, Helicon, JEB 002, 1987, Jeb Records.
- THE TITAN, Helicon, DORIAN Discovery, DIS-80115, 1989, re-released, JEB-003, 2006.
- HORIZONS, Helicon, DORIAN Discovery, DIS-80103, 1992.
- WALKING STONES: A Celtic Sojourn, Ken Kolodner with Laura Risk and Robin Bullock, DORIAN, DOR-90248, 1997, re-released 2006.
- GREENFIRE: A Celtic String Ensemble (Ken Kolodner, Laura Risk and Robin Bullock), DORIAN, DOR-90321, 1998.
- A WINTER SOLSTICE CELEBRATION, Helicon, DORIAN, DOR-90531, 1999.
- A ROOF FOR THE RAIN, Greenfire, (Ken Kolodner, Laura Risk, and guests Keith Murphy and Joseph Sobel) DORIAN, DOR-90598, 2001.
- A JOURNEY TO THE HEARTLAND, Ken Kolodner (with guests Laura Risk, Elke Baker, Robin Bullock, Paddy League) MAGGIE'S MUSIC, MM231, 2005.
- OTTER CREEK, Ken and Brad Kolodner (with guests Elke Baker and Paul Oorts), FENCHURCH MUSIC, FM05, 2011
- SUNRISE, Mark Grobner and Ken Kolodner, SUNRISE MUSIC, 0011, 2011
- OUT OF THE WOOD, Ken Kolodner and Elke Baker (with Brad Kolodner and Eric Eid-Reiner), FENCHURCH MUSIC, FM06, 2011
- SKIPPING ROCKS, Ken and Brad Kolodner (with guests Elke Baker, Alex Lacquement and Robin Bullock), FENCHURCH MUSIC, FM07, 2013

Instructional Book/CDs:

- OLD-TIME FIDDLE STYLE: A Collection of 35 Tunes, Ken Kolodner, Catalogue #MB21992BCD Pacific, MO: MEL BAY PUBLICATIONS, August, 2010 (1-800-8MELBAY)

Instructional CDs:

- HAMMERED DULCIMER ARRANGEMENTS: FIDDLE TUNES (REELS), VOLUME I, Ken Kolodner, Fenchurch Music, 2004.
- HAMMERED DULCIMER ARRANGEMENTS: WALTZES AND SLOW TUNES, VOLUME I, Ken Kolodner, Fenchurch Music, 2004.
- HAMMERED DULCIMER ARRANGEMENTS: FIDDLE TUNES (REELS) VOLUME II, Ken Kolodner, Fenchurch Music, 2005.
- HAMMERED DULCIMER ARRANGEMENTS: WALTZES AND SLOW TUNES, VOLUME II, Ken Kolodner, Fenchurch Music, 2005.
- HAMMERED DULCIMER ARRANGEMENTS: SEASONAL MUSIC, VOLUME I, Ken Kolodner, Fenchurch Music, 2005.

IV. ABOUT KEN KOLODNER

Ken Kolodner is recognized as "one of today's most accomplished, musical hammered dulcimer artists...A hammered dulcimer player of great taste and sophistication," (Elderly). Ken is known for his improvisational and expressive style that has been described as "nothing short of astonishing" (The Connection), "outstanding" (The New York Times), "marvelous" (The Washington Post), "virtuosic" (Audio) "stunning in its musicality" (Dulcimer Player News) and "not to be missed" (USA TODAY). In more recent years, Ken has received greater recognition as an Old-Time fiddler and in 2010 completed a book/ CD for Mel Bay on Appalachian fiddling.

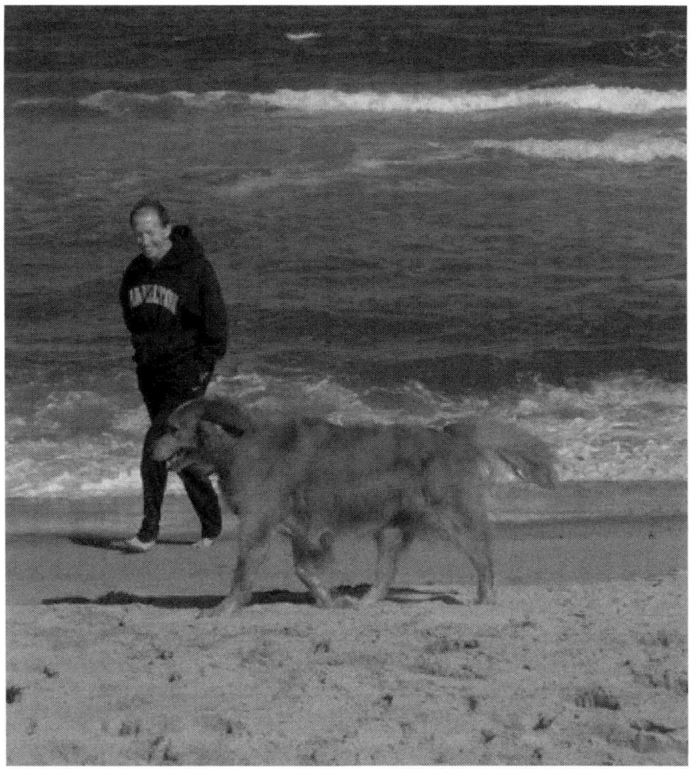

With Caspian at The Sandbridge Dulcimer Retreat, Sandbridge, VA 2012 Photo: Alison Brown

For over 30 years, Ken toured widely including many years of touring with the world-music trio Helicon (with virtuosos flutist Chris Norman and string wizard Robin Bullock) and with Quebec fiddler Laura Risk. In more recent years, in addition to much solo work, Ken's playing partners have included Scottish National fiddle champion Elke Baker and Ken's son, clawhammer banjo and fiddle player Brad Kolodner. In 2011, the father-son duo released Otter Creek featuring primarily original and American old time music. Performing and recording with his son has been the most satisfying highlight of Ken's performing career. Otter Creek was the most played instrumental recording on the national Folk Charts in 2011 while the title track (written by Brad) was the most played instrumental. In 2013, father and son released a new CD called Skipping Rocks. Among Ken's other credits are Walking Stones which sold over 55,000 copes and hit the top of the World Music charts and Helicon's A Winter Solstice (1999) which was awarded an "Indie" for Best Seasonal Recording. He has been featured in nationally broadcast concerts on NPR, German National Radio, The Thistle and the Shamrock, the CBC, Performance Today, All Things Considered, and on The Voice of America, as well as countless television and radio broadcasts around the U.S. Kolodner was the first American to be featured at the International Hackbrett Festival in Germany and was the featured soloist in an Emmy-nominated CBS-TV Christmas special.

Below: Rick Thum, Karen Mueller, and Ken Kolodner, just about to perform, Mt Dora, Florida, 2012.
Photo: Carol Scholten

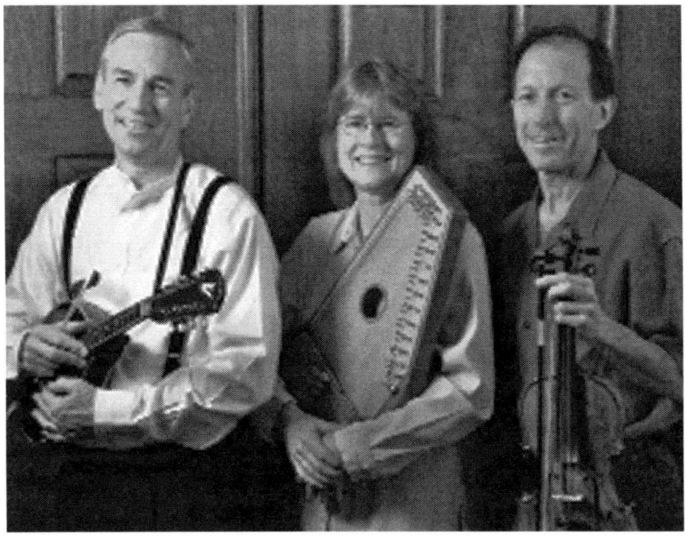

In addition to maintaining 60+ private fiddle and hammered dulcimer students, Ken is one of the most highly sought-after teachers of the dulcimer and more recently the fiddle, having taught at countless festivals and music camps throughout the U.S. including The Swannanoa Gathering, Common Ground, The John Campbell Folk School, The Augusta Heritage Festival, Meadowlark, The Mountain Arts Gathering, Kentucky Music Week and numerous others. Ken now runs his own three week-long master classes in Sandbridge, VA for 50 intermediate and advanced players from around the U.S. and beyond.

Without any formal music background, Ken began learning to play the fiddle at age 23 by listening to recordings of bluegrass and American Old-Time or Appalachian music. A few years after picking up the fiddle, Ken discovered the hammered dulcimer while in graduate school. Ken's interest in the two instruments developed into an ever-expanding musical appetite beginning with Celtic music and eventually into music spanning many cultures ranging from South American music to Chinese music. While he has mastered the fiddle and hammered dulcimer without formal musical training, he has had plenty of schooling. Along with his hammers, Ken holds a PhD in public health from Johns Hopkins. While most of Ken's professional career is devoted to music, Ken enjoys consulting as a very part-time epidemiologist (with over 100 publications). www.kenkolodner.com

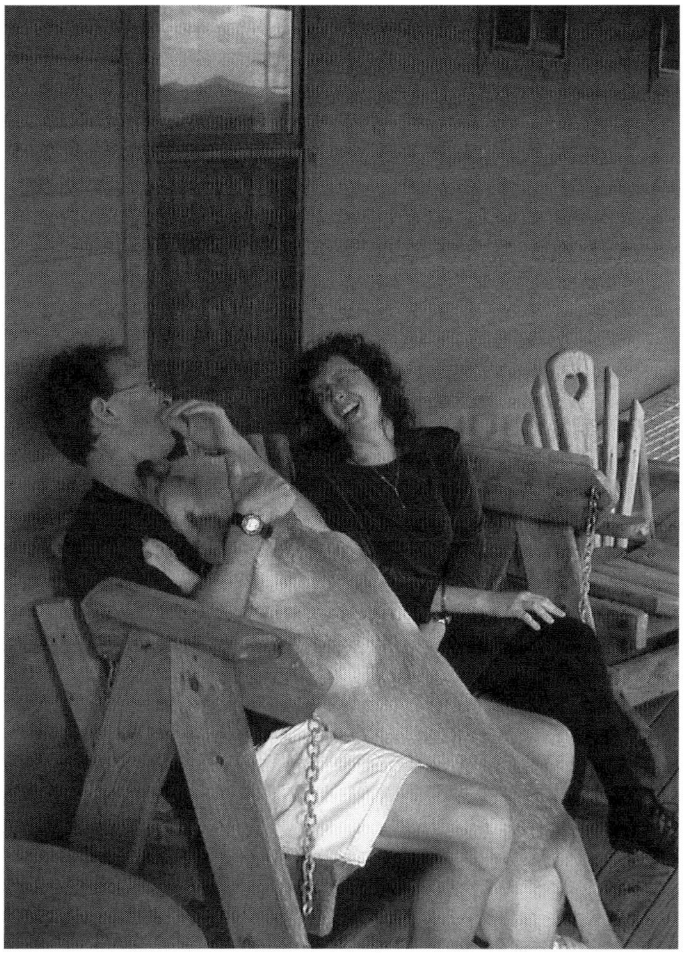

Above: Ken Kolodner, Karen Ashbrook and unamed friend, relaxing at the Southwest Dulcimer Festival, 2002, in Arizona

Below: Brad and Ken Kolodner jamming at Caspian Lake, Greensboro, VT in 2012. Photo: Erin Irby

"Mastering the mechanics of playing a tune is only part of the battle. The real art of playing comes when we master how we play each note and communicate a story with that phrasing."

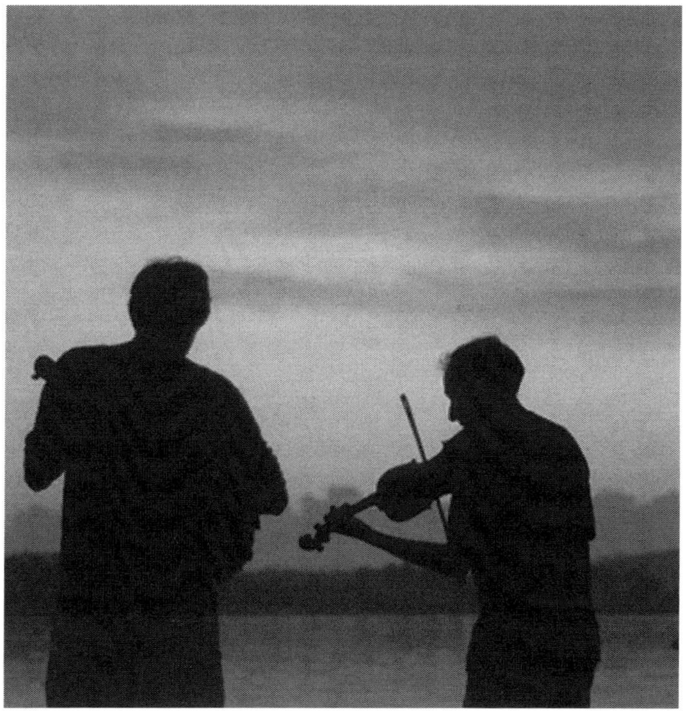

WHAT OTHERS SAY

"…without a doubt, Ken Kolodner is one of the hammered dulcimer's top exponents, playing with a dexterity which would stun many a would-be hammerer." *Folk Tales Magazine*

"When Ken Kolodner plays the hammered dulcimer, something special happens; he makes it sing…inspiring...a tremendous musician…a tremendous album [Journey to the Heartland]..." *Irish Edition, March, 2005.*

"Outstanding…soulfully beautiful." *NY Times*

"…a fiddle and hammered dulcimer virtuoso…just the right amount of fire…totally delightful…"
Sing Out, March 2005

"…joyous…reminiscent of Joe Venuti's work… [Journey to the Heartland] makes for a CD that you can live with all day." *Celtic Beat*

"He's a master at finding what Alasdair Fraser appropriately calls the "rhythmic underbelly" of a tune."
Potomac Valley Fiddle Club Newsletter

"…stirring…evocative…" *The Washington Post, April, 2005.*

"This is just about all anybody could ask for in an instrumental recording. The tunes are all great…Ken's playing positively sizzles …delightful…wonderful... Ken makes great use of syncopation…The up-tempo rhythms are really infectious…" *Dulcimer Player News, 2005*

With Brad Kolodner:

"Father and son have reached that musical telepathy that family members can sometimes achieve. The blend of the hammered dulcimer and banjo is exceptional."
The Old Time Herald January, 2012

"This is old time music played in the purest way: at home, with family, with heart, and with a creative curiosity that lets all listeners know that a passion for traditional music yet thrives in every generation."
Dulcimer Player News April 2011

"Ken Kolodner is a world class multi-instrumentalist...Otter Creek is a joyous recording featuring two fine musicians who playing excellently. There must be something special to that father-son thing.
Sing Out! April, 2011

"Ken is regarded as one of the finest hammered dulcimer players today. What makes this recording special is that Ken collaborates with his son Brad who plays the banjo and banjola. It is what folk music is all about…"
DJ Mark Pederson, WOJB Folkways, Barron, WI

With Laura Risk (Greenfire):

"This is the exceptional group that has raised a standard by both sheer musical expertise, and the love they share which allows for the spontaneous creativity that makes their music special"
The All Music Guide

"The trio plays with the soul, emotion, inspiration, and (when needed) the oomph that should be the envy of many a Celtic band. Greenfire can burn red hot! The repertoire runs the stylistic gamut from hornpipes to polkas to slow airs to jigs to strathspeys, and the geographic gamut from Ireland to Cape Breton to Scotland to Chicago, and even to Finland. Fresh, authentic, invigorating... "
Dirty Linen

"[Greenfire] explores the spirit and soul and mysticism of Irish music and kindred styles... The beauty and the beat of Celtic music are always well served."
The Washington Post

"Exceptional musicians... Greenfire's approach combines a loving respect for tradition and a thoroughly playful sense of creativity. The result is controlled artistry that should appeal to all fans of Celtic music... Clearly this is a 'must have' album for Celtic fans."
Dulcimer Player News

"...inspiring...the interplay between the hammered dulcimer's precise percussive qualities and the graceful fluidity of Risk's fiddling was a real treat."
Rambles: A Cultural Arts Magazine

With Helicon:

"...the multi-instrumental performances of Ken Kolodner and Robin Bullock are virtuosic."
H & B Recordings Direct

"...Quite wonderful! The musicians of Helicon have a deep feeling for an amazing variety of styles. This group is introducing a lot of people to some remarkable music they might not otherwise get to know. They respect the music they play, they play with spirit and sparkle, and they obviously love what they do. So do I. So will you."
Stereo Review

"All three of these guys rank at or near the very top of their profession. The musicianship is uniformly outstanding"
Dulcimer Player News

Notes

Notes

MEL BAY ®